STUDIES IN CULTURE AND COMMUNICATION

General Editor: John Fiske

The Ideological Octopus
An Exploration of Television and its Audience

STUDIES IN CULTURE AND COMMUNICATION
In The Same Series

The Ideological Octopus
An Exploration of Television and Its Audience

Justin Lewis

Routledge

New York and London

Published in 1991 by

Routledge
An imprint of Routledge, Chapman and Hall, Inc.
29 West 35th Street
New York, NY 10001

Published in Great Britain by

Routledge
11 New Fetter Lane
London EC4P 4EE

ISBN 0-415-90287-8
0-415-90288-6 (pbk.)

Library of Congress
Cataloging-in-Publication Data available.

British Library of Congress Data also available.

Contents

Acknowledgments

My principal debt of thanks goes to Janice Gillian, who cast a critical eye over the first draft of this book, and who was an invaluable source of suggestions and advice. Thanks also to my general editor, John Fiske, and to those members of the Department of Communication at the University of Massachusetts with whom some of the ideas behind the book were discussed; in particular, Sut Jhally (my co-researcher on the Cosby project) Ian Angus, Elenora Patterson, and Harold Schlechtweg.

A number of people were involved in the research on *The Cosby Show*; most notably Betsey Chadwick, Glynda Christian, Leslye Colvin and Ernest Green, who carried out the interviews and provided fascinating feedback during the first stage of the project. My thanks to them, to Bill Cosby, who funded the research (without the faintest hint of a string dangling from the check).

Last but not least, I am grateful to all those people who took part in the two audience studies, for giving me their time and their words.

Preface

This is a book about television audiences. While writing it, I was conscious of another audience, every bit as important to me as the one under discussion: the audience of which you, dear reader, are a member. I was keenly aware of how unfortunate it would be if a book that purports to know something about the television audience should be written in a way that ignores the needs and interests of its readers.

I have tried, as best I could, to keep two people in mind throughout. The first knows very little about TV audience research, or the theoretical work (such as semiology and cultural studies) behind the more recent developments thereof. The second knows a great deal about both. This book is an attempt to go as far as possible while assuming as little as possible.

The book is divided into two parts: Part 1 is a journey through developments in audience research, focusing on some of the more recent theoretical advances and the ideas that have informed them; Part 2 is the presentation of two empirical qualitative audience studies, based upon television news and television fiction.

My main concern throughout is with one of the most mysterious and elusive aspects of watching television: how, in the most precise and intricate sense, does television actually influence us? What ideological role does it play in contemporary culture? I shall investigate what television means by examining *how* it means what it means, by exploring the complex relation between the message and the viewer.

Chapter 1 introduces the reader to television audience research and takes a critical look at some of the research traditions that dominated the field from the 1940s to the 1970s. In so doing, the chapter confronts some of the basic questions to be resolved about the television audience.

Chapter 2 provides the reader with a short interlude, placing the inquiry into the TV audience in its contemporary theoretical context. The study of the audience is briefly considered in relation to modern media studies, semiology and cultural studies.

Chapter 3 takes up the story where Chapter 1 left it, examining what I have called the "new audience research," much of which has evolved from the theoretical traditions touched on in the previous chapter. It considers the relation between media criticism (or "textual analysis") and audience research, and proceeds to a discussion of the most recent work in the field.

Chapter 4 analyzes some of the practical and methodological questions that confront the audience researcher, concentrating on the qualitative approach to the subject.

Chapter 5 opens Part 2; it introduces the reader to two empirical studies, one carried out in Britain, the other in the United States. The chapter uses the studies to tackle the methodological problems that surround the analysis of interview transcripts.

Chapter 6 is an analysis of television news based upon the findings of an audience study. In the light of these findings, the ideological role of TV news is radically reconsidered.

Chapter 7 is an analysis of *The Cosby Show* based, like Chapter 6, one the findings of an audience study. The findings are used to shed some light on recent debates about the show's meaning and significance.

The title of this book is, I admit, a little enigmatic. By the end of Chapter 7 its meaning will, I hope, become clear. Happy reading.

PART 1

1

An Introduction to the TV Audience

INTRODUCING TELEVISION

Imagine, for a moment, that you have been magically transported back in time to the 1930s, anywhere in the industrialized world. Imagine also, if you will, that you have been transported for a particular reason: you are a journalist who has been asked to write a feature article on changes in everyday life between now and then. Your editor has wished you luck, leaving you by yourself to settle back into the comfortable padded seating of the time capsule.

What are your feelings as you slither backwards through recent history? Do you have any sense of danger or foreboding? Not really—your destination is, after all, vaguely familiar. It is the world your grandparents grew up in, a world you have seen pictures of, a world you have been told about by people who were there, a civilized, sophisticated, twentieth-century world. It is not as if you are being transported back to somewhere unpredictable and strange, before enlightenment, reason or the steam engine. No, you feel secure and just a little curious.

You are looking forward to seeing men dressed in baggy suits, women wearing hats and art deco furniture that isn't sitting in an overpriced antique shop. Maybe you will be able to pick something up to take back? You think nostalgically about an age before microwave ovens, shopping malls and T-shirts boasting unwitty slogans.

When you arrive, your first impression is one of absences. There are no ugly post-war high-rise buildings, no three-lane highways and no travel agents. There are fewer shops, fewer cars and a much smaller selection of vegetables in the market stalls. There is no multitude of brand names offering to cure your headache, clean your hair or wash your socks, and nothing appears to be "additive free" or "low in cholesterol".

As you begin to probe deeper into the 1930s world, however, this impression begins to change, to be gradually replaced by a sense of historical continuity. The basic social structures you observe (through the many telescopic windows of the time capsule) do not really appear to be that different. There is less money and less technology certainly, but people's daily lives don't seem to have altered that much. They work a little longer, but only a little, they eat a little less and they sleep at roughly the same times. There are hospitals, schools, movies, daily newspapers, buses and postage stamps. People go to bars, theaters and restaurants, they hang out on street corners and play the same kind of games.

As you return back to the 1990s, you reflect upon what you have seen. The gap between then and now, you muse, is, perhaps, more style than substance. And yet, people's behavior *does* seem to have changed. There is a presence now that was not there then. It is something ubiquitous, something that dominates what we now call leisure time. There used to be two activities we could name that dominated huge chunks of most of our lives. Now there are three: sleeping, working and watching television. In the average home in the United States, the TV is on for more than seven hours a day, and by the time many children finish high school, they will have spent more hours watching TV than in school. Similarly in Britain, the lengths of the average working week and of the average "viewing" week creep closer and closer.

It is not unusual for technological developments to occur more rapidly than our ability to understand their social consequences. In the last century, industrial societies pursued technological advance with scant regard for the social disruption it unleashed upon the working class. Our societies may have become a little less brutal, but, even in the twentieth century, there are few instances of social considerations determining the shape of technological development. It is possible that we have, as individuals, become more self-analytical. As societies, we have scarcely bothered to pause, even for a brief moment, for reflection.

The development of television is no exception. Television began life, not so long ago, as a gimmick, an amusing diversion from the radio. Its prodigious growth in the 1950s and 1960s turned it into a monster, a creature whose tentacles squirmed into almost every avenue of our cultural life. Now, in the 1990s, it would be difficult for us to find many more hours in the day to watch TV than we do already. Our energy has been channeled into the technologies of production, distribution and reception. We have laid cable, launched satellites, equipped viewers with video recorders and sought to improve the quality of production, sound and vision. And yet, what do we know about the practice of watching television itself? The answer is, unfortunately, very little.

The breadth of our ignorance is remarkable. We do not really know what role television plays in the formation of attitudes and beliefs about ourselves and our world. We are aware that it does play a role—as advertisers or political campaign consultants will testify—but we are uncertain about how or why. The story of TV viewing is a tale of mystery and imagination.

I do not promise, in the pages that follow, to get to the bottom of this mystery. I shall nevertheless attempt a few tentative steps into some of the more enigmatic aspects of television watching. I shall argue, moreover, that we have, as social scientists, reached a point of theoretical sophistication that allows us to understand more about the practice of watching television than ever before.

Before setting off on such an uncertain journey, we need to establish two things: first, what do we already know, and second, what remains unknown?

MASS CULTURE, POPULAR CULTURE

One assertion frequently made, by a surprising variety of people, is that media researchers invest television with too much power. The truth is, on the whole, quite the opposite. The history of TV audience research is characterized more by understatement than by bold and sweeping claims. Here we have a machine that sits in the corner and pumps out messages to people hour after hour, year in, year out—and yet media researchers, like circumspect lawyers, are prone to muffle statements about its influence with caveat upon caveat. Some, such as Conrad Lodziak (1986), have argued that television's main effect is not on our consciousness at all, but on its tendency to monopolize our leisure time.

The explanation for this rampaging caution has more to do with the nature of academic inquiry than with any social realities. The bold are necessarily taking more risks than the cautious. The more aware we have become of those risks, the more tentative we have become. It is, after all, much more difficult to build a positive case than it is to knock it down.

We are also, it must be emphasized, dealing with a complex semiotic phenomenon when we take on the study of television. There are no straightforward solutions to its mysteries. Unlike other forms of scientific investigation, there are, as we shall see, no agreed measures for evaluating the practice of TV watching.

Perhaps the most radical claims about television come from a body of work that preceded and anticipated the age of mass TV viewing. This was the work of Theodor Adorno, Max Horkheimer and Herbert Marcuse from the Frankfurt School. Capitalism, empowered by technology that could reach whole populations, was, they argued, in a position to restrict and control cultural life as never before. Mass cultural forms (like television) would create a "mass culture" that was uniform and banal, reducing cultural life to the lowest common denominator available in the marketplace. Anything dynamic, innovative or creative would be deemed unsuitable for the mass market, to be replaced by a mundane repetition of bland superficiality.

The Frankfurt School has, since then, been criticized from a number of quarters. The beauty of its generality concealed a number of flaws. The "mass culture" thesis was seen, first of all, as an expression of aesthetic values that were traditional and elitist. It appeared to contain the implicit assumption that popularity necessarily degraded and impoverished culture—a view that seemed to say more about the authors than about the culture they condemned. Indeed, the more the theory was applied to contemporary society, the more shaky it appeared. Were "the masses" really that passive? And weren't the new cultural industries, at least on occasion, producing things as innovative and creative as anything hitherto?

My own feeling is that, by and large, the critics are right: television—or, for that matter, any other popular cultural form—is *not* that simple. I am, however, wary of being too dismissive. For all its simplicity, there are elements of the Frankfurt School's grand cultural theory that strike a disturbing chord of truth. The deregulation of television and radio that has characterized government policy in the U.S. and many parts of Europe in recent years, does seem to suggest that free market capitalism will, ultimately, suppress cultural innovation and diversity (see Richeri, 1985; and Lewis, 1990). There is also no doubt that the age of television, like the age of religion, provides us with a common cultural currency, a set of ideas and images that most of us share. This gives television the power to create a degree of ideological uniformity, whether about a soft drink, a politician or a social issue, with greater speed and force than ever before.

At the heart of this debate is a tension between the viewer and the viewed. Where does power—the power to create and solidify meanings—*really* lie? Does it rest in the hands of the TV producer or the TV consumer? Do we create our own meanings, or are they passed on to us, prewrapped in an attractive, well-designed package? As we examine the fruits of over forty years of inquiry into TV watching, it will become clear that this tension underpins the whole history of audience research. The quest to resolve this tension could not be more serious. The meaning of television, no less, is at stake.

OF MICE, MEN AND WOMEN

The history of television audience research is almost as old as the history of television viewing itself. Whereas the study of television today encompasses textual and content analysis, political economy and rhetorical theory, television research from the 1940s to the 1970s was dominated by audience studies.

The first question to be asked about television—and asked repeatedly—was refreshingly simple: what was the effect of television upon people who watched it? Throughout the 1950s and 1960s, this question revolved around two recurring themes: could violence on television induce violent behavior in viewers, and what effect did TV have on people's political attitudes? While both these questions are of enduring fascination, they had the advantage of allowing researchers to enter "television" as a key variable into social statistics that were readily available. Was this the variable that lay behind shifts in political support at elections? Was it the missing link in attempts to explain the increasing crime rate?

Thus began what became known as the "effects" school of research. Studies were commissioned, surveys carried out and findings analyzed. Anyone who has ever been involved in experimental research of this kind will understand the sense of excitement and anticipation that surrounds the gathering of data whose results are unknown, data with the power to prove or disprove a theory. Discovery, as the saying goes, is no accident: it is the culmination of empirical research. So, what did they find? What mysteries did they uncover?

Without wishing to belittle a number of interesting individual studies, two words can sum up the experience of reading through the many published studies of the period as a whole: inconclusive or confusing. It is a little like reading *Hamlet*; a number of questions are thrown into the air, the reader follows the hero's quest to try and resolve them until, finally, when all the action is over, the questions are . . . left hanging there. For every "proof" of TV causing attitudes to change, there is another study disproving it. Perhaps, you wonder, these questions can never be answered?

The disappointment felt by those in the discipline was so profound that, by the 1960s, the "effects" approach to the TV audience was, to all intents and purposes, abandoned. What went wrong? How do we interpret the failure to find conclusive results?

The problem does not lie with the basic question of "effects," but with the particular formulations of that question and the means used to try and answer it. The effect of watching TV is bound up with complex social processes. It is not like giving mice small electric shocks to modify their behavior—even if it sometimes feels like it.

The difference between the TV viewer and the mouse is not simply (Douglas Adams notwithstanding) that we'd put our money on most human beings to outwit the average mouse, but in the whole nature of the experiment. Suppose an over-zealous animal behaviorist wanted to measure the effect of mild electric shocks on a mouse's preference for gorgonzola over cheddar. The methodology required to pursue such an inquiry is fairly straightforward: our cruel but thorough researcher would probably take the following steps.

First, inscribed within the study are a limited range of possible responses. These responses are behavioral and measurable: the mice will or will not change their cheese preferences, and the nature of these changes can be observed and enumerated by the researcher.

Second, it is possible for the researcher to eliminate other variables (such as a mouse's possible tendency, over time, to develop and shift preference from one type of cheese to another) by setting up a "control," involving mice free to choose their cheese as they please, without any painful deterrents. The two sets of mice can be compared and conclusions drawn.

The final problem the researcher needs to overcome concerns possible differences in response between different kinds of mice. It may be, for example, that Italian mice will stick with gorgonzola rather more tenaciously than British or Belgian mice. The researcher will simply test this variable by repeating the experiment with different kinds of mice.

The TV audience researcher, on the other hand, faces a whole range of complications, complications that many of the "effects" researchers either failed to overcome or fully appreciate. We can, with the benefit of hindsight, identify six principal difficulties.

1. Unlike the unfortunate mice, the "effect" of watching television will not necessarily be manifested in our behavior. Political coverage may not change the way we actually vote, but it may influence the way we *think* politically. Such changes, because they go on inside people's heads, will be difficult for us to observe. Similarly, the fact that TV violence does not appear to generate

homicidal tendencies in most viewers does not mean it is of no consequence.

2. Inscribed within the behaviorist's study are a limited and predictable range of responses. The significance of TV watching is more enigmatic. We can hypothesize that TV will induce certain effects, but we may be wrong and end up discovering nothing. If this happens, it will appear to us as if television has no effect.

3. While the behaviorist's mice live in a controlled environment, most of us are unaccustomed to watching television in uniform laboratory conditions. A study by Collett and Lamb (1986) in Britain placed video cameras in the front rooms of various homes, in order to find out *how* people actually watch TV. Do they watch it, completely absorbed, in total silence? Do they use it as a conversation piece, programs competing with family or friends for attention? Does it provide background entertainment or noise during other activities, from eating to ironing to newspaper reading? The answer, they discovered, was that people might be doing any one of those things while "watching television."

   Since we are all viewers ourselves, we will not find this particularly surprising. A number of researchers have, indeed, reported on the different types of viewing we engage in, particularly in relation to women using television as a secondary activity during housework (McQuail, Blumler and Brown, 1972; and Hobson, 1982). The problem for the researcher is that "watching television" becomes not just one activity but many. How we watch TV may be a variable that determines the nature of its effect upon us. This point will become particularly cogent when we consider the distracted practice of watching TV news.

4. Perhaps the most frequently made criticism of the "effects" approach is its tendency to treat TV viewers as empty vessels, passively absorbing the preconstructed meanings in television messages. For a mouse, an electric shock is a relatively (though not completely) unambiguous message. Watching television, on the other hand, is rich in ambiguity: the viewer is engaging with a myriad of complex sounds and images. These sounds and images are not delivered into our homes like neatly tied up packages, with meanings firmly attached to them—it is our *engagement* with them that generates meaning. If we come from similar social and ideological backgrounds, it is *possible* that we will generate

9

the same sets of meanings from television. We cannot, however, make this assumption without investigating the process of meaning construction itself—something that most of the "effects" studies were not equipped to do.

5. Once we acknowledge that human beings are not empty vessels, but, like TV itself, bearers of sophisticated meaning systems, we are faced with the problem of the "intervening variable." Suppose, for example, we compare persistent viewers of violent TV shows with people who prefer soaps and sitcoms, and, upon analyzing our data, we discover that the two groups exhibit different attitudes toward real violence. While the evidence might seem suggestive, we are unable to say that these differences are an effect of watching violence on TV. It is possible, for example, that the more violent viewers are violent because of other factors in their psychopathological history, and their predilection for violent TV *and* their attitudes toward violence are *both* the effect of a childhood trauma. The behaviorist is less likely to have these problems because he or she will be able to isolate these intervening variables with controls built into the experiment.

   While it is true to say that only the most näive "effects" studies ignore the question of intervening variables altogether, the history of the discipline is fraught with debates about the failure to consider one variable or another. The problem is that the process of meaning construction, for most human beings, embraces almost every aspect of their lives—from their education and social environment to those elusive childhood traumas. For the researcher, it is a veritable nightmare of intervening variables. Locating effects means locating causality, which, in turn, means delving into the murky depths of the history of the human psyche. This is not, to put it mildly, a very straightforward procedure.

6. The problem of intervening variables is compounded by the resources available to the researcher. The behaviorist can play God, placing mice into a totally controlled environment. The TV researcher is not so omnipotent. We cannot pluck human beings out of their worlds and subject them to a lifetime of controlled activity. In the original *Max Headroom*, the executives at Network 23 appear to have solved the problem of channel switching during commercial breaks (and the subsequent dip in ratings) with the invention of "blipverts"—thirty seconds of advertising processed into only three seconds of TV time. Unfortunately, the

blipverts have a troublesome side effect: some slothful TV viewers become so overstimulated that the blipvert causes them to internally combust. The effect of television is, needless to say, not usually this immediate. As Gillian Dyer points out, when writing about the influence of advertising:

> It is more than likely that an advertisement's effects are diffuse and long-term, and there is some evidence that advertising plays a part in defining "reality" in a general or anthropological sense ... For instance, the sex-role stereotyping common to many advertisements—the "little woman" as household functionary thrilling to her new polished table or whiter-than-white sheets, or the masterful, adventurous male–act, many social scientists argue, as agents of socialization and lead many people, young and old, to believe in traditional and discriminatory sex roles. (Dyer, 1982, pp. 77–78)

So it is with television. We enter the world of television at around the tender age of three or four, and we thereby begin a relationship that will accompany us to the grave.

If the effects of television are, as Dyer says, "diffuse and long-term," how can they be measured in a short-term research study? Even though many studies were carried out during the early days of television, this was a problem that many of the "effects" researchers had, perhaps not surprisingly, some difficulty in overcoming.

TREADING CAREFULLY

There is an undoubted tendency in academic writing for large bodies of research to be dismissed because of various problematic tendencies within them. It is not simply that research traditions have become unfashionable, but that anything of value that may have been produced within these traditions is subsequently forgotten. In a recent overview of the history of media studies, James Curran notes the tendency for media researchers to ignore the more useful work carried out within older research traditions: we tend to remember the pitfalls rather than the advances (Curran, 1990). In this regard, he suggests, we should be wary of "rediscovering the wheel," thereby parodying the efforts of those who have gone before.

Considering the obstacles the "effects" researchers were facing, it is, perhaps, both unfair and simplistic to dismiss their work, *en bloc*, out of hand. It is also easy to understand TV researchers' increasing tendency to be circumspect about the nature and influence of television. There are, nevertheless, two conclusions we should be careful to avoid at this early stage in our quest for the secrets of the television audience.

The first is to simply conclude that television does not affect or influence us. This would be misguided, since the failure of many of the "effects" studies to demonstrate clear and unambiguous influences appears to have more to do with theoretical and methodological shortcomings than anything else. The second conclusion is rather more half-hearted. Since the process of TV viewing seems to be so elusive, perhaps we should abandon any attempt to illuminate it, consigning it to the category of "unsolved mysteries? Given the dwindling role of audience research in the study of television over the last decade, this would seem to be a popular option. As I hope the more patient reader will discover, there are, I believe, reasons to persevere.

It is also important to remember that while the "effects" studies were, on the whole, too theoretically inadequate to deal with the complex subject matter that faced them, they were not all completely redundant. There is also something to be learned from the differences between them. Writing in 1959, as the popularity of the "effects" approach was beginning to wane, Carl Hovland reviewed the conflicting results in an attempt to make sense of them. His findings proved very interesting: he demonstrated that many of the conflicting results produced by the "effects" studies could be traced back to the way the research was done. Briefly, those surveys which were able to measure a controlled exposure to media (i.e., "before and after" exposure) yielded more positive results than those sample surveys that simply attempted to draw correlations between exposure to media and attitude, where "before and after" controls are difficult or impossible (Hovland, 1959). So, for example, an advertising campaign with specific goals to achieve in the world of meaning construction could be evaluated in a way that television in general could not. Of the two tasks, the former is closer to the one faced by our behaviorist than the latter. It works within a limited range of response, and it is more subject to the use of controls.

An example of research of this more directed and specific kind was an analysis of the media's role in promoting racist attitudes. Hartmann and Husband's study was able to isolate two discrete sections of the population in Britain: those white people who lived in areas with significant black immigrant communities, and those living in all-white areas, with no contact with black people at all.

Their study identified a number of highly particular racist attitudes about specific ethnic communities among those whose with no experience of those ethnic groups. These attitudes could be directly traced to a succession of media images on television and in the press. This led them to conclude that, in all-white areas, the media play a crucial role in gradually building up a collection of racist images, attitudes and stereotypes. This is not to suggest that these populations would otherwise be incapable of racist attitudes—the media images and stereotypes may simply have built upon a deep residual racism, lending it an ugly historical specificity (Hartmann and Husband, 1973).

While it is possible to identify flaws in Hartmann and Husband's case (they may, for example, have overlooked intervening variables, such as the more informal communication networks), the strength of their research lies in the specific nature of their inquiry. The regional concentration of post-war immigration to Britain enabled them to isolate the media as a variable, over both space and time.

It was, in this sense, the preoccupation with more general areas, like the effects of television on violent behavior or political attitude, that facilitated the downfall of "effects" research. These are questions that require us, methodologically speaking, to move on.

USES AND ABUSES

The failure of most of the "effects" studies to unambiguously demonstrate the nature and influence of television led social scientists to become disenchanted with the questions being asked, and to search for new questions within new frameworks. Thus began

> the functional approach to the media, or the "uses and gratifications" approach. It is the program that asks the question not "what do the media do to people?" but, "what do people do with the media." (Katz, 1959, p. 2)

This change in direction shifted power away from the television screen toward the viewer, who was understood as using television in order to gratify certain needs. Television was seen as serving, for example, an "information" or an "entertainment" function. McQuail, Blumler and Brown put it thus

> Our model of this process is that of an open system in which social experience gives rise to certain needs, some of which are

directed to the mass media of communications for satisfaction. (McQuail, Blumler and Brown, 1972, p. 144)

For those who had become frustrated with the failure of the "effects" model to deliver, this new approach was like a breath of fresh air. The "uses and gratifications" approach became, accordingly, extremely influential in Britain and the United States, from the late 1950s to the 1970s. As Joseph Klapper proclaimed joyously in 1963: "Viva los uses and gratifications studies, and may their tribe increase" (Klapper, 1963, p. 517).

This radical new approach represented, at its worst, one step forward and two steps back. Rather than develop a sophisticated critique of "effects," the more zealous converts were quite happy to throw the proverbial baby out with the bathwater. In its most functionalist moments, "uses and gratifications" oversaw, theoretically speaking, a complete transfer of power from the TV message to the TV viewer. If the "effects" approach was guilty of treating the television message as univocal and uncontested, then some members of the "uses and gratifications" school were equally culpable in giving the viewer the power to consciously accept, reject and manipulate the meaning of the message at will. In this brave new world, television could no longer influence us because it was totally under our control.

The more sophisticated advocates of "uses and gratifications," on the other hand, used the new methodological approach to broaden the scope of the "effects" model. The "effectivity" of television (see Fiske, 1987, pp. 19–20) was reconceived: the power of the television message was not negated but *mediated* by active, socially constructed viewers.

While this was clearly a step forward, the notion of an active viewer raised a number of new problems. Adding living, breathing, thinking human beings into the equation opened up a theoretical Pandora's box for the troubled TV researcher. The world of British and North American communications research was still in a pre-semiotic age. Semiology has dramatically advanced the study of meaning in recent years. The era of "uses and gratifications" had no recourse to this body of knowledge. The human subject, having made such a dramatic entrance into the theoretical arena, still had no recognized role to play in the constitution of meaning. The first script, hurriedly provided by the "uses and gratifications" researchers, was bound to be flawed.

The idea that people possess the capacity to determine their own environment may still be enthusiastically espoused in popular mythology, but in the human, social, and political sciences it belongs to the Dark Ages. We do not invent the way we dress, behave or think—we are the products of our environment. We are, as Louis Althusser put it, ideological beings by nature (Althusser, 1971). What complicates the picture—and feeds popular mythology—is our capacity to engage with the social and material environment, to create and recreate meanings and ideas. We may not be free to choose our own destiny, but we are active in our own formation.

This may no longer be a contentious proposition, but it is both difficult and extremely delicate. It lies at the heart of the tension between the television message and the television viewer. What role do we play in this complex relationship? How much power do we have, and what is the nature and origin of that power? These are big questions and, as I have already hinted, it would be premature to attempt to answer them in the opening chapter of this book. What marks "uses and gratifications" from "effects" is a willingness to deal seriously with such problems.

The perceptive reader will have already noticed that inscribed within the "uses and gratifications" model is a very precise conception of human agency. Our engagement with the world is seen in terms of our "needs," and our meandering path through life is guided by our desire to gratify those needs. These needs are not limited to the primitive demands of sustenance, rest and procreation—quite the contrary. They lie behind the whole way we make sense of the world. Our motivations are, accordingly, more elaborate than the crude instinctive variety (no one is claiming that, for example, people have an innate and insatiable need for soap opera). They are shaped by the social world that we have the luck or misfortune to stumble through; or, as Elihu Katz puts it:

> The uses approach assumes that people's values, their interests, their associations, their social roles, are pre-potent and that people selectively "fashion" what they see and hear to those interests. (Katz, 1959, p. 3)

This is a dexterous attempt to resolve the problem of human agency within a socially determined world. It contains, nevertheless, two significant flaws.

The first problem rests upon a central contradiction it embraces. People are, on the one hand, shaped and determined by the social world, instilling them with certain "values," "interests," "social roles" and "associations": and yet, when it comes to watching TV, they appear to suddenly develop the ability to "select" and "fashion" what they see and hear in accordance with their interests. It is a kind of conjuring trick, where the notion of social determination appears and disappears in the blink of an eye. Television, in this formula, becomes the weakest of all ideological agencies, deprived of the power to shape the "pre-potent" needs of the viewer.

The second problem is more deep-rooted, for it concerns the nature of human agency. The notion of human desire may lie at the bottom of many of life's enigmas, but it does not explain, on its own, the way we think. Meanings slip and slide into our brains inadvertently and surreptitiously: they may or may not be a source of gratification. To understand television as a purely functional entity—we see and hear what we *need* to see and hear—is like reducing the world of sex and sexuality to the moment of orgasm.

John Fiske makes the same point in relation to the role TV plays in our oral culture—the world of gossip. Television programs, for example, often provide the material for our conversations the next day—"Did you see so and so last night?" "Wasn't so and so great?" and so on. Soap opera, in particular, allows us to discuss the vicissitudes of characters that have become part of our own lives. The "uses and gratifications" approach would see this social use of TV programs as an end in itself, a phenomenon that explains the meaning of TV programs. This means, as Fiske points out, that they

> all too frequently assume that such a social use is in itself an adequate explanation, and they fail to ask further how gossip can be read back into the program, can activate certain of its meanings, and can become part of a critique of its values. (Fiske, 1987, p. 77)

So, while you and I may watch *The Cosby Show* for the same reasons, this does not mean (as we shall see later) that we see the same things or give the show the same meanings. This general "function" scarcely touches the whole process of meaning generation.

This problem becomes clearer if we look at how "uses and gratifications" explains what television means to different people. The work of Blumler and McQuail on the influence of political television is particularly interesting, because it spans both the "effects" and "uses and gratifications" approaches.

Their first attempt to discover the influence of political television was conducted within the "effects" tradition. They wanted to see whether the Party Political Broadcasts (PPBs) made by the major political parties during the 1959 General Election campaign in Britain influenced people's political inclinations. Their findings were not untypical of "effects" studies of this kind. They concluded, rather anticlimactically, that

> within the frame of reference set up by our experiment, political change was neither related to the degree of exposure nor to any particular programme or argument put forward by the parties. (Blumler and McQuail, 1970, p. 457)

Undeterred by this deflating result, they continued their research, using a more sophisticated "uses and gratifications" model. Their second study incorporated the idea of "need" into the analysis, distinguishing between strongly motivated and weakly motivated voters. The two sets of voters were seen as needing different levels of information, and, therefore seeking different levels of gratification. They discovered, this time, a subtle trend that their earlier study had overlooked:

> The strongly motivated voters had responded in one direction and the less keen in another. Whereas opinions of the strongly motivated voters were influenced by major (Labour and Conservative) party propaganda, the politically less keen electors responded favorably to the presentation of the Liberal case." (*Ibid*, p. 473)

The use of the "uses and gratifications" model allowed Blumler and McQuail to detect that there are differences in the way people watch television, and that these differences determine the effect it has. So far so good. The problem comes when we try to make sense of these findings.

What is it about the Liberal PPBs that the weakly motivated voters found so effective? Why did the strongly motivated voters resist this form of political persuasion and succumb to another? It is, within the framework provided, difficult to say with any precision. Related as it is to the concept of need, the notion of "motivation" is too clumsy an instrument to discover the secrets of political communication.

It is possible that if we disentangle the many political attitudes that distinguish the two categories of voters, we might be able to begin to explain these findings. Suppose, for example, the "strongly motivated" voters shared a set of political priorities that revolved around "issues," like the balance of payments or unemployment: if the Labour and Conservative PPBs addressed themselves to these problems, the "strongly motivated" viewers are likely to respond. The "weakly motivated" viewers, on the other hand, may not have been familiar with these kinds of political discourses. An idea like the "balance of payments" may have seemed both incomprehensible and remote. They may have found these forms of political discussion both alienating and irrelevant to their own experience. If the Liberal PPBs spoke with a more "commonsense" political voice, the "weakly motivated" viewers may have been a little more receptive. Those in the "strongly motivated" category, contrariwise, may have dismissed the Liberals for their failure to address what they saw as the political issues of the day.

This speculative account forces us to think about *meaning* and the *communication of meaning*. Why are some messages more persuasive than others? The equation *message + viewer = meaning* invites us to explore a complex interaction between an intricate display of sounds and images and a message carrier with the capacity to think. Once we come to terms with this, we can analyze the generation of meaning in specific encounters between TV programs and those who watch them. The "uses and gratifications" approach reduces this equation to one dimension. The viewer is reduced to a set of needs, the message to a set of gratifications. We have, consequently, only one way of understanding what meaning is: meaning is gratification.

It is difficult to develop this point much further without introducing some of the principles of semiology into the equation. Semiology is, after all, the science of meaning: to proceed without it would be like exploring an underground cavern with only a box of matches to guide us. The matches give forth only a feeble light and we would probably run out of them fairly early on our journey. Suffice to say that "uses and gratifications" has at least led us to the entrance of the cavern.

THE CULTIVATION OF MEANING

Although the "effects" school of research had dug itself into a methodological hole, not everyone looked toward "uses and gratifications" as a way out. In many ways, the shift made by "uses and gratifications" avoided any serious re-evaluation of the "effects" model: it simply dumped "effects" and substituted it with a whole new theoretical framework. Some resisted this temptation in order to set about a transformation of "effects" from within, to criticize and advance the analysis of television's influence. The most fruitful work in this area involved the development of an approach known as "cultivation analysis."

One way to understand cultivation analysis is as a mature, more sophisticated version of the "effects" model. Some would argue that cultivation analysis has grown into a different creature altogether. That may be so: but it is useful to see how a thorough auto-critique of "effects" might lead you to the cultivation approach.

The "effects" model made frequent assumptions about the nature of the TV message. It was often assumed, for example, that television violence was, essentially, like any other kind of violence. The cultivation approach makes the considerably more modest assumption that violence on TV should be seen not as violence itself but as messages *about* violence.

When it came to influencing the audience, the cultivation researchers abandoned the behaviorist tendencies in the "effects" model. To use the same example, TV violence was no longer seen in terms of its ability to induce violent behavior, but simply as a possible influence on people's *perceptions* of violence.

I have already described the methodological minefield facing the "effects" researcher. Watching TV is a ubiquitous long term activity over which the researcher has little or no control. It is very difficult to anticipate and isolate intervening variables, and to clearly attribute particular correlations between TV watching and attitude *to* television. Cultivation analysis overcomes this problem by deliberately limiting its field of vision. It avoids the particularities of television, focusing instead on TV in general. In its purest form, this means that TV viewing is measured in the simplest possible way, reducing the possible intervention of other variables to the absolute minimum. After they have been differentiated in terms of appropriate socio-demographic variables, viewers are simply distinguished on the basis of how much TV they watch.

The theoretical and methodological rigor of the cultivation approach has, to use an appropriate metaphor, reaped significant rewards. It has spawned studies that have clearly isolated TV viewing as the influential variable in the "cultivation" of certain attitudes about the world. Whereas the findings of traditional "effects" studies are ambiguous about the influence of television violence on viewers, cultivation analysis has revealed that, in certain countries (notably the U.S.), the more TV you watch, the more likely you are to have a fearful or distrustful attitude to the world outside (Gerbner and Gross, 1976).

Another area that proved elusive to the "effects" studies is the influence of television on political attitudes. It may be comfortable for TV producers to conclude, as many "effects" studies did, that the hearts and minds of voters are not subject to their influence (thereby granting the newsmaker power without responsibility), but cultivation studies have suggested otherwise. In the United States, the heavy use of television appears to cultivate a set of attitudes that are seen as "middle of the road" but actually embrace conservative thinking on most social and political issues (Gerbner, Gross, Morgan and Signorielli, 1980). This suggests television draws us to a conservatism masquerading as moderation. As Morgan puts it:

> Some people are to the left of the television mainstream, and others are to the right; in order to maximize its audience, television attempts to steer a middle course—and in the process absorbs and homogenizes people with otherwise divergent orientations. This process of convergence is called mainstreaming. . . . On the surface mainstreaming looks like a "centering" or "middling" of political tendencies. But if we look at the actual positions heavy viewers take on specific political issues, we see that the mainstream does not run down the "middle of the road." . . . Mainstreaming means not only a narrowing of political differences but also a significant tilt in a conservative direction. (Morgan, 1989, pp. 246, 248 and 250)

Many analysts have described how TV news's use of "balance" employs an implicit logic that situates the "correct" or "truthful" position in the middle of the two "extremes" (see, for example, Jensen, 1987a). Morgan's findings suggest that this logic actually structures the way we think. For students of ideology (from the Frankfurt School onwards), this may not come as a surprise; it is nonetheless, no less alarming for that.

Cultivation analysis has isolated television viewing as a variable that coincides with a number of other ways of thinking. The heavy TV viewer is, for example, significantly less likely than those who watch less television to vote in elections. On one level, this may seem to simply confirm Lodziak's argument, that television leads to inertia and withdrawal from other, more socially involved activities (Lodziak, 1986). Morgan, instead, suggests that television plays a more active role. It does more than divert our attention away from other activities, it *promotes* a profoundly depoliticized view of the world. It is not merely that the TV provides a distraction away from the polling booth; it induces a view of the world in which the polling booth becomes increasingly irrelevant.

Those who have criticized cultivation analysis for its failure to explain the mechanisms behind these effects, for its refusal to deal with the specificities of television or the activity of the audience, have, in many ways, missed the point. Cultivation analysis, unlike "uses and gratifications," does not pretend to deal with these things. It is its concern with only the generalities of television viewing that gives cultivation analysis its methodological strength. It has *demonstrated* at long last, that television is a powerful ideological agency in contemporary society. Given the ambiguities that preceded it and the skepticism that still persists in both the academic and television worlds, this is no small feat! It is the responsibility of other forms of analysis to fill out the picture, to answer the many questions that cultivation analysis can raise but cannot answer. Therein lies the scope of this book.

TELEVISION: KNOW THYSELF

The direction of the path ahead, in the quest to solve some the mysteries of the television audience, has, I hope, begun to look a little clearer. Before continuing onward, it is worth pausing for a moment to ask what the television industry knows about itself.

The basic answer is disturbingly brief and straightforward: very little. Once it has passed out of the hands of the program makers and onto the screen, television passes into the world of the unknown. Program makers are the modern cultural equivalent of Dr. Frankenstein: they have created a monster that, once unleashed into the outside world, they can no longer control or comprehend.

What is, perhaps, most extraordinary, is that so many people who work within television either assume they already know what influence it has (or doesn't have), or don't particularly care. For many television professionals, the most important audience, the audience whose attitudes and opinions are sought after, consists of their peers in the industry. Whether or not a program has a deleterious effect on the political education of its audience is a minor matter when compared to the plaudits of other professionals.

The more cynical among us would not find this particularly surprising: most TV companies have commercial imperatives and competing careers to guide them. As long as the ratings are good, revenue keeps rolling in and programs score well in "appreciation indices," why *should* anyone care?

The character of most audience research within television would seem to justify this cynicism. Within the industry, TV audience research is seen as "in-depth" if it asks audiences to score a program on a scale of one to ten. The only question that you and I are likely to be routinely asked is: did we watch? There are exceptions to this (usually involving the "product testing" of programs, using focus groups) but they are not the rule—particularly within a commercial system (as in the United States).

The problem is not, however, simply a result of limited commercial horizons. There is a widespread assumption among television professionals that viewers are "rational" individuals who will unproblematically understand the meaning of what they see and hear. Meaning, in this sense is not the result of complex negotiations between the viewer and the TV screen, but something *inscribed* by the program makers into the very fabric of the message. If we do not interpret or understand the messages as we were intended to, well, that's our own fault for not paying proper attention.

Commercial television companies can perhaps be forgiven for ignoring the social meaning of their product: in a capitalist system, the quest for profit will always precede ethical considerations. The failure to carry out any serious audience research suggests, nevertheless, a little complacency even in commercial terms. The struggle to communicate meaning and appeal to viewers would be greatly facilitated by an understanding of the mechanisms of TV viewing.

The recent industrial history of many developed countries suggest that investment in *any* kind of research and development, despite its long-term benefits, is usually deemed too costly and unproductive in the medium and short term. The cultural industries, including television, are no exception to this. The most innovative and experimental periods in the development of our popular cultural industries tend to occur in the early stages of their economic development. Once it becomes apparent what sells and what doesn't, and the market has settled down under the control of large corporations, stagnation sets in.

The research and development that does take place commonly does so outside the major corporations. It is usually initiated by small, independent companies, like independent record labels or independent filmmakers, who are prepared to introduce new ideas regardless of their immediate commercial viability (see Mulgan and Worpole, 1986).

When it comes to audience research, we should, perhaps, be grateful for this. It is questionable whether most TV companies would use a sophisticated knowledge of the TV audience to improve cultural life and political education. It may be that we should not *expect* television to understand itself. Perhaps this is something that should be left to those of us quirky enough to believe it is of enormous social significance.

2

Rethinking Television

THE END OF AN ERA

The 1970s marked a turning point in the study of television. At the beginning of the 1970s investigation of the TV audience still dominated television research in Britain and the United States. By the end of the decade, with the possible exception of some cultivation studies in the United States, audience research was in grave danger of becoming an almost moribund area of media studies.

Had we been blessed with the power of foresight, we would probably have been surprised by such a dramatic decline. This was, after all, a decade in which people continued to watch more and more TV, and yet interest in the phenomenon undoubtedly waned. How can we explain such an anachronism?

Part of the explanation certainly lies in the failure of the "effects" and "uses and gratifications" studies to cope with the complexity of the subject. This was a decade when a number of sophisticated theoretical ideas were introduced to the study of culture, ideas that provided social scientists with the means to be highly critical of both approaches. These criticisms may have been incisive, but they were not usually very constructive. In this age of "high theory," the empirical necessities of audience research were neglected in the meandering search for theoretical splendor.

It was also a period when students of television discovered a number of preoccupying new concerns. As television became big business, social scientists were obliged to address questions of political economy. Even if the magical quality of off-air broadcasting gave us illusions to the contrary, TV programs did not fall out of the sky. Their particularities could be traced to the production process. The professional ideologies and the economics of production were thus the subjects of increasing scrutiny. Who owned and controlled the media? How was production organized? How did the economic structure of the television industry determine programing and program content? Did certain professional codes intervene in the portrayal of the world? (See, for example, Murdock and Golding, 1973.)

This field of inquiry was also stimulated by an increasing interest in the nature of program content itself. As audience researchers had inadvertently discovered, the meaning of television was neither obvious nor straightforward. Television had constructed a reality of its own, a new world that needed exploring and evaluating. While the forms of television became more familiar and routine, the image of society TV offered us became a matter of increasing concern.

The analysis of content took two principal forms. The first, rather literally termed "content analysis," was comparative and quantitative. Researchers would measure presences and absences in the TV world in order to see how television represented or distorted the world beyond it. How, for example, did television portray men and women? Did the portrayal of sex roles involve sexual stereotyping? Such questions were pursued by establishing a coding frame and counting relevant appearances across a number of programs. So, for example, sexual stereotyping might be measured using an analysis of the occupations men and women were allowed on TV. If women were routinely portrayed as mothers, models, nurses and dancers, while men were given jobs that demonstrated control, power or toughness, it would seem to confirm the hypothesis that television emphasized traditional notions of masculinity and femininity. (See, for example, Fiske and Hartley, 1978.)

While this form of content analysis could be applied to all forms of television, it seemed particularly appropriate to the coverage of news and current affairs. Television fiction could, perhaps, be granted a certain amount of poetic license. News and documentary programs, on the other hand, were clearly in the business of reproducing specific realities. Since people were becoming more reliant upon television news for their information about the world, any systematic bias in the coverage of events was seen to be critical. The quality of a democracy is, after all, dependent upon the quality of information people receive about the world.

Perhaps the most extensive content analyses of bias were the Glasgow University Media Group studies (*Bad News, More Bad News* and *Really Bad News*). These studies drew upon exhaustive samples, based upon months of television news coverage that was painstakingly coded and analyzed to investigate the contention that news was systematically biased against the trade union movement and the political left. Their findings did, indeed, confirm this hypothesis, causing a defensive stir within British television—a depth of reaction that academic research rarely succeeds in provoking.

The second form of television content analysis, developing, on the whole, a little later than the first, was less enumerative and more qualitative. It straightforwardly challenged the assumption that the meaning of TV messages was explicit and unambiguous. Borrowing from approaches recently introduced into film and literary criticism, it interrogated the form and structure of television in order to understand the mechanisms behind the generation of meaning. How, in other words, did television actually work as a meaning system? Partly because of its literary background, this mode of exploration has been called "textual analysis."

Although these two forms of analysis proved to be a distraction from audience research, their findings were still clearly of consequence to the study of television viewing. Audience research had, as we have seen, been guilty of making unwarranted assumptions about the complex nature of meaning on television. It was now presented with the opportunity to develop a more sophisticated approach to the generation of meaning among TV viewers.

Was this a challenge that fueled the energies of television researchers in the 1980s? Were we on the verge of an exciting new era of audience research? Was the study of the television audience finally able to free itself from the theoretical and methodological limitations that had held it back for so long? I shall, in this chapter, try and address these questions. Before I do, it will be necessary to retrace our steps, in order to consider the relevant theoretical developments of the 1970s and 1980s in a little more detail.

THE USE AND ABUSE OF SEMIOLOGY

There are a number of potted histories of "semiology" or "semiotics" (the two terms have become more or less interchangeable), and I do not intend to increase their number here. Suffice to say that semiology is the study of meaning. It was introduced into the study of popular culture in Britain and the U.S. in the 1970s, following a trail blazed by, among others, Umberto Eco, Christian Metz, Julia Kristeva and, perhaps most notably, Roland Barthes. Like other related disciplines that started to become influential in this period (such as psychoanalysis, Marxism and discourse analysis), semiological literature has remained elusive to most people. The main reason for this is fairly simple: its advocates have written in a style that ranges from the obscure to the incomprehensible. While semiologists may not be the most guilty of such unnecessary obfuscation, they have, in recent years, created more frustration than enlightenment. If satirical novelists like David Lodge or Malcolm

Bradbury have taken liberties in ridiculing semiologists and their like, it is well deserved.

The problem cannot *entirely* be blamed upon willfully pedantic academics. The basic principles of semiology do require new ways of thinking. This, in turn, has meant introducing new words into the language—what is pejoratively referred to as "jargon." As Ellen Seiter has commented:

> Learning the vocabulary of semiotics is certainly one of its most trying aspects. This vocabulary makes it possible, however, to identify and describe what makes TV distinctive as a communication medium, as well as how it relies on other sign systems to communicate. (Seiter, 1987)

Jargon, unfortunately, has a tendency to proliferate like mosquitoes in hot wet weather: it is difficult to control and makes most people extremely uncomfortable. I shall endeavor, in the pages that follow, to keep this firmly in mind.

The founding principle of semiology is of profound analytical significance. Its profundity has, I shall suggest shortly, frequently been lost in the study of popular culture, overwhelmed by the use of semiotic trickery in textual analysis. This principle can be translated into a simple formula:

the signifier + the signified = the sign.

Explaining the meaning of this formula is not straightforward: there are no precise synonyms we can substitute for these terms. They are, in their semiological sense, new words with new meanings. In order, therefore, to appreciate their full significance, it is necessary to be a little long-winded.

The signifier is the "thing" *before* it has been given a meaning. It could be any "thing"; an object, a word or a sound. It is always a *material* entity. By this I mean that its presence can always be felt by sensory means: we might see it, hear it, touch it, smell it or taste it. Something that we refer to by a single name could refer to a number of different signifiers. So, for example, we might use the world *clock* to refer to the thing we see mounted on the wall, the thing we hear going "tick tock, tick tock," a photo or a drawing of a clock, the spoken word *clock*, or the five letters you have seen repeated in this paragraph. What makes all these things signifiers is that they do not, yet, have a meaning.

Meaning comes along with the help of the signified. The signified is the concept we use to understand or interpret a signifier. It is what we—or any other animal species, for that matter—*think* in response to a thing. The signified, as opposed to the signifier, is never material: beyond, at least, the squirming of grey matter in the brain. It has an ineffable quality that makes it hard to describe. Unlike the amiable gremlins that sit inside the brains of comic-strip characters, we are unable to watch these concepts materialize and reduce them into neat concrete entities. Since communication necessarily takes place on a material level (usually through language), the best we can do is to refer back to another signifier. So, I might say that when I see a clock I think "clock" (or "time," or even, "Why hasn't he/she phoned yet?"). This is as close as we can get to realizing the signified. Unless you believe in what has been called the "transcendental signified" or in the ability to read people's minds, we cannot communicate without returning to the level of the signifier.

When a tree that nobody sees or hears falls in the forest, does it really happen? It is, in fact, the arrogance of our species to countenance such a question: the chances of no animals, birds or bugs being around to witness such as event (and give it a meaning) are fairly remote. Even if we accept this unlikely occurrence: at the level of the signifier, the answer must be yes. Objects do not have to have a meaning to exist. Sound waves, for example, have a physical presence even if there are no ears there to receive them.

At the level of the signified, on the other hand, the answer is a qualified no: or, to be more precise, *its existence has no meaning*. This is a philosophical distinction that the founding principle of semiology allows us to make.

For most practical purposes, the separation implied by the signifier and the signified is an analytical one. As the "tree in the forest" example suggests, it is hard to think of many instances of signifiers existing free of signifieds. The two normally go together—hence the nomination of a third term, the "sign." The sign incorporates both signifier and signified: it is the material entity made meaningful. As Ferdinand de Saussure, one of the founders of semiology, put it, the sign is like a piece of paper: we can analytically distinguish between its two sides, but we cannot separate them.

Before going any further, it is worth dispelling two misconceptions. The first derives from the development of semiology from linguistics. This derivation is founded not only in Saussure's seminal *Course in General Linguistics* (Sassure, 1984), which introduced semiology to Europeans (a role played by Charles Peirce in the United States), but in its widespread use in the discipline of literary criticism. Subsequently, the sign and its component terms are usually described in relation to one particular semiological system: language. Here the signifier is the written or spoken word. While this is, in itself, as good as any other example of a signifier, it can lead to a common misunderstanding. This is to see the object (or the thing the word refers to) *not* as simply another signifier, but as the word's signified. This misunderstanding is partly encouraged by a tendency to call the object or thing we associate with a word the "referent." For many, this implies the thing or object is not quite a signifier, but almost a signified.

This misconception is not always confined to students of semiology: I have read many accounts that frequently lapse into this misreading. The word, it should be emphasized, is just as much an object as a piece of furniture. If we do relate the word to the object, we are relating two different *signifiers*.

The second misconception is rather more complicated. It also concerns the relation between signifiers. It has become commonplace in semiology to assert that meaning is derived from the *difference* between signifiers. So, for example, the meaning of a chair is understood in relation to those things it is not, like a table or a chest of drawers. It is this system of differences which is seen as determining meaning, or, as Coward and Ellis put it:

> The determinant then is to be understood not by a link between the thing and the sign, but by the relation of signifiers: Saussurian linguistics does not look for identity, but for difference; each element [is] ... different at each new instant of its repetition, and similar or identical only in opposition to other elements in the signifying chain. (Coward and Ellis, 1977, p. 97)

This is reminiscent of Sartre's argument in *Being and Nothingness*: our conception of being or "things" is based upon our ability to distinguish objects from an "otherness" (nothingness) that surrounds them. Deprived of this ability, the world becomes an existential nightmare where objects lose their distinctive quality and merge into one another (the fate of the fictional Rocquentin in Sartre's *Nausea*). In the same way, babies can be described as reaching cognition through the distinction between the signifier "absence" (of mother) and the signifier "presence" (of mother). The presence of mother therefore only has meaning in relation to that which it isn't, which, at this stage, is likely to be the mother's absence.

The problem is not that this is wrong, but that it cannot, alone, account for the derivation and development of meaning. While this may seem a long way from understanding the meaning of TV programs, it permits me to introduce an analytical point that will crop up later. Meaning is derived not only through difference between signifiers, but through their *association*. Our semiological baby may understand the signifier "mother" by distinguishing between her absence and presence, but he or she will also do so by establishing associations, such as mother/breast/food. The meaning of a thing, in other words, derives from what it is *like* as well as what it is *not like*.

The idea of association is useful in clarifying the first misconception. We can now say that the meaning of the word *clock* is partly generated by its association with another signifier, such as the object clock or the sound "tick tock." We are taught to make these connections, and our minds will learn to translate the relations between things (signifiers) onto a conceptual level (signifieds).

This brings us to the final part of semiology's founding principle: the character of the relation between the signifier and the signified. Despite appearances, there is no natural or inevitable relation between the two. The sign does not appear automatically, fully inscribed with meaning; it is something we construct.

With a semiological system like language, this is an easy enough point to grasp. The word *dog* usually bears very little relation to what we think of when we read the letters D O G. French people, for example, are likely to think roughly the same thing (signified) when presented with the completely different signifier, *chien.*

This does not mean that, in language, the relation is *completely* arbitrary, as most semiologists suggest. We may, when confronted with the letters D O G, simply construct a mental image of those three letters, without so much of a thought for friendly domestic quadrupeds. This may seem both unlikely and pedantic, but the possibility is usually discounted for the wrong reason. This is the tendency, described earlier, to confuse the signified with the "referent" (i.e., when the signifier is the word *dog*, and the signified is confused with the animal itself). If we do discount the possibility, it should be because the images we tend to construct, in response to a word, are based upon non-linguistic rather than linguistic objects.

When it comes to a non-linguistic object, like a plank of wood or the vice president of the United States, the relation between the signifier and the signified does *appear* to be much closer. We may construct mental images (signifieds) of these objects that look very much like the objects or persons (signifiers) themselves. The same goes for representations of objects, like photographs or television:

it is, in fact, quite conceivable that the images (signifieds) we construct are more like TV images than anything else. Pat Aufderheide argues that pop videos are structured (or unstructured) like dreams (Aufderheide, 1986). We might extend this argument to suggest that less surrealistic forms of television bear the structures of conscious thought.

Either way, these are instances that might lead us to suppose that the relation between signifier and signified can be direct and unambiguous. An anthropologist could quickly dispel us of this cultural illusion. Objects do not automatically represent themselves to us—they have no essential meaning for us to discover. What is the essence of an apple? What meaning lies at its core? There is none. If an apple "means" a sweet juicy edible object, that is because we "know" the apple predominantly through the practice of eating. If we came from another culture, we might think of an apple as an object to throw at people we dislike. In both instances we are constructing a relationship between an object and a practice. Terence Hawkes makes this point briefly and succinctly:

> The true nature of things may be said to lie not in things themselves, but in the relationships we construct, and then perceive, between them. (Hawkes, 1977, p. 17)

We are not free to determine these relationships as we please: we are part of a prearranged semiological world. From the cradle to the grave, we are encouraged by the shape of our environment to engage with the world of signifiers in particular ways.

This deterministic environment includes everything from the words and objects offered by parents, teachers and friends, to the way a shopping center is designed. The structure and layout of a supermarket, for example, are something we take for granted, and yet, like everything else in our environment, they shape our perceptions and our actions; or, as Eco puts it, they "frame" our cognition:

> The supermarket frame would involve virtually the notion of a place where people enter to buy items of different types, pick them up without mediation from any vendor, pay for them all together at a terminal counter, and so on. Probably a good frame of this sort also involves a list of all the commodities one can find in a supermarket (brooms: *yes*; cars: *no*). (Eco, 1979, p. 21)

Our view of shopping and the world of commodities is, therefore, highly coded by these signifying structures (see, for example, Chaney, 1983, on the development of the department store as a cultural form). As we learn more, we slip into familiar routines and practices, and this carefully constructed world begins to seem natural and inevitable. Each culture is, in this way, able to generate a common stock of shared meanings.

While this is true of all cultures, the commonality and homogeneity of shared meanings will vary. In a society that inculcates its subjects within a single dominant ideological system, there is likely to be a high level of agreement about the meaning of things. Some have argued, for example, that the church played this dominant ideological role in less secular times.

As cultures become more complex and sophisticated, the range and diversity of semiological systems increase the permutations available and cause meanings to fragment. Twentieth-century postindustrial societies are usually described in this way. Meaning becomes a battleground between folk cultures, class subcultures, ethnic cultures and national cultures, between different communications media, the home and the school, between churches and advertising agencies, between different versions of history and political ideologies. The sign is no longer inscribed within a fixed cultural order. The meaning of things seems less predictable and less certain.

The founding principle of semiology (the signifier + the signified = the sign) gives us a more comprehensive and systematic understanding of this chaotic world. It establishes the status of meaning itself. It allows us to appreciate the nature of ambiguity, and provides us with an analytical framework for investigating why things mean what they mean. We can begin the search for the source of meanings on a surer footing.

The consequences of this for the study of TV viewing are profound. We can now define the nature of the relationship between the viewer (signified) and the screen (signifier). The meaning of the television message is not fixed, but neither is it arbitrary. It will be determined by the viewers' semiotic environment—which includes their history, their neighborhood, their class, and of course, television itself. It takes us beyond the confines of "effects" and "uses and gratifications," allowing us to evaluate the process whereby television signifiers become television signs. These signs can be taken apart in order to see what binds them together.

THE TYRANNY OF THE TEXT

You could be forgiven for thinking that the introduction of semiology to the study of television would have rekindled interest in the study of the audience. The audience is, after all, inscribed within semiology's founding principle—in the form of the signified. The TV sign only exists because the viewer has sealed its meaning. Without the viewer, it is like the tree falling in the uninhabited forest—it only exists on the level of the signifier.

This does not mean the viewer is free to construct whatever meaning he or she likes—TV viewers are constrained by their semiotic environment (of which the TV message in question is a key element). Neither does it mean, even though we cannot peer inside people's heads, that the audience is beyond us. We can attempt to reproduce the television sign by talking to the viewer and analyzing the semiological structures of the society that surrounds them.

These possibilities seemed, at the beginning of the 1970s, to open up a whole new field of enquiry. Umberto Eco wrote, with an enthusiasm tinged with a sense of urgency:

> When I send a message, what do different individuals in different environments actually receive? A similar one? A totally different one? Questions of this kind are common to all research in human communication; but they are particularly pressing in the field of mass communication. (Eco, 1972, p. 104)

Or, as Stuart Hall carefully put it:

> Beginnings and endings have been announced in communications research before, so we must be cautious. But there seems some ground for thinking that a new and existing phase in so-called audience research, of a quite new kind, may be opening up. (Hall, 1980a, p. 131)

So, did the floodgates open, spilling forth a deluge of semiological explorations into the TV audience? The answer is unequivocal: no, they did not. In the 1970s, as I have indicated, there was almost complete silence on the matter. There were too many theoretical distractions and, despite the prescience of Eco and Hall, semiology did not make serious headway into television studies until the end of the decade. And yet, even in the 1980s, research of this kind appeared only in trickles. Why?

One explanation is very simple and practical. Audience research, even of the quick-and-dirty variety, is expensive. It is, moreover, always more difficult to get funding for experimental forms of research in the social sciences. The funding climate for innovative non-commercial research in Britain during the 1980s was particularly dismal.

Despite this significant material obstacle, perhaps the main reason for the comparative silence is the enduring preoccupation with
television messages. Explorations into the content of television and
other forms of popular culture, and, in particular, the use of textual
analysis, have continued unabated into the 1980s and 1990s. The
literary style of many of these analyses has created a new termi-
nology: TV programs are increasingly referred to as "texts."

The popularity of this form of research (as opposed to investigations of the audience) is not entirely a product of the urgency
of the inquiry: there is, unfortunately, a more mundane and un-
impressive explanation. The rapid spread of cheap, efficient video-
cassette recorders (VCRs) has made the whole thing very much
easier. Carrying out content or textual analysis without such technology is extremely difficult. The widespread acquisition of VCRs
allows us to store and recall programs, to fast-forward, freeze-frame
and manipulate them at will. This changed everything. Suddenly,
media research could be done in our living rooms or offices at the
touch of a button. Audience research, by comparison, remains difficult and time-consuming.

The preponderance of textual analysis in the study of television
has certainly had its uses. It has allowed a number of debates to
take place about how TV messages might generate meaning, thereby
creating a new analytical lexicon for describing what happens on
the screen. It has allowed us to explore the minutiae of camera
angles, cuts, graphics, sets, narrative and other structural and ideological details of the television world.

At its best, textual analysis has been liberating, opening up the
dark and secret mechanisms of messages. Armed with the tools of
semiology, it has removed the air of inevitability that enshrined the
meaning of TV programs. Messages have been broken down into
structural components, so that we might better understand how they
can be built up again into the particularity of meaning. These discursive structures were appropriately called "codes," and it is our
ability to recognize and unravel these codes that offers the necessary
clues to the mysteries of viewing, reading, listening or other forms
of "decoding."

As invigorating an enlightening as this has sometimes been, the
tendency to overindulge in textual exploration has produced a number of harmful side effects. Perhaps the most damaging of these has
been the way in which textual analysis has captured semiology for
itself. Like other forms of captivity, the result has been restricting
and limiting.

The semiology of the "text," whether it is *Dynasty* or *Finne-*

gan's Wake, is necessarily speculative. Textual semiotics allows us to open up the possibilities and machinery of meaning, to identify the "codes" through which we make sense of television's sounds and images. Textual analysis has, unfortunately, become alarmingly presumptuous. Throughout its brief history, there has been a tendency to distort the semiological endeavor, to show not what the text *could* mean, but to assert what it *does* mean. The founding principle of semiology, no less, denies the credibility of such an assertion: to unravel meaning we need to explore not only the level of the signifier (the message), but the level of the signified (the audience). Instances of this distortion have become so commonplace that they have undermined the credibility of semiology itself.

The most well-known example of this indulgence is associated with the British journal *Screen*, particularly during the late 1970s. The journal, shielded by layers of impenetrable and awkward language, frequently granted films, programs or other discourses more power than was dreamed of by even the most misguided member of the "effects" tradition. Audiences disappeared from the construction of meaning altogether, to be replaced by a witless creature known as the "textual subject." The textual subject, like the unfortunate mouse in the behaviorist's experiment, was manipulated and forced (by the text's structures and strategies) to adopt particular positions. Once in position, the inexorable meaning of the message (produced with consummate wizardry by the analyst) would manifest itself.

A friend of mind, asked if he had any idea what "semiology" meant, replied ingeniously that it might mean "half an ology." This is precisely what this kind of textual analysis amounts to: it interrogates the sign from the point of view of the signifier and ignores the realities of the signified. This adoption of this half-baked semiotics may have been convenient (it meant you didn't have to cite any evidence), but it dramatically failed to exploit the radical insights of semiology's founding principle.

While there were those who were critical of the worst excesses of the *Screen* position, the tendency was to modify rather than reappraise it. Paul Willeman, for example, criticized the *Screen* position for its failure to distinguish between

real readers/authors and inscribed ones, constructed or marked in and by the text. Real readers are subjects in history, living in social formations, rather than mere subjects of a single text. The two types of subject are not commensurate. (Willeman, 1978, p. 48)

34

He accepted, in other words, that the message did construct its meaning (via the "inscribed subject"), but reserved the right of a real subject (reader or viewer) to refuse it. This may be an improvement on the crudity of the *Screen* approach, but it still misses the radical semiological point: signs do not come prepackaged; they are produced by the engagement of people with things.

The damage, unfortunately, has been done. Textual analysis has repeatedly reverted to assertions about what the text means, rather than what and how it could mean. If these analyses offered some evidence, some sociological analysis of the ideology of the audience, this might be not only forgivable but revealing. It is, sadly, a rare thing for textual critics to let such harsh realities interrupt the flow of their journey through the text. We are *told*, consequently, what films, TV programs or other cultural artifacts are "really" about. We are told how so and so really represents the phallus, or capitalism, or post-modernist angst. This may be intellectually stimulating—just as literary criticism is intellectually stimulating—but it leaves us, semiologically speaking, little wiser about contemporary culture.

This has created a new (though certainly not improved) semiology, a semiology with a partially obscured signified. The signified is simply reduced to a set of assumptions carried by the analyst—it is not investigated or questioned. This misrepresentation of semiology has, ironically, led to criticisms of the discipline itself. It is semiology, critics allege, that has failed to move beyond the text. Ellen Seiter's remarks to this effect are typical:

> Semiotics frequently speaks of a text as though it were understood in precisely the same way by everyone. At worst, it operates as though all meanings were translatable and predictable through the work of a gifted semiotician. Such an approach is nowhere more deficient than in television criticism. (Seiter, 1987)

What is being criticized here is not semiology but the semioticians who use and abuse it. It is like saying that the history of the Soviet Union demonstrates the inevitable failure of socialism. Both statements mistake the distortion of a theory for the theory itself. It is the tyranny of the text that has blunted semiology's radical potential and reduced it to this impoverished state.

Textual analysis, nevertheless, remains an important part of audience research, and it will be considered further in the next chapter. For the time being, if we accept its inevitably speculative status, we may have reached a point where the textual analysis of television can go little further. The absence of anything other than a hypothetical TV viewer imposes an increasing strain upon the analysis of meaning in the television message. Debates about the production of meaning, whether they revolve around the notion of political/cultural "bias" or the precise construction of that meaning, are inevitably limited because they require more detailed knowledge of *how* the TV viewer reads and understands what appears on the screen. John Hartley's description of this gap in our knowledge, in relation to TV news, remains apt for all forms of television:

> The growing areas of semiotics and communication studies developed largely out of textual analysis of various kinds . . . and as a result, there is currently a gap in research into social discourses like the news. Most of what happens when the text is "realized" as a "live" discourse, when it is read by the consumer is a mystery. As Patrick Moore says about other mysteries of the cosmos, "we just don't know." (Hartley, 1982, p. 138)

It is this gap that we need to fill if we are to begin to really understand the meaning and influence of television.

DETERMINATION AND CULTURAL STUDIES

I have concentrated, thus far, on the nature of the encounter between television and the audience. The social and cultural world in which this encounter takes place has, hitherto, only been suggested and implied. It is now time to start sketching in a few details: the practice of TV viewing cannot be treated as if it takes place in a vacuum, impervious to the world outside.

We cannot investigate the specific mechanisms of the audience without a more general understanding of culture and society. Readers of Agatha Christie will know that while the mystery will revolve around the murder, Miss Marple's ability to solve it came not only from her understanding of the facts of the case, but from her intricate understanding of the social environment. So it is with audience research, where the practice of viewing is simply the focal point in the vast ebb and flow of social and cultural determinations.

The theoretical shortcomings of the "effects" and "uses and gratifications" approaches were part of the more general failure of mainstream sociology to deal with culture and cultural meaning. It was in response to this failure that the new tradition of "cultural studies" emerged, emanating from the Centre for Contemporary Cultural Studies in the 1970s in Britain. The Centre's approach was both innovative and eclectic, drawing from semiology, history, feminism, Marxism, post-structuralism, ethnography, literary criticism and any other discipline that seemed to throw light on the study of culture. Despite the indifference of the academic establishment and habitual underfunding, this theoretical *glasnost*, under Stuart Hall's directorship, began to spawn an exciting body of work. Cultural studies (or British cultural studies, as it has become known elsewhere) has, since then, become increasingly influential. It is within the broad rubric of cultural studies that some of the more innovative audience research has come.

Cultural studies freed the study of culture from two intellectual dead-ends. The first of these was a notion of culture as a separate and cultivated domain, with its own rules and organic momentum. Culture, in this sense, was above and beyond the society it commented upon. This is the culture of the "high arts" and artistic genius, of Matthew Arnold and F. R. Leavis, of an aesthetics untouched by the grubby world outside. It is the kind of culture that governments prefer to subsidize.

Cultural studies took a more anthropological approach to its subject. The cultural domain was no longer the hallowed ephemeral world of the "cultured": it was inscribed within the practices and symbols of everyday life. It was the culture of nightclubs and shopping malls, of pop music and television, of the beliefs and practices of the suburban middle class or the urban working class, of fashion and sexual identity. It did not, moreover, exist in isolation, but was bound up with the social and economic world.

The second notion cultural studies avoided was more sophisticated. This was an orthodox Marxist conception, where culture or ideology (ideology being, in most definitions, a close relative of culture) was seen as a product or a function of a society's economic system. This form of economic determinism was seen as too rigid to explain the complexities of cultural life, which, though related to economic life, has a dynamic of its own.

Liberated from these restrictions, the study of culture became a specific and detailed enterprise; one that, in Europe or the United States, could not take place without a broad understanding of late twentieth-century capitalist societies. Television viewing is a cultural practice alongside a range of other cultural practices. Since these inevitably interact, we cannot study one without reference to the others. These cultural practices are interwoven into the whole fabric of economic and social life. The study of culture means untangling these strands, examining how they touch and mingle.

There is, throughout this venture into the specificities of cultural meaning, a central idea. It is an idea that lurks behind every corner of social inquiry, an idea that despite its almost frightening simplicity, can adopt a baffling array of shapes and forms. This is the idea of determination. Why do things happen? How do we explain the meanderings of history? Why, in a certain time and place, do things take on one meaning and not another? Why does a TV program mean x to Jack and y to Jill? From the very beginning, it is these secrets of determination that have lain behind our quest for the audience.

Nearly all audience research contains some notion of determination. In traditional market research, it takes the form of basic demographic correlations. A sample of people will be asked attitudinal questions and details about their socio-demographic background. Their responses will then be broken down and analyzed to see if certain attitudes can be correlated with particular socio-demographic characteristics. It may be, for example, that there is a correlation between income and political attitude, or between gender and the response to beer commercials. These correlations will then be assumed to reveal some form of determination: so, something about your material wealth appears to determine your political attitudes, or, alternatively, there is something about the experience of being male or female that determines your view of beer commercials.

This method of investigation is common to nearly all forms of audience research, with varying degrees of sophistication. It brings with it a whole range of methodological considerations. When, for example, does a correlation become statistically significant? How can we isolate the important determining variables, at the expense of those that simply intervene? Unfortunately, answers to these questions cannot, on their own, lead us cantering enthusiastically toward the fountain of knowledge.

There is, in fact, nothing intrinsically wrong with this straightforward method. Problems arise when it is couched, as it has tended to be, within an empiricist framework. *Empiricism* is a word that tends to get bandied around academic circles rather too easily these days, so we should be careful how we use it. There are those, for example, who will condemn any excursion beyond the pristine world of theory as "empiricism" (the belief that the world will reveal itself through the rigorous use of theory is as misguided as the empiricist notion that the world reveals itself to us automatically through experience). The empiricist is a little like the feckless police inspector pitted against the superior wit of Miss Marple. The inspector is in possession of all the facts, he just doesn't know how to make sense of them. To Miss Marple, who knows about the world of human determination, the solution is a matter of using her knowledge to explain the relation between the mysterious series of events.

The history of audience research is steeped with a residual empiricism. An example that sticks in my mind involves a study whose impressive set of correlations produced a number of curious revelations. It was discovered, for example, that first born children demonstrated a penchant for TV quiz shows. The mind boggles at such a curious discovery. Since the study had been conceived within a largely empiricist framework, the meaning of this rather baffling statistic could neither be anticipated nor explained.

Those working within the cultural studies approach were well aware that determination will not be discovered simply by scanning the cross-tabulations of a computer printout. We need to have a theoretical framework to understand which questions to ask and how to make sense of the answers. So where, theoretically speaking, do we begin?

We have a vast body of accumulated evidence to draw upon. Cultural studies began thinking through the question of determination on a general level. Social life could, for example, be analytically separated into economic, ideological and political spheres. By applying these kinds of generalities to specific historical instances, they could be to be refined and adapted to the realities of contemporary society.

We might begin, for instance, to analyze the relation between ideological, political and economic practices by describing them, as Louis Althusser does, as relatively autonomous. So, for example, an ideological practice, like women listening to Barry Manilow records, could be seen as the articulation of an economic practice (the political economy of the music industry and the role of women in this particular market place) through a political practice (such as the contemporary politics of sexuality) and another ideological practice (such as the recent history of popular music). These multiple layers of determining instances point the limitation of any simple notion of determination (like "the economic level determines the ideological"), giving rise to (again borrowing from Althusser) the concept of "overdetermination."

Within cultural studies, perhaps the most important of these generalities is the concept of "hegemony." This was developed by Antonio Gramsci as a way of understanding the organization and distribution of power within civil society. It is, as Stuart Hall has written

> an enlarged and complex idea. In essence it refers to all those processes whereby a fundamental social group (Gramsci speaks of alliances of class strata, not a unitary and unproblematic "ruling class"), which has achieved direction over the "decisive social nucleus," is able to expand this into a moment of social, political and cultural leadership and authority throughout civil society and the state." (Hall, 1980b, p. 35)

Although developed as a way of understanding the historical development of capitalist societies, the concept of hegemony is not, ultimately, tied to any particular form of power or social formation. What hegemony is and how it works has therefore developed within cultural studies to embrace a sophisticated understanding of social determination.

The development of feminism was particularly influential in refining the analysis of hegemony. Because of the concept's development in Marxism, there was an initial tendency to focus upon those social hierarchies that revolved around the distribution and organization of capital and wealth (such as "class"). There is nothing necessarily wrong with this analysis (the ideological and political practices—like the use of Old Glory or the pervasive myth of social mobility—that sustain the capitalist class in the U.S. are undeniably one of that country's defining characteristics), there is much that it does not explain. As feminism developed analyses of patriarchy, it became clear that hegemonic power was organized on a number of different planes. Being male entitles you to membership of a dominant group, just as being the head of a major corporation does. If you happen to be a highly educated, white, male, able-bodied, heterosexual head of a major corporation (and, inevitably, most of them are), you have simultaneous membership of a range of dominant groups.

Martin Allor, writing about the cultural studies approach to audience research, has complained that

> the levels of determination brought to bear on the site of the audience within cultural studies are . . . somewhat less complex than they first appear. Class, discursive competencies, and the practices of decoding were investigated in relation to only one axis of power: the reproduction of dominant representations of the social formation. (Allor, 1988, p. 225)

Allor uses this critique to dismiss what he calls "the sociological pull of the problematic of hegemony." This may or may not be a fair appraisal of work within cultural studies: the main problem with this criticism is its failure to appreciate how hegemony can apply to the organization of power at a number of different and discrete points. These points may come together at certain unified moments (of which the white, male, able-bodied, heterosexual head of a major corporation is a perfect example), but they do not necessarily do so. These "dominant representations of the social formation" are not, therefore, conceived "in relation to only one axis of power."

Inscribed within the concept of hegemony is the idea of struggle. If history teaches us anything, it is that there is nothing inevitable about the acquisition of power (this is a feudal idea that is, like feudalism, a little out of date). Power needs to be won over and over again—since victory can never be absolutely certain.

The struggle for economic or political power (whether over the state or the household) takes place alongside the struggle for meaning. It is possible to hold economic or political power without winning, in one form or another, hearts and minds. Military dictatorships, for example, substitute the control of the semiotic world with raw physical power. The struggle for hegemony is, however, usually a more complex business, one that will involve serious engagements in the battleground of meaning. The semiotic environment for the support of free market capitalism or patriarchy takes place in all sorts of places, from the supermarket to the cinema.

Audience research, in other words, does not take place in a vacuum. We are surrounded by the mighty structures of our cultures and our economy: to exclude these structures from our analysis would be like taking a close-up shot of a figure standing in the Grand Canyon—we risk missing the bigger picture. I would, along with Clifford Christians and James Carey,

> make an appeal for sociologically spacious studies here. The texture of a cultural system at large, the Zeitgeist of an era, must be understood for an immediate event to be appraised accurately ... Humans create science, art, religion, cities, laws and institutions. All these are meaningful contexts that need clarification for behavior to be intelligible, for us to understand what people intend and the reason they have for their actions. (Christians and Carey, 1989, p. 364)

I would simply add that we need to be aware of the power relations involved in these "meaningful contexts" if we are to assess the political consequences of, in this case, watching TV.

Once we begin to study the struggle for semiotic hegemony, we become aware of its many ambiguities and contradictions. John Fiske has argued, for instance, that the signifier "Madonna" (the one who sings, not the one who is sung to) signifies both for and against dominant representations of women. She appears, on the one hand, to exemplify female sexual freedom and power, while simultaneously being the "sex kitten" permeated by layers of patriarchical meaning (Fiske, 1987). It is also a struggle in which meanings do not always or straightforwardly fit within the major hegemonic battlegrounds. The aesthetic battles that take place in architectural design or popular fashion may have ramifications within the large hegemonic structures of capitalism, patriarchy or racism, but they also work at discrete aesthetic levels. The changing meaning of blue jeans, for example, orchestrated by advertising campaigns, works within the dominant aesthetics of fashion and our visual environment.

The semiotic universe is not, therefore, a series of coincidences; it is manifested through a series of fluctuating hegemonic structures. These structures are never absolute, never complete; they can rise, fall and transform the history that sweeps them along. The more we begin to understand the specificity of these structures, the more able we are to understand what determines meaning in contemporary society.

As TV viewers, we are usually innocent of our inevitable part in the struggle for meaning. As we put our feet up in front of the television, our mood is more likely to be relaxed than combative. And yet, like it or not, our regular encounters with the kaleidoscope of words and images that flow in to our living rooms form an inexorable part of our semiotic universe. It is inextricably linked to the complex of determinations that produce the particularities of the society we live in. The study of the audience is not politically innocent; it forces us to consider the power structures that shape social reality: as Klaus Bruhn Jensen puts it,

> Because the reception of communication is a crucial site for the struggle over the definition, and re-definition, of social reality, audience analysis raises critical political questions. (Jensen, 1987b, p. 22)

While this struggle is often simply between us and the TV screen, it is most graphically illustrated when we argue with others about what something means. These arguments are not limited to the analytical ponderings of sophisticates, who will debate with one another about what a film or program was "really" about. They are articulations of the semiotic battles that *define* the whole activity of television viewing. Because arguments between people can be heard, recorded and transcribed, they allow researchers a glimpse inside people's heads.

An interesting example comes form the Katz and Liebes cross-cultural audience study of *Dallas*. In an extract from an interview with a group of Moroccan Jews, the meaning of a particular incident on the story is clearly informed by a struggle between matriarchy and patriarchy. The group are discussing Miss Ellie's refusal to comply in her son's (JR's) kidnapping of her grandson:

ZEHAVA: She [Miss Ellie] knows how it feels to be a mother. If her own son were taken away how would she feel? She would feel it keenly. She doesn't want others to suffer that way.

YOSSIE: You're talking as a mother? How about talking like a father?

ZEHAVA: That's my opinion, and that's what I said. Let me explain to my husband. He's saying, "Why should the father be the only one to suffer? Why should we be defending only the mother?" My answer is that the mother gave birth to the child and suffered for him. She loved him better than the father because the child is of her flesh. A father is a father; OK, so he loves the child.

MACHLUF: And not of his flesh? Isn't his father a partner in the child?

ZEHAVA: The child's from his seed, but not of his flesh.

MACHLUF: What do you mean his seed and not his flesh?

ZEHAVA: It's not the same thing. She suffered at the time of birth, and not the father.

MACHLUF: Don't they have half and half in the child . . . ? In the government you [women, feminists] say you want 50 per cent, but you really mean you want 75 per cent.

(Katz and Liebes, 1985, p. 193)

The meaning of this fictional incident (and the characters within it) is inflected by a semiotic universe that has generated competing versions of what motherhood and fatherhood mean. The situation is further complicated by the unspoken feminist discourse that Machluf refers to (pejoratively) in his final remark. The meaning of *Dallas*, and the meaning of this interpretation, both depend upon our ability to appreciate the terms of this discursive struggle.

Our search for the audience has, by now, become a little less aimless. We are beginning to form a much clearer idea of what we are looking for, and we now have a map—albeit a hastily drawn sketch of a map—to guide us. Like the explorers of old, our task is made a little easier by the trails of the few that have come this way before. It is to these that we shall now turn.

3

The New Audience Research

IN AND OUT OF HISTORY

Alienation is not always a state of awareness. Like stupidity, alienation is a condition we may suffer from without realizing it. There are some forms of alienation, indeed, that are characterized *by* a lack of awareness. Many of us, for example, will spend large amounts of time doing jobs without ever thinking, in any broad social sense, what we are doing them for. Academics and researchers are as prone to this condition as anyone else. It is easy to get lost in the intricacies of study and inquiry. The abundance and diversity of theoretical intrigue can become a quicksand into which we slowly and helplessly sink. The more we struggle, the faster we become submerged, until we forget why we were treading this path in the first place.

One way to avoid this confusing state of affairs is to periodically pause to reflect upon the purpose of our endeavors. Or, to put it another way, what exactly are we doing when we are doing what we are doing? This question is, I think, particularly pertinent in the study of popular culture, where the search for cultural meaning can get lost in the exploration of the cultural object. The recent focus on pop video as a cultural form is an illustrative case.

The emergence of the pop music video as a major expressive form in contemporary culture has quickly become the subject of considerable critical scrutiny, both within and outside the academy. Part of its appeal as an object of study is the opportunity it presents to those schooled in film and literary theory to practice their critical art upon a genuinely popular cultural genre. To students of textual and filmic form, pop video was a fascinating development. Here, after all, was a cultural form that appeared (whether through artiness or laziness) to break all the rules and conventions of the traditional realist narrative. *And*, unlike avant-garde film, many people actually seemed to enjoy it.

Analysis of music video (and the most well-known player in its success story, *MTV*) has, accordingly, become the latest episode in various traditions of textual criticism. Writers such as Ann Kaplan (Kaplan, 1987) and Pat Aufderheide (Aufderheide, 1986) have, for example, explored its post-modernist and psychoanalytic nuances. While many of these analyses have been ingenious and provocative, we should be clear about what is, and is not, going on here. An exploration of the textuality of music videos does not, on its own, bear much relation to an analysis of the significance of pop video in contemporary pop culture. How could it? A consideration of the cultural significance of pop video requires looking beyond the writhing bodies and fast cuts of the video to the world in which it makes its impact. Unfortunately, academics often behave as if textual exploration and cultural meaning were the same thing. They are not.

Andrew Goodwin has commented upon the curious reluctance of analysts and critics to approach pop video from a cultural perspective (Goodwin, 1987 and 1988). Pop videos, are, after all, commercials made to sell records, and their place in our world is closely bound to the music they promote. And yet, as Goodwin points out:

> Postmodern analyses of music video generally have very little to say about pop music itself, or the music industry. This is very serious, because MTV and music videos are consumed as part of a pop culture that lacks any one dominant discourse, in which the different sites of meaning production (records, cassettes, posters, gigs, films, newspaper articles, music video, etc.) are interdependent. (Goodwin, 1987, p. 38)

There may be people who watch MTV who don't read music papers, don't go to concerts, or don't listen to records, tapes or CDs, just as there may be those who fast-forward the programs between TV commercials. Such people, even if they exist, would tell us very little about the nature and meaning of contemporary culture.

Goodwin, in a rigorous critique of Ann Kaplan's book on MTV, (*Rock Around the Clock*), develops this point with poignant simplicity. Kaplan argues that an analysis of the film *Gentlemen Prefer Blonds* is the key to understanding the Madonna video of *Material Girl*. Goodwin responds by acknowledging the possibilities of such an analysis, but questions how appropriate or useful it is for understanding what the video means to the majority of viewers, whose cultural reference points are rather different:

> And why pick a text—a thirty-four-year-old film—that MTV viewers and Madonna fans are likely to be least familiar with? The references to the movie are fascinating for those of us interested in film, but the analysis has little to tell us about the meaning of "Material Girl" for Madonna fans and MTV-watchers—many of whom have probably never seen *Gentlemen Prefer*

Blonds and thus may have no idea that the clip is a pastiche. The "Material Girl" analysis is symptomatic of the postmodern approach in many ways: it's clever and extremely interesting for people who read *Screen*, but needs to be grounded more firmly in a consideration of the actual processes of meaning-production undertaken by MTV audiences. (*ibid.*, p. 40)

The problem Goodwin has unearthed is not a question of right and wrong, a good method and a bad method. As a form of literary or textual criticism, there is nothing wrong with an approach that treats the text as it likes, free from the specificities of the audience's cultural constraints. As David Lodge mischievously suggests in the novel *Small World*, literary criticism would be intellectually impoverished by any such methodological requirements. The problem comes when we infuse this literary endeavor with any wider historical or sociological purpose. As Goodwin argues, if we are concerned with the meaning and significance of popular culture *in contemporary society*, with how cultural forms work ideologically or politically, then we need to understand cultural products (or "texts") as they are understood by audiences.

This is a political distinction, and one that is not generally acknowledged. Literary criticism allows you to do what the hell you like (analytically speaking) with a cultural product, but it limits the political consequences of the exercise. Janice Radway makes just this point to explain her move, in a literary discipline, toward the analysis of audiences.

> I continue to believe that in-depth, qualitative analysis of the way an audience encounters, interprets and uses mass media should be included as a necessary part of a larger investigation into the manner of its production and distribution as well as into its internal organization. The argument offered here will have less to do with the "accuracy" of the results the method will produce . . . and more to do with the political consequences or potential of those results. (Radway, 1986, p. 99)

It is only by understanding the meanings constructed by audiences, she argues, that we can "understand how that (cultural) form functions within the larger culture," which is the only effective basis for making a political intervention to *change* that culture.

This is not to say that any analysis that is not grounded in audience research is necessarily politically impotent. Audience research is simply a means to an end, a way of collecting evidence about common cultural meanings. There are other forms of evidence we can draw upon to the same purpose—including other cultural products and forms. To return to Goodwin's point, what is important here is that we recognize which forms are appropriate in contemporary culture and which are not. The other cultural forms that help most viewers make sense of a Madonna video, such as magazines, records, TV interviews and other popular representations of female sexuality, are all clues to the contemporary meaning of that video.

Cultural forms do not drift through history aimlessly, they are grounded in an ideological context, and therein lies their historical significance. This does not mean they are unambiguous—far from it. The ambiguous sexuality of Madonna herself is a case in point. On the one hand, Schwichtenberg has illustrated how Madonna provides an image of an assertive female sexuality, in control and unoppressed (Schwichtenberg, 1989). On the other hand, she expresses this sexuality in a style that bares more than a passing resemblance to the more traditional image of the female sex object, the sex kitten performing for the pleasure of the male gaze. So, to teenage girls, Madonna's assertive sexuality may be a liberating departure from the images of passive subordination that fill the pages of teenage girls' magazines, while male readers of *Playboy* may see nothing more than an attractive young woman displaying herself for their pleasure. As John Fiske puts it:

> When Madonna's primary texts are "linked" to the subordinate culture of young girls in patriarchy they "speak" quite differently from when they are "linked" with the sexist masculine culture of *Playboy*. Reading the secondary and tertiary texts can help us see how the primary text can be articulated into the general culture in different ways, by different readers in different subcultures. (Fiske, 1987, p. 126)

So, the cultural objects that surround Madonna at a particular moment in history, what Fiske calls "secondary and tertiary texts," give us an insight into her cultural significance. Sut Jhally's video *Dreamworlds*, for example, argues persuasively that music video in general is typified by acutely sexist representations straight out of the pages of *Playboy*, placing Madonna in a context, for MTV viewers, where she ends up negating rather than promoting assertive female sexuality.

This brings us back to the point reached at the end of the last chapter: audience research does not take place in an intellectual vacuum. The analysis of the complex mechanics of the history in which we live provides us with a wealth of evidence about the world of cultural meaning. By talking to the audience, we are simply gathering more evidence. Or, to put it another way, we are fashioning a cultural product (the voice of the viewer) with which to contextualize and evaluate another cultural product (or "text"). The question that should be put to textual analysis that purports to tell us how a cultural product "works" in contemporary culture is almost embarrassingly simple: where's the evidence? Without evidence, everything is pure speculation.

THE ETHNOGRAPHY OF THE AUDIENCE

In Chapter 1, I described how the "uses and gratifications" approach to media audiences opened up a whole new vista. The viewer was no longer seen as a passive recipient of messages, but as an active participant in the production of meaning. The problem with the audience research spawned by this new tradition, I suggested, lay in its inadequate conception of the process of meaning construction. At its worst, it conceived TV viewers as creatures with a pre-given set of attitudes and beliefs who could pick and choose to interpret television as it suited them. The disciplines of semiology and cultural studies, outlined briefly in Chapter 2, reinstated both the power of television *and* the activity of the audience. Television becomes one meaning system among many, part of our semiotic environment. Our interaction with that environment is, in turn, shaped by that environment, or, to quote David Morley paraphrasing Sartre, "It is a question of what we make of what history has made of us" (Morley, 1986, p. 43).

One consequence of all this is that it complicates the whole process of television viewing, which becomes more than simply sitting down, pressing buttons and watching. TV viewing is a cultural practice, and like all cultural practices, it involves not only "doing it" but "ways of doing it." So, we don't just engage with the sounds and pictures on the screen, we engage with them in *particular* ways. How we watch television is therefore part of the cultural context in which programs, commercials and other televisual paraphernalia are placed. This calls our attention to what we might broadly call the ethnography of television viewing, in order to gather what Katz and Liebes call "ethno-semiological data" about the audience (Katz and Liebes, 1985, p. 189).

There is, as David Morley has put it, "more to watching TV than what's on the screen" (Morley, 1988, p. 47). James Lull's work,

49

for example, has explored some of the ways in which we incorporate television into our social world, introducing "processes of interpersonal communication . . . into the domain of mass communication" (Lull, 1988, p. 15). The television set, like the respected elder in an extended family, fits comfortably into our domestic environment and tells us stories about the turbulent world outside. It brings the outside inside and, to quote Roger Silverstone,

> These two worlds juxtapose at the screen, both a domestic nodal point and a frame for the display of the limited, vicarious and often crucial experiences that television makes constantly available. (Silverstone, 1981, p. 12)

The places where these two worlds intertwine are the sites, quite literally, where television makes sense.

The exploration of the ethnography of television viewing has been one of the richest areas of audience research in recent years. Studies have usually focused on two broad areas: the domestic and family context of viewing, and the subcultural uses of television programs by specific groups (such as Jenkins's work with the "Trekkies"—cult followers of the show *Star Trek*). These studies describe how the social conditions of TV viewing contextualizes how and what television means. Perhaps the most interesting area of exploration has been the unraveling of the politics of gender in front of the TV screen, or what David Morley has called "the politics of the living room" (Morley, 1986). Morley's analysis of family viewing in South London reveals the power struggles that take place between men and women in front of the TV set. The remote control device, giving viewers the pleasant smell of power at their fingertips, becomes a source of cultural hegemony. The (largely successful) attempt by men to capture this diminutive box of tricks represents more than their symbolic power within the household; it means they really do run the show. As one woman complained of her husband:

> I don't get much choice, because he sits with the thing beside him and that's it. I get annoyed because I can be watching a programme and he's flicking channels to see if a programme on the other side has finished, so he can record something. So the television's flicking all the time, or he's flicking the timer. I just say, "For goodness' sake, leave it." (Morley, 1986, p. 69)

Such is the display of male megalomania in this case that the woman is happy to relinquish power over the set if only her trigger-happy husband would be less ostentatiously in control. The hint of a threat in her final plea suggests that, like the French aristocracy in the eighteenth century, such ostentation might backfire and breed outright revolt.

It is not surprising, in this context, that gender differences tend to coalesce around specific program preferences. James Lull, commenting upon research around the world, notes that

> Men everywhere prefer sports, action-orientated programs, and information programming (especially news), while women prefer dramas (including serials, soap operas and films) and music/dance/comedy-based programs. (Lull, 1988, p. 248)

While TV audience ratings give us clues about some of these differences (although preferences are not always translated into viewing figures), ethnographic findings suggest that program preference is linked to specific ideologies and cultural practices. This is particularly the case for soap opera, generally characterized by both producers and viewers as feminine, and news, which is rather more subtly demarcated as male territory.

Studies by McQuail, Blumler and Brown (1972), Dorothy Hobson (1980 and 1982), Morley (1986) and others (such as the studies contained in Lull, 1988) have explored the nature of these differences. For many women, the world of soap opera, with its chronological realism and emphasis on everyday concerns (see Dyer et al., 1981), provides entry into a world of gossip, local community (see Rosen, 1986) and intriguing social relations. The pleasures of this world are both vicarious and real. The range of characters whose lives and loves we can talk and speculate about is extended, by soap operas, beyond our own social circle, to incorporate the worlds of *Neighbours, Eastenders, Dallas* and *General Hospital*. If we miss a few episodes, we might ask friends or family to fill us in, much as we would inquire after a friend who had been away somewhere interesting. The pleasures of gossip and the oral cultures that accompany it are deeply enriched.

It is men's refusal (in public, at least) to acknowledge the world of gossip, a world denigrated by the voice of machismo for its "femininity," that contextualizes their attitude to TV soaps. Tulloch and Moran take one step further to argue that

> it is males' refusal to be open in their emotions, and to gossip, which is a major reason for their put down of soaps. They displace their own inadequacies onto the viewing habits of women. And in asserting the value of gossip and emotional release, women are insisting on their own personal and social

space, in the face of male dominated culture. (Quoted in Fiske, 1987, p. 78)

This view resonates with Radway's study of women and popular romantic fiction (Radway, 1984) and Hobson's study of *Crossroads* viewers (Hobson, 1982). Both studies describe how women create and protect this "personal and social space" (by, for example, watching soaps on the second TV in the kitchen), so that they might be free to express themselves through it.

Since this space is often found within the confines of the domestic environment, we would expect to see different patterns of TV viewing in societies where the domestic domain—television and all—is controlled by women rather than men. Leoncio Barrios's analysis of family viewing in Venezuela (Barrios, 1988) provides us with an opportunity to make just such a comparison. While the world outside is profoundly patriarchal, domestic space in Venezuela, according to Barrios, is organized by women. Battles over the TV set, unlike those battles described by Morley in the living rooms of south London, are played out on matriarchal territory. Consequently, prime-time television in Venezuela is dominated by their own version of soap opera, the "telenovela" (watched by more than 80 percent of the primetime audience). Lull describes a period in Venezuela when

> programmers attempted to put male-orientated programs on during this time, but the shows were miserable failures in the ratings since women, who control nighttime viewing, were watching the telenovelas on the other channels. (Lull, 1988, p. 254)

The lesson here is simple enough: in order to understand television, we must understand the rules of the domestic setting in which it finds itself.

The point can be developed by considering male preferences for news and current affairs programing. While research (Hobson, 1980; Morley, 1986; and Loomis, 1990, for example), repeatedly indicates that both men and women regard news and current affairs as primarily men's business, they do not suggest that it is incorporated into male culture in the same way as soaps are used by women. The image of blokes down the pub, chewing the fat over the issues of the day, is, on the whole, nothing more than a comforting male myth. As Chapter 5 indicates, my own research suggests that most TV news washes over both men and women. Its style, for most people, is undiscriminatingly obtuse.

Amy Loomis (1990), in a study of people's responses to an hour-long documentary (about the sinister role of intelligence organizations in the recent history of the United States, up to the Iran/Contra affair) discovered that although men and women differed in their professed level of interest, these differences had little to do with their levels of comprehension. In accordance with other studies, men claimed to be interested in news and documentary, while women admitted that it usually bored them. In discussions following the program, Loomis observed that what this meant, in practice, was that the women who watched the documentary confessed to finding it confusing, while men, as equally confused, tended to conceal the fact.

If men were as committed to news and current affairs as they profess, we would expect them to demonstrate far more involvement with these television discourses than women. Yet a careful reading of the evidence suggests that the attachment they proclaim does not usually translate into an appropriately attentive practice of viewing. They watch, but they do not see. They hear, but they do not listen. Why?

The answer requires a sophisticated understanding of the practices of patriarchy and the place of television within those practices. News and current affairs television deals with the public rather than the domestic sphere. It does not require a detailed knowledge of history to see how notions of masculinity are closely bound up with perceptions of the public domain. The fact that proletarian men won the right to vote before bourgeois women (as opposed to say, rights over private property) in most Western countries tells us a great deal about the ideology of patriarchy. To deny access to this domain is to emasculate.

This is a point illuminated by Lull when he describes how men will tend to see TV viewing as "work" rather than play (Lull, 1988, pp. 252–253). Watching the news becomes a necessary responsibility, even if, deep down, they would rather be watching *Dynasty*. It also becomes a "more important" type of viewing, enabling men to justify the precedence it takes over less "worthy" programs, like soap operas. The man is able to say to his wife: "I'm watching out of sense of public duty, while you're only watching so you can gossip about it." To relinquish this responsibility would be to give up a little piece of patriarchy. So men will fiercely protect their right to sit and watch and be bored mindless by news and current affairs on TV. Like much of patriarchal ideology, it is as disingenuous and self-deceiving as it is powerful.

This may be a slightly pathetic story, but it is an important

53

one. It tells us a great deal about the context in which men and women watch news and current affairs, and allows us to interpret what men and women say about the world they see portrayed, in a more sophisticated way than hitherto. The attempts made by men and women to grapple with the complexity of the discourse of news will be determined by different ideological forces. What they make of what they see is, therefore, likely to be different.

The same can be said for soap operas. The way people watch *Dynasty* or *General Hospital* will be changed by their involvement (or lack of it) in an oral culture where the characters are the subjects of gossip. The fact that one of our friends thinks that one particular character is a nasty piece of work will affect how we interpret episodes in which he or she appears. Ien Ang, in her study of *Dallas* watching in Holland, points out that

> women watch *Dallas* in a different way from men. Dutch women seem to be most interested in the mutual relationships within the Ewing family and in the love complications in *Dallas*, while they respond much less to the business relations and problems, the cowboy elements and the power and wealth represented. It is not surprising that for male viewers exactly the opposite is the case. (Ang, 1985, p. 118)

Men and women, in other words, are ideologically constrained to watch the program in different and particular ways.

This idea is a significant one, because it takes the ethnography of TV viewing beyond the rubric of "uses and gratifications" research. It is, in other words, not enough to say that people use TV programs for various purposes: we need to understand that this changes the nature of what is being watched.

SOLIDIFYING AMBIGUITIES

Nothing, semiology tells us, is unambiguous. Something as intricate as a TV program is seeped in potential ambiguity, or what semiology calls "polysemy" (many meanings). This should not surprise us—indeed, the televisual message is so extravagantly coded it is amazing that any two people should respond to it in the same way.

Even something as simple and innocent as a close-up shot can operate as a highly coded sign, signifying—to those with access to the appropriate cultural codes—different things in different televisual contexts. In the TV interview an extreme close-up may signify that the person being interviewed is probably hiding something, the camera "interrogating" his or her face for clues (see Brundson and Morley, 1979). In the TV drama, it may signify depth of feeling (the camera forcing us to consider the meaning of the smallest facial expression as significant), or the point of view of another character who is within an intimate distance. To someone who has never seen a photographic image, it may simply signify that a character's face has, mysteriously, grown extremely large. These ambiguities will then intertwine with the many different meanings we may have already given the subject of the extreme close-up. A whole minute of interchanging images and sounds increases the number of permutations still further. During an hour-long TV program, the chance of us coming up with the same reading as the person sitting next to us would seem to be as remote as our chances of winning a national lottery.

And yet, despite the almost infinite complexity of the televisual discourse, many of us will routinely experience television in much the same way. Not only will most of us find our way out of the labyrinth of sounds and images, we may well choose roughly the same path through it. Semiology teaches us that nothing has a fixed or inexorable meaning—commonality is rooted only in culture. We have, it would appear, been well-trained. The capacity of societies to create such levels of cultural uniformity is remarkable.

The problem with a society that nurtures and guides its citizens toward common meanings is its tendency to suppress not only the ambiguity of things but the very *idea* of ambiguity. We behave as if the meaning of things were natural and inevitable. The failure to come up with the socially agreed meaning is often interpreted as stupid or troublesome. In many societies, the very act of digression from this semiological control is seen as subversive and, because it challenges the fixity of the sign, threatening. Herein lies the resistance to cultural diversity, and, by degrees, the breeding ground for racial or religious intolerance.

Our reluctance to accept ambiguity has had profound consequences in the study of television. It would have been logical to start with the premise of polysemy, so that we might trace the social roots of commonality. The history of television audience research has done precisely the opposite: it is commonality of meaning that has been assumed and ambiguity that has to be explained. So, if something meant the same to X, Y and Z, it remained uninterrogated. Only when X, Y and Z responded differently were questions asked.

The corollary of this is that the nature and roots of television's ambiguity have only recently been explored. The most interesting of these recent explorations have rooted the analysis of ambiguity in cultural difference. In particular, the global distribution of TV programs and commercials has inevitably raised a number of questions about the ambiguities of TV messages across different cultures. Or, as Katz and Liebes put it: "Consider the worldwide success of a programme like *Dallas*. How do viewers from another culture understand it?" (Katz and Liebes, 1985, p. 187). Their analysis of discussions among groups from five different ethnic/cultural backgrounds (Israeli Arabs, new immigrants to Israel from Russia, immigrants from Morocco, kibbutz members and North Americans from Los Angeles) explores the culturally generated ambiguities of *Dallas*.

One of the many cultural differences in the way the varied groups talked about the program concerned the cultural location attributed to the world of *Dallas*. The non-Americans saw it as a story about the U.S.A., generating a stream of specific cultural references that were less likely to occur to the North Americans. The non-Americans were, consequently, more willing to interpret the program as realistic, while the North Americans were far more playful in their interpretations. Ien Ang's study of Dutch attitudes to the program (Ang, 1985) suggests that viewers in the Netherlands are closer to the North American readings than the ethnic groups in the Katz and Liebes study. From their cultural position, it would appear, the world of *Dallas* seems less culturally specific and closer to home. This allows them to develop the playful responses that Ang describes in her book.

This point is developed by Hodge and Tripp (1986) in a slightly different way. They discovered that Australian Aboriginal children were able to identify with particular representations of black Americans on television. In an interpretation ridden with historical irony, black Americans were "transformed" by these children into Australian Aboriginals. They were, in so doing, able to transcribe their own disadvantaged ethnic minority position onto the black characters in U.S. TV shows, and interpret them accordingly.

If the ambiguities revealed by these cross-cultural studies are not especially surprising, we should not forget their semiological implication. Ambiguity is not simply "added onto" a straightforward message by people from different cultures; it was there already—like the secrets of the universe, waiting to be discovered. They demonstrate that the meaning of *Dallas* to a group in Los Angeles is as culturally defined as it is to a group of Israeli Arabs.

The emergence of ambiguity within cultures clarifies this point.

Hodge and Tripp's analysis of the way children "play" with television is illustrative. The popularity among Australian schoolchildren of *Prisoner* (not to be confused with the 1960s British cult series), a soap opera set in a women's prison, had, they discovered, little to do with conventional adult readings of the show. They discovered that children had constructed a whole range of associations between the representation of prison life on the show and their experience of school. Shut in the school and forced to obey a set of rules imposed by authority figures, they were able to identify with the prisoners. The wardens—good and bad—became teachers—good and bad; there were gangs and bullies, secret forms of communication among pupils/prisoners, strategies for breaking rules and other parallels between school and prison life.

The experience of school and the world of *Prisoner* fit together so neatly that, to use a rather whimsical phrase, they might almost have been intended for one another. In other words, if we, as adults, interpret the program from a different cultural perspective, perhaps we are missing something? To realize this is to comprehend the inevitable—our culture confines us—we are *always* missing something. Roland Barthes's concept of the "writerly" or "writable" text, unlimited by the cultural closing down of possible meaning, is, as he reluctantly admits, a purely theoretical object (Barthes, 1974). To develop his analogy, you would neither find such a text in a bookstore nor see it on the TV screen—the act of reading or interpreting can solidify its ambiguity. Audience research allows us to see how ambiguity is frozen by time and place.

Meaning is potentially endless and historically fixed. As students of contemporary culture, we must acknowledge its potential but explain its fixity. What, in our recent history, are the ideological forces that freeze the flow of ambiguity? What cultural glue that binds so many of us together in clusters of common interpretation?

Some audience researchers have been self-conscious in their confrontation with ambiguity. Peter Dahlgren has, for example, analyzed his (and other researchers') own readings of TV news using what he calls the "discrepancy method" (Dahlgren, 1985). The researchers watch the program in two ways—first as they would as normal citizens, and subsequently with the critical distance, time and space that textual analysis allows. This self-psychoanalytic procedure allows us to glimpse at our own role, as viewers and researchers, in the construction of meaning.

Janice Radway's analysis of the way women read popular romances (Radway, 1984 and 1986) is also deliberately self-conscious. Her awareness of the ideological origins of her own reading of these texts allows her to evaluate the interpretations of her audience with a similar level of scrutiny. The discrepancy between the two readings becomes, for her, a political question: what is the ideological source of these readings, and what, in contemporary society, is their effect?

The existence of ambiguity has often been used to argue that the power of television in our society is weak and intangible. This is to misunderstand the enormity of the gap between the potential and actual meaning of cultural forms. If ambiguity is interesting in its presence, it is even more revealing in its absence. When the complex semiological encounter between television and its audience produces a narrow rather than an infinite range of meanings, when ambiguity is limited by history, then television has power.

ENCODING AND DECODING: POWER AND DETERMINATION

It is, in the wake of semiology and cultural studies, difficult to conceptualize the delicate encounter between television and television viewers. We now know that the power to produce meanings lies neither within the TV message nor within the viewer, but in the active engagement between the two. This is a complex idea. It is much easier to conceive the relationship as controlled by one or the other—particularly if we are trying to evaluate the political or ideological influence of television.

The most influential description of this encounter has been the "encoding/decoding" model, developed by Stuart Hall (1980a) and David Morley (1980). The model saw the production (encoding) and consumption (decoding) of television as two distinct semiological processes. Television programs were no longer seen as reflections or distortions of reality, but as a set of highly coded *significations*, the product of specific aesthetic, political, technical and professional ideologies. The program, once produced, was a powerful but ambiguous structure of signs. The producers of the program could use their semiological skill to encourage the viewer to "prefer" certain meanings, but, since decoding is an active process, this "preferring" was a bid for power rather than a guarantee of it. In *The Nationwide Audience*, Morley defined the TV message as:

> a complex sign, in which a preferred meaning has been inscribed, but which retains the potential, if decoded in a manner different from the way it has been encoded, of communicating a different meaning. The message is thus a structured polysemy. It is central to the argument that all meanings do not exist

58

"equally" in the message: it has been structured in dominance, although its meaning can never be totally fixed or "closed." (Morley, 1980, p. 10)

Viewers, or decoders, though active, are not free to interpret this "structured polysemy" as they choose. They are limited both by the message and by their own ideological world.

Members of the academic world are, in some respects (and *only* in some respects!) dedicated followers of fashion. The haphazard use of new ideas tends to be more de rigueur than the rigorous use of older ones. To use a rather grotesque phrase, this has meant that too many interesting babies have been victims of premature dismissal, flushed out on a tidal wave of bathwater. The encoding/decoding model, developed in the 1970s, is, even after this short space of time, no longer as fashionable as it was. We should not, however, underestimate its significance.

Morley's first attempt to apply the encoding/decoding model, published in *The Nationwide Audience* in 1980, was an extremely important event in the history of media research. The study involved a series of in-depth interviews with a variety of different groups, following the viewing of the then popular British news/current affairs program *Nationwide*. For many, this empirical use of a sophisticated model of TV viewing revitalized interest in empirical questions about the audience. Not only did it move beyond the limitations of the "effects" and "uses and gratifications" traditions; it positioned the audience within what Kim Schroder has called the "socio-semiotic" world (Schroder, 1988). Audiences did not simply come to the TV set with a history, they were part of history, shaped by social, economic and cultural forces.

Like any piece of innovative work, *The Nationwide Audience* was not without its problems, many of which Morley has addressed in subsequent work (Morley, 1980 and 1986). It has been criticized for its tendency to neglect other hegemonic structures, like patriarchy, in its focus upon class structure (see Allor, 1988). In so doing, it also over-simplified the relationship between someone's class position and the meaning he or she gave to the TV program. Morley addresses this point in *Family Television*:

There is a tendency in the *Nationwide* book to think of deep structures (for instance, class positions) as generating direct effects of the level of cultural practice. That is a tendency I would want to qualify more now, to examine in detail the different ways in which a given "deep structure" works itself out in particular contexts, and to try and reinstate the notion of persons actively engaged in cultural practice. (Morley, 1986, p. 43)

We cannot, in other words, press a sociological button marked CLASS and expect a pre-packaged ideological view of the world to pop out. That does not mean that class structure plays no part in people's conception of their environment. We need, as Morley suggests, "to formulate a position from which we can see the person actively producing meanings from the restricted range of cultural resources which his or her structural position has allowed them access to" (*ibid.*, p. 43).

This is a significant point. While critiques of certain forms of Marxist theory have shown the dangers of a crude theory of social determination, to abandon the concept altogether would diminish our capacity to explain why the world works as it does. We do not arrive at an ideological position through self-will or coincidence. The chain of causes and effects that operates the vast social machinery in which we live may be intricate and sophisticated rather than crude, but it is no less effective for that. It is only by understanding these mechanisms that we can see how power is structured and distributed throughout our social and economic system.

The work of Pierre Bourdieu is illustrative here. Bourdieu has reconceptualized the relation between social structure in general and cultural expressions in particular, introducing the idea of "cultural competence" (Bourdieu, 1980). He has traced ways in which people's economic and social position, through the educational system, gives them access to certain knowledges and discourses about the world. This creates hierarchies of "cultural competence." Someone from a wealthy background, for example, will often acquire the cultural competence necessary to understand high art forms, like opera or abstract painting. Someone from a working-class background, on the other hand, is likely to acquire a very different set of cultural competencies, thereby excluding him or her from the world of high culture. It is, in other words, not only the cost of the seat that keeps working-class people away from a classical music concert.

To use a rather different example, the last few decades in most Western countries have seen the development of a news media that discusses politics in terms of vague associations rather than the historical processes rooted in people's experience. So, for example, in the U.S., the association between totalitarianism and communism or socialism has created the association "democracy equals capitalism." This misleading platitude provided the theoretical framework for much of the media coverage of events in Eastern Europe in 1989 and 1990. Apart from negating the history of social democracy in Europe, it is an association that has little to do with the history of democracy as experienced by nations and citizens.

Tempting as it is to dwell on this example, it will suffice to say that the reduction of the political world to a series of abstract associations shapes the cultural competence of those who rely on the news media for information. This makes other forms of political discourse seem unintelligible or irrelevant. So, when political candidates address the public in terms of broad associations rather than historical exigencies, it works. The attempt by candidates like Reagan or Bush to associate themselves with vague notions like "patriotism" or "prosperity" is successful because people have acquired the cultural competence to accept this form of political discourse. Harping on about social causality or the relation between capitalism and social problems will, in this political culture, get you nowhere.

We can, moreover, trace the shape and form of the news media back to the specific ideological (see, for example, Cohen and Young, 1973) and economic (see, for example, Herman and Chomsky, 1988) conditions that produced it. We have, in other words, a whole string of determinations that, at appropriate moments, make sense of the encoding/decoding model, placing it within a whole range of power relations.

This example demonstrates that, when analyzing the power of television, we cannot simply allocate power to the message or to the audience as if we were sharing out jelly beans. Television's power lies in the specificities of its encounter with the audience. One cannot exist without the other. While this idea has been implicit throughout this book's argument, it is often difficult to grasp empirically. The section that follows will attempt to lay a path through the confusions that arise when we consider how such an idea works in practice.

PREFERRING MEANINGS

The power of television is necessarily deferred until the moment of decoding. Like any object in the semiological universe, it makes no sense until someone looks at or listens to it. This is an uncontroversial proposition: to deny it, after all, is to deny the founding principle of semiology. It is, however, a complex idea to fully grasp.

The source of this complexity is the contradiction it *appears*, at first glance, to embrace. I am arguing, on the one hand, that television is a powerful ideological instrument, with the power to influence the way we think about the world. I am also saying that this power cannot be realized without the viewer to make sense of it. The message is meaningless without the audience. Does this mean, as it seems on the surface, that I am no better than a disingenuous politician, giving power with one hand and taking it away with the other?

Behind this question (and the appearance of the contradiction) lies our ability to distinguish between the object (the TV message) and its meaning (the TV message plus its audience). The TV program, after all, *exists* whether we watch it or not. Because we are able to make the analytical distinction between message and audience, it is easy to assume that we should be able to allocate power between them. The problem with this assumption is that meaning is the combination of two *dependent* terms: we can separate them analytically but not physically. Take away either object (message) or subject (audience) and there is existence but no meaning.

If we want to drill a hole, we need a drill and a surface to drill into. The drill's power is dependent upon the surface it penetrates: without the surface, its power is meaningless. Although we can still talk about the drill and speculate fairly accurately the likely outcome upon different surfaces when it meets them, its power is still contingent upon its relationship with those surfaces. The relationship between TV and its audience is similarly dependent but, needless to say, far less predictable.

The situation is complicated further by the fact that TV researchers are, regardless of the skill or knowledge they might possess, still an audience. To pretend otherwise is to claim godlike omnipotence. This raises the question of how the "preferred meaning" is inscribed within the encoding/decoding model.

In order to maintain the delicate relationship between the message and its audience, the encoding/decoding model sees the structure of the message as infused with potential rather than actual power. Most versions or developments of the model therefore come equipped with devices to grant the audience the power to submit to or resist the meanings thrust at them through the screen. The audience will either endorse the preferred meaning, oppose it, or produce a response that negotiates between acceptance and rejection.

As a system for evaluating the ideological power of messages, this is a useful conception. However, it contains within it a major problem: as Morley succinctly puts it, "Is the preferred reading a property of the text, the analyst or the audience?" (Morley, 1981, p. 6) I have, in the past, argued that, since meaning is contingent upon the audience, the answer must be the latter (Lewis, 1983). This is, in retrospect, a little misleading. What the question requires us to address is how and when the preferred meaning is constituted.

Television is not produced in an ideological vacuum. The producers of programs or commercials share a whole range of ideological and aesthetic assumptions with the people who watch them. Some of these assumptions have been created by television for television. Television, through forms like the commercial and the pop video, has, for example, developed an audience with the cultural competence to watch a succession of moving images, each lasting little more than one second. Even when the connections between these images are unstated, the culturally competent audience will often have little difficulty in understanding what is going on. Many commercials we now accept as normal would, nevertheless, have been unintelligible to us thirty years ago. Television has, in this sense, taught its audience a new set of aesthetic rules, a visual grammar shared by producers and consumers.

There are, in a similar but more general sense, vast areas of homogeneity within a culture about the form and content of meaning. The home, the school and the mass media are cultural apparatuses that generate a whole world of common associations, associations that become inscribed within our social environment. So, in this culture, pigs are there to be eaten, cats to be petted and spiders to be avoided. None of these meanings are inevitable: there is no reason why pigs shouldn't be sacred, cats eaten and spiders kept as pets. If such a cultural redefinition seems unimaginable or profane, it merely demonstrates how powerfully common associations become fixed in our minds.

These common meanings may be extremely delicate, even if they are often difficult to shift. In many cases, a fairly subtle change in the association can, within a culture, look quite ridiculous. Imagine, for example, seeing a picture of a slim woman in a bikini draped over the bonnet of a new car. We have, within this culture, learnt to accept the association of these images as normal. We turn the page of the magazine without batting an eyelid, yet we only need to tinker with the image to make it look strange and incomprehensible. Add a small moustache to the woman's face, and it looks ridiculous. Change the car into a rusty old banger, and it looks ridiculous. Make the woman fat, and it looks ridiculous. Even if we accept the culturally agreed definitions of what makes people and cars look sexy and attractive, we only need to substitute an attractive woman in a bathing suit with an attractive man in a bathing suit, and, once again, it looks ridiculous.

This playful approach to the associations that become the common currency of cultural communication can tell us a great deal about the assumptions we were able to make within a culture. The woman on the car illustrates that as semiologically precarious as these assumptions may be, we are trained to accept and reject a very particular order of things. The interesting question then becomes: what is it about our society that makes one association look acceptable and another silly? What conditions do these associations depend upon?

The answer is both qualitative and quantitative: they rely upon a precise series of ideological presuppositions (about, in this instance, sexuality, gender and power) and upon their shared acceptance. This is the basis for investigating the "preferred meaning" of the televisual message.

The "preferred meaning" is the exercise of power within a set of shared cultural assumptions. The TV message, produced and transmitted within these semiological confines, is able to guide the viewer's consciousness along carefully defined paths of meaning. We cannot find the "preferred meaning" by studying the message alone. We need to study the message in terms of the shared assumptions it articulates and manipulates.

This, of course, makes the task of the researcher much more difficult. The "preferred meaning" of a message is not simply the product of prolonged scrutiny. What differentiates analysts from any other TV viewers is not their cleverness or critical distance, but their ability to use the evidence available to demonstrate the quality and quantity of shared associations in a message. Sometimes this evidence can be fairly straightforward. A superficial study of advertising and patriarchy could tell us that the woman on the bonnet of the car is an image based upon ideological presuppositions that resonate throughout our culture, and one that is, in advertising terms, fairly successful.

Having established its cultural power, we could proceed to examine the commercial in terms of an endorsement of the preferred meaning, a negotiation with it (you might, for example, broadly accept its ideological presuppositions, but find it, nonetheless, a stereotypical and uninteresting ad), or a rejection of the preferred meaning (dismissing the ad as sexist).

The preferred meaning model, with its three categories of response (preferred, negotiated and oppositional) works in this instance, for two specific reasons. There is, first of all, evidence to substantiate it. It is, second, at this moment in our culture's history, a fairly straightforward and unambiguous image. Most people, whether they accept or reject it, will be culturally competent enough to understand the symbolic nature of the association between the car and the woman.

The preferred meaning model is, therefore, appropriate to specific messages and at a specific stage in the analysis. Once a culture allows a message a greater degree of ambiguity, it can no longer be reduced to a single plane of meaning. Even the image of the woman on the car is not as ideologically simple as it first appears. Suppose, for example, someone objects to it strongly on the grounds that it is a salacious and improper way for a young woman to behave. This rejection may come from an ideological position that is fiercely traditional in its support for patriarchy. To lump this response with those who would dismiss it as sexist would be extremely misleading. Both are discrete readings of the advertisement based on radically different ideological perspectives. The pragmatic anti-pornography alliance between feminists and members of the right-wing Moral Majority is untenable in the same way. It is simplistic to say that both groups are objecting to the same thing for different reasons. Both groups are, in fact, objecting to something quite different.

The three responses are, therefore, useful at a *secondary* stage in the analysis, after the commonality of the preferred meaning has been established. This point is made by Celeste Condit in a discussion of audience responses to an episode of *Cagney and Lacey* (Condit, 1989). Using an episode that dealt with the issue of abortion, she focuses on two particular interpretations—one from a woman in favor of legal abortion ("Jill") and one from a man against it ("Jack"). While their readings of the program, are, fairly predictably, very different, they both agree about the program's preferred meaning. Their plot summaries are very similar, and they both see the program as sympathetic to the maintenance of abortion rights (Jill's position). The differences between their readings come at a secondary level: Jill agrees with the program's message while Jack rejects it.

The preferred meaning/three response model is, for Condit's audience, an appropriate way to proceed: Condit is able to investigate the nature of Jill's preferred reading and Jack's oppositional reading. This is, nevertheless, only possible because at a more primary level, they interpret the program in the *same* way. If Jack and Jill had both endorsed the program as supportive of their different positions, it becomes much more difficult to use the concepts of "preferred" and "oppositional" readings. They would simply be preferring different meanings.

There has been a tendency in recent audience research to stretch the analytical limits of the preferred meaning/three response model by lumping together any readings that do not in some way endorse or negotiate with the preferred meaning in the same category. So, for example, what Umberto Eco calls an "aberrant" decoding (Eco, 1972), where the viewer understands the program in a different way from that intended (my analysis of news watching in Chapter 6 is full of such "aberrant" readings) is seen as merely another oppositional reading (see, for example, Sigman and Fry, 1985, p. 311). So, for example, someone (who, for the sake of alliteration, I shall call "Jo") who interpreted this episode of *Cagney and Lacey* with scarcely a reference to the abortion issue, concentrating instead on what the program says about the dangers of political extremism, would be put in the same oppositional category as Jack. This is profoundly misleading. Jo's reading cannot be evaluated on the same scale as Jack and Jill's—it is based upon a set of semiotic constructions that are qualitatively different.

The existence of the preferred meaning is dependent upon the suppression of ambiguity. To give something a preferred meaning is to fit into an agreed range of semiological responses, as Jack and Jill do. The differences between Jack and Jill have little to do with the program's ambiguity. They not only agree that the program is "about" abortion, but agree on the ideological position it takes on that issue. Their different responses are not struggles over the substantive meaning of the program's narrative or symbolic structure— a struggle that *would* have occurred if Jack had interpreted the program as anti-abortion. Indeed, as Condit points out, Jack is forced to draw upon other discourses, outside the program, to support his oppositional reading.

The problem with the preferred meaning/three response model is that it is only appropriate in these circumstances. We cannot, moreover, assume the existence of a preferred meaning without evidence. How far and in what circumstances our culture is able to display the homogeneity of response required for the recognition of preferred meanings has yet to be established. It is a question that will be taken up and explored in the second part of this book.

THE POLITICS OF VIEWING

I have, so far, argued that television programs are, potentially, a source of considerable ideological power. I have also suggested that a study of the television audience addresses questions—in a way that textual analysis often does not—about the political and ideological role of television in contemporary culture. If, for example, as Herman and Chomsky or the Glasgow Media Group have suggested, television is promoting particular political or ideological views of the world, how effectively is that message being communicated? This is, as I suggested in the opening chapter, neither a new question nor a particularly easy one to answer. We are, nonetheless, in a better position to answer it now than ever before.

One of the more recent debates within audience research concerns precisely this issue. The cultural studies tradition, so influential to recent developments in the discipline, placed the study of television firmly within an analysis of contemporary ideological and economic power structures. Once we examine the exercise and distribution of power, we need to ask some basic questions. Who possesses it and who does not? Who benefits and who loses? How is power used? How do those who have it hang on to it, and how does television fit into this scheme of things?

These are political questions and they inevitably lead us into some controversial areas. What is less controversial is the idea that we live in a society in which the distribution of power and resources are, to say the least, unequal. We are able to speak of dominant and subordinate groups and ideas. We will go on to see how, in the complex struggle between dominant and subordinate groups and ideas (complex because they can both coalesce and cut across one another), television, as one of the most important ideological mechanisms in our society, plays a significant part.

The nature of television's role in this maelstrom of competing interests is the subject of considerable debate. Television, it has been argued, is a mechanism used by the dominant groups in our society (such as the wealthy, men or white people) to promote ideologies and meanings that sustain their hegemony. Whether this point has been made with crudity or great finesse, it has certainly been made many times, and the evidence to support some form of this argument is extensive. It would be very surprising, indeed, if this were not the case. This argument has, nonetheless, two principal shortcomings. The first is that there is also evidence to demonstrate that television does not *always* work this way. Programs that question capitalism, or patriarchy, or other features of the status quo, may not appear as often as programs that do not question these things, but they crop up just the same. There are also a great many things that we see on TV that bear, at most, only an ambiguous relation to dominant ideologies. To cast, for example, *The Cosby Show* or *Roseanne* in this mold would be to miss a great deal. There is, at the very least, enough political ambiguity in these shows for us to argue about their political meaning.

The second shortcoming concerns the audience. We may accept that the content of television appears to support some views over others, but we need evidence before we can guarantee that these meanings are transmitted unscathed. We cannot, in other words, assume the existence of a firmly inscribed preferred reading. Programs, even in our relatively homogeneous symbolic world, may well contain other, quite different, readings.

This second point has led to the development of a theory of "popular" or "resistive" readings. This is not the same as an oppositional reading, since it works *with* the message, not in opposition to it. In her research on women and popular romantic fiction, Janice Radway found that books that appeared to promote patriarchy were read by women in ways that, albeit subtly, did not endorse this dominant ideology (Radway, 1984). This allowed her to appreciate the ambiguities in the texts, ambiguities that created the space for a reading that resisted the dominant ideology. She has, consequently, been able to argue that

> if mass culture does indeed allow for differential interpretation and use, if particular groups can adapt messages for their own purposes, it is conceivable that the ideological control achieved by any particular mass culture form may not be complete. (Radway, 1986, p. 97)

John Fiske has developed a similar line of argument, suggesting that the ambiguities that inevitably permeate popular culture create what he calls a "semiotic democracy" (Fiske, 1987). He cites a number of varied instances of groups using popular culture for their own subcultural interests, and concludes that television

> is the plurality of its reading practices, the democracy of its pleasures and it can only be understood in its fragments. It promotes and provokes a network of resistances to its own power whose attempt to homogenize and hegemonize breaks down on the instability and multiplicity of its meanings and pleasures. (Fiske, 1987, p. 324)

This idea is developed in an audience study of *The Newlywed Game*, a popular game show in which partners have to guess how their spouses responded to a question. In the show Fiske uses, four men are asked whether their wives' response to their "romantic needs" were best summarized by the phrases: "Yes, master"; "Get serious, man" or "No way, Jose!" While all four men, rather predictably, responded with the first answer, only two of the women obliged them by agreeing. One, to the considerable embarrassment of her husband, gave the third response, referring to his recent "operation."

Now, this is not the sort of TV material that is going to win any feminist awards. It is, on one level, a nakedly patriarchal discourse, yet Fiske's audience suggest that the pleasure generated by moments like these are much more subversive. The show's pleasure comes not during those moments when spouses agree, but when they don't. In this instance, the pleasure comes from seeing the moment when patriarchy is, figuratively speaking, caught with its trousers down. The pleasure, in other words, comes not from seeing patriarchy confirmed, but from seeing it exposed.

We cannot, in the light of this, assume any one preferred reading. What Fiske's audience tells us is that *The Newlywed Game* both endorses and exposes patriarchy. Different audiences will prefer different interpretations. Fiske's audience are *not* recognizing a patriarchal preferred reading and opposing it; they are simply exploiting the message's ambiguity as they see fit. There is, therefore a great deal that distinguishes the "popular" or "resistive" reading from an oppositional one. The oppositional reading *assumes* a preferred reading (which it subsequently questions), while the resistive reading questions the very idea of a preferred reading.

In Condit's example, Jack "recognizes" that the show he is watching is unsympathetic to his own views. He therefore works hard to oppose this preferred reading, drawing upon other discourses to support his case. (This is in line with Morley's *Nationwide* study, in which, for example, a group of shop stewards construct an oppositional reading of *Nationwide* based upon the leftist political discourses involved in their trade union activity.) Condit argues that Jack's interpretive task is much more difficult than Jill's. Jill does not need to go outside the program's narrative—she is able to relax into what she sees is the show's ideological flow. The preferred reading is, therefore, a more pleasurable viewing experience than the oppositional reading.

This might appear (as Condit, in fact, claims) to be in contention with Fiske's suggestion that "resistive" interpretations of messages are, in fact a source of pleasure to the viewer, a celebration of the audience's power to exploit the message's ambiguity for their own interests. Once we appreciate the difference between the popular/resistive and the oppositional reading, however, we can see that the contradiction vanishes. The popular/resistive reading may be in opposition to a dominant ideology (hence "resistive"), but it works *in league* with the TV text, not against it. There is no need (as there is with an oppositional reading) to self-consciously draw upon other discourses—the material for the resistive/popular reading is already there in the program. Part of the problem here is a semantic one— the terms *resistive* and *oppositional* are so close that they appear to embrace the same idea. They have, nonetheless, developed particular and discrete meanings in audience studies, and we need to appreciate the difference in the viewing practices they refer to.

The discovery and celebration of these popular, resistive or subversive readings is important for audience studies, but we should not let them go to our heads. Morley's *Nationwide* project (1980) or Condit's study of *Cagney and Lacey* (1989), paint very different pictures of the politics of viewing. They offer few examples that mirror Fiske's popular readings. We should also note that the space the audience of *The Newlywed Game* are allowed to ridicule patriarchy is a small one. We are allowed to laugh at the collapse of a parody of machismo, but there is no real alternative on offer. The three responses allowed by the program, for example, assume that sex is a male, not a female, pleasure. Resistance can only deny male pleasure, it cannot assert female sexuality.

Ann Gray makes a similar point when commenting on Jane Root's celebratory analysis of *The Price Is Right* (see Root, 1986). She warns us that

> what seems to be happening here, and it is a worrying trend, is that by celebrating on the one hand an active audience for popular forms and on the other those popular forms which the audience "enjoys," we appear to be throwing the whole enterprise of a cultural critique out of the window. (Gray, 1987, p. 28)

In other words, while there are shortcomings with the idea that television unproblematically transmits dominant ideologies, we should not let those shortcomings obscure the accumulated evidence in its favor.

Similarly, while Fiske and Radway are also correct to point out that the ideological experience of TV viewing can be highly contradictory, we should remember that these contradictions can cut both ways. Harold Schlechtweg's study of *Roseanne* gives an interesting instance of this (Schlechtweg, 1989), in relation to an episode that ridiculed the rules imposed by authority figures (and were obeyed for their own sake). A traveling salesman has dropped dead in Roseanne's home, but the policeman who is called to deal with the body refuses to move it until the coroner (who is playing golf, and therefore unavailable) certifies what everyone knows already—that the dead man is, in fact, dead. While Schlechtweg's viewers found the ridiculing of this absurd situation funny and enjoyable, they still argued, when pressed, for the necessity of such rules. So, although they found pleasure in the "subversive" elements of the program, they remained ideologically unmoved by it.

Condit, in response to Fiske and Radway, has argued that these kinds of

> audience studies and the theories they are generating offer a useful counterbalance to the flat assertion that messages produced by elites necessarily dominate social meaning-making processes. Nonetheless, the scope and character of audience power have not yet been delimited . . . It is clear that there are substantial limits to the polysemic potential of texts and decodings. (Condit, 1989, p. 105)

Exactly what those limits are, and how they suppress the kinds of ambiguity that Fiske and Radway reveal, is one of the focal points of Part 2 of this book.

We are also, I have argued, becoming theoretically well-equipped to answer a whole range of more specific and detailed questions about the politics of TV viewing. While audience studies have not exactly flourished in the last decade or so, those that have been published (the material that has fed this chapter) have covered a great deal of theoretical ground. There is still, however, much to be discovered.

4

Gathering Evidence

MEANINGS IN THE METHOD

Doing audience research is a messy and slippery business. It is difficult to avoid being speculative rather than precise when delving into the murky world of thought, meaning and desire. No matter how clever or fastidious we are, we have to accept that we receive most of our information second-hand. We cannot, in other words, watch meanings as they are being made or transformed in someone's brain: we are forced to rely on the account people are prepared to give us. There is, as psychoanalysts testify, a gap between what people think and what people tell us about those thoughts.

This gap is an inevitable one. In the signifying chain described by semiology, the concept (or signified) can never be communicated without changing into something more material, like a word (or some other signifier—see Chapter 2). Surgeons may be able to put their hands inside our bodies and pull out a heart or an appendix for all to see, but they cannot reach inside our heads and pluck out an idea.

If we are also interested in what determines why people think what they think, the problem becomes more awkward still. We cannot *see* the connection between people's thoughts and their social history, we can only surmise. The researcher will need to rummage through the tangled and confusing social and semiotic worlds that make up people's environment in the search for clues. Like a jury in a murder trial, since we did not witness the event we are examining, the best we can do is interpret the evidence in an attempt to reconstruct it. A vital part of that evidence will be what people choose to tell us.

We would be ill advised to blunder into this speculative world without a sophisticated set of methodological tools to assist us. Unfortunately, however sophisticated our approach, the methodology we use will further complicate an already muddled picture. People do not normally watch or talk about television in research conditions, so our quest for information is likely to intrude into the private worlds of the people we interview. However delicately we tread, our intrusion will inevitable change those worlds. A private world is unlikely to become public without some alteration. We need, as far as possible, to be able to anticipate how people will behave under such scrutiny.

Before reviewing our methodological options, a useful maxim to adopt is that we should be rigorous without being dogmatic. It is hard to think of a methodology that, however crude or flawed it may be, will not tell us something useful. Methodologies, like any other set of tools, are not intrinsically good or bad. Our job is to understand what those tools can and cannot do, to know the potential and the limits of the method we choose.

A great deal will stand or fall on the devices we use to gather evidence. As I pointed out in Chapter 1, the main problem with many earlier attempts to investigate the influence of television was a lack of methodological sophistication. The process of meaning construction was treated as if the relation between stimulus and response was straightforward, rather than diffuse and overdetermined. In short, you do not use a nutcracker to crack a safe.

It is difficult to explore the ambiguities and enigmas of television viewing without talking to people in some depth. I shall, for this reason, focus upon the more qualitative research methodologies. It is no coincidence that nearly all the innovative work I have discussed thus far (with the exception of cultivation analysis) is based upon a qualitative rather than a quantitative approach. I do not want, nonetheless, to dismiss quantitative approaches too summarily—there is much to be learnt from considering both the scope and the constraints of larger attitude surveys.

One final cautionary note: the terms *quantitative* and *qualitative* are, at times, rather vague. In TV audience research, "quantitative" suggests using large samples to generate general and broadly defined data, while the term "qualitative" implies dealing with smaller samples in much more detail. There is, of course, a substantial grey area in between these two categories. The two terms are therefore descriptive rather than mutually exclusive.

CRUNCHING NUMBERS

There are two contrary schools of thought on the use of quantitative surveys. There are those for whom samples are only meaningful if they are made up of hundreds, or even thousands, of respondents. This is understandable in some circumstances—the statistical accuracy of a survey, as a representation of a more general population, may depend upon the size of the sample. The preference for quantity rather than quality is sometimes based on the rather more amorphous idea that the bigger the sample, the more "scientific" or "objective" the survey. Consequently, the qualitative survey, because it is based upon too small a sample to be "representative," is seen as of little value. Suffice to say that if the quality of information is suspect, the merits of a large sample are fairly dubious.

There are those, on the other hand, who tend to dismiss quantitative surveys as too superficial and clumsy a mechanism to reveal anything of substance about a complex practice like television viewing. Without wishing to sound like a self-consciously "balanced" editorial writer, I would suggest that this view, despite its merits, can be as intransigent as the "number crunchers" it opposes. It is also slightly disingenuous—there are few researchers who can resist using a quantitative survey that supports the case they are making. The question we should ask when evaluating any research method is: what can it tell us?

The potential of quantitative surveys

The standard qualitative survey will involve interviewing a sample large enough to be an approximate statistical representation of the population or sub-group within that population. The data will usually take the form of responses to a questionnaire: responses that are, in most cases, among a predefined list of options. The temptation to ask open questions—allowing the respondents to answer as they please—will be tempered by the technical difficulties involved in post-coding (rather than pre-coding) responses. Post-coding a questionnaire means reading all the responses and then organizing them into appropriate groups. It is a cumbersome and time-consuming procedure that is usually avoided by the use of a pilot study to anticipate likely categories of response.

In any social science, numbers are important. As complex as the practice of TV viewing is, we are still able to gather a great deal of information about it from responses to fairly simple questions. In the study of television, the numbers of people who choose to watch a program is significant. As crass as it sounds, the fact that people in our culture are more likely to watch a sitcom than a political documentary suggests, on one basic level, that the sitcom is a more significant cultural phenomenon.

If we are interested in contemporary culture, we have to acknowledge our interest in numbers. While we cannot reduce notions like "popular" or "dominant ideology" to a precise numerical formula, we cannot disregard the proportion of people involved. We can redefine the concept of a dominant ideology to suit our purposes, but we would be foolish to ignore the fact that, at some point, it contains assumptions about the number of people subject to its influence. Christians and Cary make this point well:

> Counting, even the more elaborate forms of counting, are among the extraordinary and indispensable tools invented by humans. No one can survive very long in scholarly research without such tools, and simple arguments about quantifying versus non-quantifying distort and obscure real intellectual problems ... The simple point here is that qualitative studies do not rule out arithmatic. (Christians and Cary, 1989)

Since qualitative data does not always lend itself to simple arithmetic, the need for qualitative studies to adopt a level of quantitative responsibility raises a number of difficult methodological questions, problems I shall address more directly in the following chapter.

In the meantime, it is worth acknowledging that the strength of quantitative surveys lies in the precision of the questions being asked, and upon our ability to interpret the meaning of the replies. This means understanding, among other things, people's levels of self-awareness. Suppose, for example, we want to investigate the existence and influence of political bias in the media: we should not begin and end our investigations by asking people their views on the matter. The very consciousness of political bias may well be an important factor in determining how influential it is.

If, on the other hand, content and textual analysis was able to locate a certain newspaper as the source of a particular perception of a political party, we might usefully compare the attitudes of readers and non-readers toward that party. Once we have eliminated other explanatory variables, we will have some evidence that suggests the possibility of a causal relationship between media use and political attitude. At this point, the question of whether people perceive the political bias of that newspaper becomes relevant. We are able to ask a question like: does awareness of bias help negate the effect of that bias?

There are, in fact, a great many things that the careful use of quantitative surveys may discover. There are also things that we can only discover with a large, statistically representative sample. Cultivation analyses of media use and attitude have been particularly revealing, demonstrating that television viewing "cultivates" particular attitudes about the world (see Chapter 1).

As useful as the quantitative survey can be, there are many things that it cannot tell us. The image of the quantitative method has not been improved by the failure of some media studies researchers (as in the "effects" studies, outlined in Chapter 1) to fully appreciate its limits. It is useful, at this stage, to briefly consider these constraints.

The limits of quantitative surveys

We can, from an audience research perspective, identify a number of shortcomings with the quantitative survey method. My concern here is not with the technical or statistical problems of "accuracy," but with some of the assumptions underlying the whole process. The limitations of quantitative surveys are particularly evident when they step out of easily quantifiable areas (like program ratings) and stray into the realm of attitudes and opinions. These problems are also, in some cases, pertinent to the qualitative method—we should be wary of assuming that we can solve them simply by interviewing fewer people in more detail.

a) The interview is a delicate model of information exchange. It can be affected by a range of different circumstances: where it takes place, how the questions are asked, who asks those questions, the mood the respondent is in, the relationship struck between interviewer and respondent, and so on. The respondents' answers might depend upon the fact they're in a hurry to get home, or that they had a bad day, or their desire to impress an interviewer of the opposite sex, or their reluctance to impart information to someone who they feel is intrusive. Even if it were possible to control these variables by reproducing a uniform set of conditions (a practical impossibility), you cannot predict that variations in response will occur uniformly. Men may, for example, have a greater propensity to tell lies to female than to male interviewers, while the sex of the interviewer might have no effect on the women who are interviewed.

While this is a problem for both qualitative and quantitative methods, the uniformity of interviewing conditions tends to be taken for granted in the quantitative survey. To scrutinize each interview in a survey of a thousand people is, in most cases, simply impractical. We have no choice but to treat each interview uniformly, and thereby rule out the possibility that individual answers might have been different in different circumstances. There is, as we shall see, greater scope for the examination of the interpersonal dynamics of the interview in the qualitative approach.

b) In the large survey the conversation between interviewer and subject will, for a number of reasons, be tightly controlled. Regardless of the conversation respondents would like to have, they are forced to follow the remorseless linear logic of the pre-designed questionnaire. The questionnaire will determine the agenda for what is discussed and how it is discussed. Our answers will then be squeezed into the appropriate box so that they can be counted and evaluated. We have no way of telling if the respondents are comfortable with the way of thinking that has been imposed upon them. It is possible, for example, that the agenda thrust upon them has little relevance to their views on a subject.

Although a good pilot study can go some way toward addressing this problem, the quantitative survey still pushes us toward the production of a general framework of response. Unless we have the resources to carry out extremely long and cumbersome interviews, this framework will inevitably suppress nuances and ambiguities.

If they fall within the same category, the responses that people give are assumed to be equivalent. Once the response has been given, there is usually little time or space in the questionnaire for further clarification. There are, for example, countless reasons for liking or disliking a TV program. The fact that 72 percent of people express a preference either way is, therefore, still fairly speculative. It is, moreover, extremely difficult to reach the diversity of meanings behind this response with a uniform pre-designed questionnaire. We cannot anticipate any single direction our questions should follow.

This problem highlights the complexities of language and meaning. The ambiguities of language mean that it is difficult to explore the precise meaning of words or sentences without giving the respondent the opportunity to elaborate. Responses to a question may subsequently raise more questions than they answer.

c) Many other problems spring from this point. Research on recall of TV news generally shows that people remember very little of what they see. This has led some researchers to argue, in the face of such apparent indifference, that TV news can have little influence on people. Morley, commenting on research by Nordenstreng (1972) in Finland, argues that "while an audience may retain little, in terms of specific information, they may well retain general 'definitions of the order of things,' ideological categories embedded in the structure of the specific content" (Morley, 1980, p. 8).

This pushes us toward a consideration of the semiotic interplay between the TV message and the viewer—something that the generalities of the quantitative survey are poorly equipped to investigate.

d) The way a question is asked, or the context in which it is asked, can be a powerful influence upon the respondent. As Trenaman points out, the "apparent objectivity of such questions is no more than an appearance, subjective judgments enter into the framing of questions" (Trenaman, 1967, p. 24). This is, by now, fairly common knowledge. It allows different political or interest groups to manufacture public opinion polls almost at will. Those in favor of maintaining the right to a legal abortion, for example, may put the question: Who should have the right to choose whether an abortion is the right decision for an individual—politicians or the woman concerned? The respondent, in a culture that emphasizes individual freedom and distrust of politicians, will naturally favor the woman's right to choose. Those who wish to restrict or end the right to a legal abortion may, on the other hand, ask: Do you favor abortion on demand regardless of the circumstances? The respondent, not wishing to appear strident or mindless of "the circumstances," will be inclined to answer no. Both groups will then be able to show that, say, 65 percent of people support their case.

One of the many absurdities of the "democratic" system in the United States is the widespread use of such questions, at state level, to determine state policy. Apart from their tendency to spawn esoteric bumper stickers, like "Question 2 is Bad For You" (seen around Massachusetts in 1988), it elevates the problem of question writing to a new level. The subtleties of language are inscribed with a frightening power: political decisions become a matter of phrasing.

Many market research professionals will, accordingly, pride themselves on their ability to formulate "impartial" questions. This is, in one sense, to miss the point. There is no such thing as a neutral question. The quality and quantity of information we give in a question will inevitably affect the answer we receive. So, for example, people will usually support the idea of cutting taxes, but are less likely to support the financial consequences in public spending cuts. To leave information out of a question about tax cuts (the consequences of those cuts) is as manipulative as leaving it in. The problem with large surveys is that the respondent is unable to arrive at an attitude in anything like a normal setting. The qualitative survey, on the other hand, allows respondents to reach positions through a dialogue that they partly control.

The use of a more qualitative approach may not automatically solve these problems, but it does, at least, force us to consider them in more detail.

THE QUALITATIVE APPROACH

Before reviewing some of the qualitative techniques used to gather evidence about the TV audience, it is worth restating some objectives. My aim, in writing this book, is to explore the meaning and influence of television in contemporary society. Many of the enduring mysteries about television's role in our society, I have argued, spring from a failure to explore the precise semiological relationship between television and the TV viewer. To focus upon the TV viewer means positioning them within two complex fields of determination: television; and their "socio-semiotic" history and environment.

Watching television involves an elaborate interplay of ideologies, activated by the viewer's engagement with the sounds and images on the screen. This is not a simple process, and researchers have been misled when they supposed otherwise. While the use of textural analysis has allowed us to appreciate both the structure and the ambiguity of television, the mechanisms that make it popular or powerful when watched by cultural creatures like ourselves remain elusive. "What," Robert Allen has asked, "is the extent of the determination of meaning exercised by the text itself?" (Allen, 1985, p. 185). What ideological or semiotic conditions do those determinations depend upon?

The methodological difficulties involved in addressing these questions are, to say the least, discouraging. I have already suggested that the processes we are investigating cannot be reproduced—we can only gather evidence that will help us piece them together. Qualitative research methods are, at this stage in our knowledge, a more appropriate means of accumulating such evidence. As Jensen has argued,

> The communication model of a qualitative approach is implicitly dialectic in the sense that the analysis traces the process of establishing the units of meaning, and it does so by studying the interplay between media codes and the audience codes and, in a wider sense, by interpreting the origins of those codes in different sectors of the social context. In sum, meaning is approached as it is being produced. (Jensen, 1987, p. 32)

There are a number of qualitative methodologies that might enable us to do this. All of them will, in some form or another, involve intruding into the viewer's world, and thereby subtly changing the very process we are investigating. Planting hidden cameras in someone's living room, even if we could do it without their noticing, would still give us ambiguous information, as Morley suggests:

> I may be observed to be sitting staring at the TV screen, but this behavior could be equally compatible with a sense of total fascination or total boredom on my part—and the distinction may not be readily accessible from observed behavioral clues. Moreover, should you wish to understand what I am doing it would probably be as well to ask me. I may well, of course, lie to you or otherwise misrepresent my thoughts and feelings, for any number of purposes, but at least you will then begin to get some access to the language, criteria of distinction, and types of categorizations through which I construct my (conscious) world. (Morley, 1988, p. 46)

The conversation, in other words, is our most obvious route into this conscious world. It is also a route that, to a greater or lesser degree, will be guided by the interviewer. While this is unavoidable, we need to be aware of the possible consequences.

There are other ways of gathering qualitative evidence. We can, for instance, ask people to express themselves not in speech, but in writing. This has advantages and disadvantages. People, by themselves, will be uninhibited by social rules, thereby able to follow a logic that is of their own design. We will, on the other hand, tend to favor those people with an educational background that makes them comfortable with the written word, since they will be more likely to participate in our survey. Most people are used to talking rather than writing about television. We are also unable to probe into areas that the writer ignores or glosses over.

Ien Ang's survey of *Dallas* viewers in Holland is based upon letters she solicited from (mostly female) viewers. Her comments about the nature of the data this provides are instructive.:

> It would ... be wrong to regard the letters as a direct and unproblematic reflection of the reasons why the writers love or hate *Dallas*. What people say or write about their experiences, preferences, habits, etc., cannot be taken at face value ... We must search for what is behind the explicitly written, for the presuppositions and accepted attitudes concealed within them. In other words, the letters must be regarded as texts, as discourses people produce. (Ang, 1985, p. 11)

While an interview allows us to explore some of these questions as the discourse evolves, Ang's approach applies equally well to the analysis of a set of interview transcripts.

THE INTERVIEW

For all its limitations and flaws, the interview will usually form the basis for most qualitative studies of the television audience. While it cannot claim to be statistically representative, it is possible to include enough people in an interview based qualitative survey to be suggestive about patterns of determination. We can also tape record (or even video tape) the interview so that it might be examined in some detail afterwards.

The interview is a type of conversation and, like a conversation, it can take many forms. We can be directive or unobtrusive. We can follow a carefully controlled schedule or we can take a more laid-back approach, letting the conversation flow freely where it will. We can conduct the interview in the viewer's own home, in someone else's home or in an institutional setting. We can interview individuals, small groups (like families) or larger groups of around six to ten people. There are no hard and fast rules favoring any of these options, we simply need to choose the most appropriate means for generating the particular information we want. We should, nonetheless, be aware of the consequences involved in our choices.

These options, as those familiar with audience research will know, are not always based upon a sophisticated theoretical rationale. There are a number of technical difficulties involved in selecting a qualitative sample that may determine our approach. Suppose, for example, we decide to base the interview upon the viewing of a particular program. Unless we have an enormous interviewing team, we will need to show the program to people on a VCR. We may find that VCR ownership is skewed toward particular sorts of people, which may make it difficult, if we choose to interview people in their own homes, to recruit the sample we would like. This means choosing to interview outside the domestic setting, or accepting the limits of our sample.

Perhaps the most significant factor influencing the decisions we make is the size of our research budget. For a variety of reasons, most of the recent qualitative studies (carried out outside the television industry) of television viewing have been funded on a shoestring. This means making a number of compromises. The most common of these are:

1. we will not have the interviewing or analytical resources to deal with as large a sample as we would like;

2. we are liable to take shortcuts in recruiting our sample, working through community contacts, institutions and organizations—thereby slanting our sample toward certain types of social network;

3. if we cannot offer the interviewee any financial inducement to take part, and unless we are blessed with uncommon powers of persuasion, we will necessarily recruit a sample that is, in some sense, self-selecting;

4. if we are organizing and carrying out all the interviews on our own, they may well take several weeks or months to complete—a potential problem if the TV program we are using "dates" because of developments that occur during our interviewing timetable.

While few of us would refuse money and resources if so offered, the possibilities opened up by a larger research budget can raise restrictions of its own. The luxury of employing an interviewing team will enable us to do more interviews more quickly, but it will raise questions about variations in interviewing style. This, in turn, will incline us toward more controlled interviews, with a series of guidelines to be followed.

Once we have fought our way through the technicalities of the research process, we need to make a number of methodological decisions about the kind of data we want to collect. These concern how we do the interview, who we do it with and where it takes place.

THE STYLE OF THE INTERVIEW

One of the main advantages of the qualitative interview is the freedom it allows the respondent to set the agenda, and the scope it allows the interviewer to probe into potentially interesting areas. Even if it is based upon a predetermined set of questions, the interview can develop and explore meanings. The dilemma we face is usually one of degree: how "open" or "closed" should the interview be?

The "open," loosely structured interview allows interviewees to move in a direction of their own choosing, and to impose their own definitions and framework of interpretation upon the subject under discussion. It gives interviewers the opportunity to delve fairly deeply into these structures of interpretation, and to establish some of the discourses they seem to draw upon. The more structured, "closed" interview allows interviewers to focus more closely on particular moments of the television message, and affords a clearer basis for comparison between different respondents' interpretations. We cannot, unfortunately, have the best of both worlds. We need to steer a path through this methodological dilemma in a way that retains key elements of both interviewing styles.

One way of achieving this is to move from the general to the specific, beginning with fairly open-ended questions in order to develop an agenda and a framework for discussing more specific aspects of a program. This is the approach adopted by Morley in his *Nationwide* study:

> The initial stages of the interview were non-directive; only in subsequent stages of an interview, having attempted to establish the "frames of reference" and "functioning vocabulary" with which the respondents defined the situation, did I begin to introduce questions about the program material based on earlier analysis of it. (Morley, 1980, p. 33)

Accommodating the viewer's and the interviewer's interests can be a rather precarious balancing act. It requires careful planning and sensitive questioning. Allowing the respondent to set the agenda at an early stage is extremely useful because, as Morley suggests, it allows us to devise an appropriate "way in" to the more specific topics we may want to pursue.

Even if the respondent's frame of reference is too divergent to allow us to do this comfortably, we are able to clearly recognize this fact, and draw conclusions from it. Morley's discussion with a group of young working-class black people in the *Nationwide* study is a case in point: he is able to pinpoint "the lack of a 'unitary sign community' in relation to central signifiers like 'family'. The representation of 'the family' within the discourse of *Nationwide* has no purchase on the representation of that field within the discourse and experience of this group—and is consequently rejected" (ibid., p. 122). His interviewing style, in other words, gave his group the space to formulate the discursive basis for a rejection of the program's whole frame of reference.

Implicit in this approach is Trenaman's proposal that questions should be used, as far as possible, to simulate "a normal conversation" in order "to elicit those elements of comprehended material which the respondent would be inclined to make use of in real life" (Trenaman, 1967, p. 26). The only problem with this idea is that it is slightly contradictory: "normal conversations" do not *usually* involve the use of non-directive questions designed to encourage someone to set the agenda for discussion. This can be particularly awkward at the early stages of an interview, when respondents may be feeling a little unsure of themselves.

This difficulty was encountered in the surveys that will be analyzed in Part 2. Interviews would usually begin with a series of "open" questions, such as "What did you think that was about?" or "What did you make of the first part of the program?" A number of respondents found opening with this rather vague style of questioning unsettling—they were not sure what was required of them. One respondent, when asked about the first item on *News at Ten*, was unusually forthright in voicing this insecurity:

Is that it? Is that the only question I get? It's a bit loose isn't it?

Most interviewees would be a little less bold, and would simply request a more specific question by asking, for example, "in what way?" or "in what respect?" This, in turn, raises the problem of pushing the agenda-setting role back onto the interviewer. The contradiction between this non-directive interviewing style and the desire to generate a normal conversation is hard to resolve. My own solution, in this instance, is to simply ask another "open" question, or to ask interviewees to describe what they saw. While this is not exactly what insecure respondents are asking for, it reassures them that you are not simply being unnecessarily coy, and that they do not need to deliver anything specific. Interviewees, in most cases, will adapt to the rules of this conversation as the interview progresses.

It is often helpful to ask respondents to reconstruct, at an early stage in the interview, the program they have just watched. This is one of the many advantages of basing a discussion on the viewing of a particular program: even if researchers aim to move into more general areas, it provides a useful focal point for initiating discussion. Interviewers are then able, if they choose, to draw upon these accounts in order to develop the discussion in relation to specific moments in the program. As the discussion develops, the interviewers' recall of the program will fill out, as moments they had overlooked gradually become relevant. There will be occasions, nevertheless, when it becomes necessary to prompt the respondent's memory, since, as Trenaman suggests,

> there is some likelihood that in free recall whole sections of programme may fail to be reproduced only because the informant has temporarily overlooked them. Part of the function of questions might, therefore, be to remind the informant of principal areas of a programme without giving too much away. (ibid., p. 25)

The use of prompting raises wider the more general issue. If we are trying to authenticate a person's everyday response to a program, we need to be wary about introducing information into an interview. Even if this information is simply a reminder of what they have already seen, we are adding to the respondents' normal discursive environment. In so doing, we are inevitably playing a manipulative role in the process of meaning construction.

This does not make the introduction of new information into a discussion a cardinal sin: we should simply be aware that we are doing it. This applies, ultimately, to the whole interview, which is a contrivance of our own making. The amount of information we give the interviewee is, in this sense, a qualitative rather than an absolute question. We cannot speak without giving something away. We should, nevertheless, be careful to distinguish between topics that we raise and topics raised by the respondent.

There will be circumstances when the provision of additional information will be a way of developing rather than shaping a discussion. It may be, for example, that we need to introduce a new "way in" to encourage someone to discuss a certain topic. People may feel more comfortable going into a subject through, (what we might call) one "discursive doorway" rather than another. An interesting instance of this is recounted in a survey designed to find out why people were reluctant to take part in local community arts activities (carried out among those social and ethnic groups the community arts wanted to involve, but found it difficult to reach). The interviewers, Sue Mia and Lynne Wardle, found that the best way in to a discussion was by a circuitous route:

> It was a striking feature of the interviews that if we began by asking people what they did in their free time and told them about some of the more "arty" activities that the community arts had to offer, we were frequently met with blank disinterest or puzzlement. It was only when we began to discuss other aspects of their lives, like children, homes, schools etc. and

developed the idea of community arts from those starting points, to illustrate its relevance to them, that they responded positively. (London Strategic Policy Unit, 1987)

In the same way, a respondent who appears to be indifferent toward a subject raised by a television program may simply feel uncomfortable using the framework offered by that program.

Perhaps the most important element of the interviewers' job is their ability to listen carefully to the interviewee. It is important to be able to pick up on statements and to probe and develop their meaning. This will involve encouraging respondents to sketch out some of the discourses that inform their reading of a program, to find out why people are responding in a particular way.

DISCUSSION GROUPS: SIZE AND SETTING

Since the very early years of TV audience studies, researchers have acknowledged that the meaning of a television program is not permanently fixed through the act of watching, but developed through a viewer's social history. Lazarsfeld's concept of "two-step flow" introduced the idea that the meaning of the message was constituted not only in the moment of watching, but again in subsequent discussions (Lazarsfeld et al., 1944). The meaning of something is always subject to clarification, redefinition and change. If we are, as Chaney suggests, to

grasp the potential implications of mass communications for social relationships, it is necessary to discover how the performance of mass communications are mediated in the social groups that constitute an individual's meaningful social environment. (Chaney, 1972, p. 18)

This qualifies any evidence that we may glean from an interview. It is extremely difficult to trace the historical evolvement of meanings in someone's consciousness, along what Straw calls "the networks of communication within and from which people arrive at the decisions required in daily life" (Straw, 1983, p. 4). All we hope to provide in an interview is a snapshot of the decoding process.

This also raises the question of the most appropriate setting for a discussion about a TV viewing program. As Jensen suggests, "we need to study the concrete contexts of decoding and the immediate ways in which the programs are used" (Jensen, 1987, p. 26), in order, as Pollock puts it, "to come as close as possible . . . to those conditions in which actual opinions are formed, held and modified" (Pollock, 1976, p. 229). We should, in other words, try to simulate the "natural conditions" in which television is watched and discussed.

In *Family Television*, Morley suggests that one of the problems with his *Nationwide* study was that interviews took place in groups outside people's normal domestic viewing environment (Morley, 1986, p. 40), a problem that leads him to conduct interviews with family groups in their own homes. Interviewing people in their own homes not only puts the interviewees in a familiar and comfortable setting, it allows the interviewer to observe the kind of discussions about TV that take place there (albeit a little more self-consciously in the interviewer's presence). The inhibiting effects of interviewing in institutional conditions are minimized.

The social setting and numbers involved in a discussion about television will inevitably change the nature of that discussion, and they have accordingly been the subject of some debate (see, for example, Brunt and Jordin, 1986). While I have, in the past, argued in favor of the one-to-one interview (Lewis, 1983), I now feel that this is not a subject that we can be too prescriptive about. We simply need to be aware of the advantages and disadvantages of the approach we adopt. We can identify three main categories of interview size: the one-to-one interview; the small group interview; and the focused group interview. Each has its merits and shortcomings.

a) The one-to-one interview

Before dealing with its practicalities, it is worth addressing the qualms that have been expressed about approaching the individual as a unit for research. Most of us are social animals, and the construction of meaning is usually a social process. We do not make up ideological positions, understandings and beliefs on our own—they are the cultural products that bind societies and social groups. In Werner Herzog's film *The Enigma of Kaspar Hauser*, we are asked to dwell on how we would view the world without social practices to shape our perceptions. As the film reminds us, it is difficult to comprehend such an absence.

Our socially determined condition does not mean we are unable to construct meanings without other people around to help us. Society has shaped our semiotic environment. As well-trained adults, we are quite capable of learning from it on our own. Society's presence, in other words, does not necessitate the presence of other people. We do not need to talk to the author to learn from a book.

If we choose to interview people on their own, we are not necessarily treating them as isolated beings in a social vacuum: we are simply concentrating on the viewer's first reading of the television message. Since the meanings within it can be endlessly mediated through a range of social networks (at home, with friends, at work, at home again . . .), we cannot privilege any particular stage in the meaning process. Nevertheless, since we may watch TV on our own, and even if we watch in company we will only actually discuss a small proportion of what we see, this first reading is an important one. It is, moreover, important to regard this reading as a social, not an individual, product. To paraphrase Roland Barthes, our interpretation, from the moment we utter it, will be a tissue of quotations from innumerable centers of culture.

The one-to-one interview allows us to explore a particular reading in some detail. It also gives us the opportunity to develop and clarify points without pausing to consider the effects of a particular set of group dynamics in the formulation of that reading. We do not, for instance, have to worry that our interviewee is finding it difficult to get a word in edgeways.

What the one-to-one interview does not allow us to do is observe the dialectics of conversations between people. The development of readings and positions through social intercourse, particularly between families or friends, can be extremely illuminating. It allows a level of social engagement that we cannot, as tentative and unfamiliar interviewers, ever hope to achieve one-to-one.

On a rather more mundane note, the one-to-one interview is a time-consuming way of gathering information, both in execution and in subsequent analysis. This will invariably restrict the numbers involved in our sample.

b) The small group interview

Interviewing people in small groups has a number of advantages. We can, first of all, choose a group of people who are comfortable watching and discussing television with one another. This may be a family or it may be groups of friends: either way the conversation should flow naturally and freely. It will also be possible to base the interview in a domestic setting.

Morley adds an important caveat to his work with families, reminding us that despite the clichés of advertising, only a minority of households contain the classic nuclear family of breadwinner husband, housewife and children. We also need to be aware of the importance of peer groups in discussions about TV, a point that Katz and Liebes acknowledge in their work on *Dallas*. Their method of recruitment involved a host couple inviting two other couples from among their friends to take part in the interview/viewing sessions. They subsequently discovered, in post-discussion questionnaires, that the program was already widely viewed and discussed among these groups. Commenting on the "social process of reading *Dallas*," they suggest that they were able to "simulate and 'sample' the high moments of this process," and that even if they

> overstated the "necessary" and pervasive aspects of such interaction, the method of focus-group discussion provides a very close look at the social dynamics of meaning-making. People seem to express themselves very freely. (Katz and Liebes, 1985, p. 189)

The point at which a small group becomes a medium-sized group is, of course fairly arbitrary. It is difficult to identify a moment when we necessarily lose the intimacy we associate with small groups. This is not purely a question of numbers. A group of people who know one another well will have an established pattern of conversational rules. A group less familiar with each other will, to some extent, need to have those rules imposed upon them by the interviewer. The more intimate groups are much more likely to let the interviewer sit back and listen during the discussion, while the less familiar groups will usually rely upon the interviewer to organize the conversation. A group's size is, nonetheless, bound to affect the social dynamics of the encounter. Suffice to say that the groups in the Katz and Liebes study are about as large as a small group can be. While six people probably stretch the informal rules of conversation to their limit, the intimacy between the group members allows them, as the transcripts from the interviews testify, to behave as a small group.

c) The focus group

A focus group is traditionally a collection of around six to ten people who will share some cultural or demographic characteristics. This applies, of course, to the Katz and Liebes study, although focus group members are usually less intimate with each other. There are two main ways of recruiting group members: they can be recruited individually (the standard market research method) or, via an in-

stitution, as an already constituted group. The institutionally constituted group will usually be recruited through workplaces, social
or community organizations (such as social club or a "keep fit"
group) or educational institutions (from schools to adult education):
this is the approach used, for example, in Morley's *Nationwide* research and Brunt and Jordin's *Newsnight* study (Brunt and Jordin,
1987). The first method of recruitment will probably be more representative in a socio-demographic sense, while the second, drawing
upon an established social network, will make discussion easier to
promote.

The use of focus groups allows researchers to incorporate a
reasonably large number of people into the sample. It also gives
them the chance to explore the constitution of meaning in a more
public setting: how do people respond when forced to confront their
familiar frameworks of interpretation, in public discussion?

While the social dynamics of the larger group may be revealing,
they also impose restrictions on the things people are prepared to
say. It is difficult, for example, to interpret the views of less confident
members of the group. It will be hard to distinguish attitudes that
are deeply held from those that are deemed by the group member
to be publicly acceptable. Perhaps the greatest danger is that one or
two dominant members of the group will frame the whole discussion
in a way that appears to produce a consensus, masking all kinds of
unspoken contradictions and ambiguities.

This leads to the second possible problem with the use of focus
groups. We have defined the groups' characteristics in a way that we
hope allows us to make statements—however tentatively—about the
role of social or cultural variables in TV viewing. There is a risk
that the apparent homogeneity within a group (or social/cultural
category) has been artificially manufactured by the most persuasive
members of that group. This might lead us to suppose that certain
social or cultural variables seem to determine readings uniformly
(among group members), when they do nothing of the kind. So, for
example, a group of white working-class men may produce, collectively, a clear and unambiguous reading of a TV program, a reading
that a majority of the group would *not* have produced without the
strong influence of two persuasive group members. There is a danger
that we may falsely characterize this as a "white, working-class, male
reading."

This risk will, of course, be reduced by doing a number of
interviews with groups from similar social or cultural backgrounds.
We should not be seduced into thinking that the fact a group contains
ten people means we are gathering the views of ten people. To put

it crudely, interviewing one group of ten is not the same as interviewing two groups of five—even if it involved the same ten people.

It is sometimes stated in the defense of focus groups that the manipulation and control exercised by dominant group members simply reflects the reality of social life. While this contains an element of truth, it is a little too glib. The focus group is, for most people, an unusual setting for talking about TV. Most people will choose social environments in which they feel comfortable to discuss such things. A focus group discussion can be an intimidating experience for people who, in other social circumstances, may be quite confident.

READING THE INTERVIEW: STORIES AND SILENCES

The easiest way of recording the evidence gathered by an interview is to tape it on sound cassette and transcribe it. As elaborate as transcriptions are, we should remember that they do not reproduce everything that happens in an interview. It is, accordingly, useful to record the more interesting non-verbal aspects of the interview. My experience is that it is helpful to make a note of these both during and immediately after the interview has taken place, when the intricacies of mood change and non-verbal dynamics are fresh in the mind.

It is sometimes useful to record interviews on video tape, particularly if it is part of a preliminary or pilot study. Watching "data" on video is most appropriate for a microscopic level of analysis, although it becomes unwieldy when we want to analyze a number of interviews simultaneously. We can, however, learn a great deal about our own interviewing style (if we can bear it!) by watching ourselves in action.

Once we have collected our transcripts and notes, we are confronted by an intimidating methodological problem: what do we do with these disorderly piles of data? It is at this point that we might begin to regret our decision to pursue a qualitative approach: how much easier it would be to have a set of responses that could be classified under, for instance, categories one, two, three, four or five. In the quantitative survey, we have a clear basis for detecting patterns of response and drawing comparisons between them. Qualitative data, on the other hand, sits defiantly on our desks, resisting any straightforward attempts to organize it into some systematic or coherent form.

Ann Gray has, in response to this problem, emphasized the

need to do more than simply resort to a descriptive account of the transcribed interview, and to "develop further more sophisticated forms of analysis" (Gray, 1987, p. 33). Part of the problem is that it is difficult to break down the interview into discrete and quantifiable units of analysis. As Elliot Mishler, in his book on research interviewing, writes:

> From transcriptions it becomes clear that the meanings of questions and answers are not ... adequately represented by the interview schedule or by code-category systems. Instead, meanings emerge, develop, are shaped by and in turn shape the discourse. (Mishler, 1986, p. 138)

Mishler proceeds to argue that interviews, particularly those that use a relatively "open" interviewing style, resemble narratives. The transcript will contain a sporadic series of stories told by the interviewee, and any attempt at systematic analysis must, Mishler suggests, involve forms of narrative analysis.

Many interviews, when regarded as narratives, will appear disjointed and incomplete. Nevertheless, once we begin to see statements as fragments of a narrative, we can begin to situate them within a wider discursive framework. Where did this statement come from? What themes emerge and link various statements? At what point do they cohere into a set of attitudes and logics? What seems to constrain or determine these attitudes and logics? The interview is, after all, merely a fragment of a person's social and cultural history.

These questions force us to consider not only what is said, but what remains unspoken. If the articulated is significant, so are the silences. The trouble with silence is that it is profoundly ambiguous. We should, however, resist the temptation to consign it to the world of the unknowable and the unknown. There are, for our purposes, two kinds of silence. The first refers to those things that the respondent deliberately or unintentionally leaves out, described by Schroder thus:

> We have to admit that even the most candid of respondents, consciously and unconsciously, mobilize filters that censor their utterances in the interview situation. Therefore, this sort of open elicitation provides an incomplete, but at the same time the *most* coherent and reliable account of viewer experiences we can get. (Schroder, 1988, p. 9)

We can, particularly if we were aware of it during the interview, search the transcripts for clues about these silences. The *Cosby* study, which will be described in Part 2, tried to anticipate this process in relation to discourses about race—a topic that is likely to involve both conscious and unconscious self-censorship. In order to make sense of respondents' possible silences on this subject during a discussion of *The Cosby Show*, the last part of the interview involved a series of possible questions designed to give the interviewee an appropriate "way in" to a discussion about race. Their responses, at this point, could be *read back* into their comments about the program, thereby providing clues about the meaning of both the spoken and the silent (this point will be developed in Chapter 5).

The second form of silence we need to consider is not so much the unsaid but what *cannot* be said. If the world sometimes appears to suffer from a lack of ambiguity, it is a product of our own semiological limits: we have only a restricted supply of knowledge and ideologies with which to make sense of it. Suppose, to develop a previous example, we understand the word *democracy* purely as a rather vague symbol that distinguishes "repressive communist states" from the "free West." The only sense we are then able to make of the description "pro-democracy," should we hear it on the news, is in terms of a desire for Western-style capitalism. Any contradictions between Western capitalism and democracy cannot, from this ideological position, be articulated.

The same process will inform those parts of a program that we "miss": the silence or powerlessness of those moments is a necessary consequence of our inability to draw upon a discourse that would make them relevant to us. Loomis (1990) found that viewers of a documentary were unable to express any great qualms about a sequence that exposed sinister surveillance by the U.S. government on members of the Committee in Solidarity with the People of El Salvador (CISPES). This sequence played no part in the respondents' discussions, and when Loomis introduced it at a later stage, reasons for this silence began to emerge. The viewers had consigned the CISPES members to a social category (political activist/protester) that felt so alien and distant to their own experience that it became impossible to identify with them.

The implication that "if it can happen to them, it can happen to you" was a connection the respondents were unable to make. The power of the sequence was therefore dependent upon a set of conditions that were, for these respondents, simply unavailable. The studies analyzed in Part 2 contain many other instances of what we might call (without wishing to be too melodramatic) the unspoken and the unspeakable.

Exploring the stories and silences in the interview are useful textual strategies with which to make sense of the transcript. The problem that remains is one of quantifying and comparing the transcripts as a whole. The greater the number of interviews in the sample, the more acute this problem becomes. There is, after all, little point in carrying out a series of interviews if we cannot establish general patterns and comparisons, thereby exploring the textual and socio-cultural determinations of television viewing.

There is an inevitable tension here, between the desire to maintain a qualitative depth in the analysis and the need to establish a systematic framework for organizing the data. This is a tension that is difficult to resolve without making fairly specific references to a set of transcripts. It is to these, and Part 2, that I shall now turn.

PART 2

5

Two Empirical Studies

INTO THE NITTY GRITTY

Having spent the first half of this book messing around with other people's audience research, I should now start messing about with my own. In the pages that follow, I will be analyzing the findings from two studies: the first was carried out in Britain, the second in the United States; the former deals with perceptions of TV news, and the latter with a piece of popular fiction.

The two studies are, methodologically speaking, fairly similar, although the second was carried out not only with the benefit of hindsight, but with more adequate funding and resources. Both involved data sets consisting of fifty taped and transcribed interviews, and, in both cases, interviews were carried out following the viewing of a half-hour videotaped program.

The first study carried the painstaking burden of overcoming some of the more difficult methodological problems that theoretical inquiry had left unresolved. As I suggested at the end of the last chapter, the most pressing of these involved devising a method for breaking down and analyzing a comparatively large number of interview transcripts in relation to the TV program. While the preliminary findings of this study have already been published (Lewis, 1985), the fairly rich material generated by the interviews allowed me to visit and revisit the data, in an attempt to refine a methodological approach to these questions.

THE NEWS STUDY

1) The program

The first study was based upon a transmission of the popular prime-time ITV news program *News at Ten*. The program provided the basis for fifty viewing/interview sessions, carried out within a three-week period following the broadcast. The timetable of the research made the choice of program fairly random. I was keen to work with a program whose content was still fairly fresh, which meant setting up a fairly tight schedule of interviews with the chosen respondents (two to three interviews a day, seven days a week) and selecting a program at the last possible moment before this schedule began. Accordingly, all the primetime news broadcasts from the two main channels (BBC and ITV) were taped in the three day period before the interviews were due to begin, allowing a further two days to decide which one to use and to make the necessary adjustments to the interviewing strategy.

Since my aim was to explore television news in general rather than specific terms, the small number of news programs to choose from was not a problem. The choice of this particular *News at Ten* was made for the typicality of its form and the variety of its content. The program consisted of one major domestic political story, four other substantial stories (two domestic, two foreign), five shorter stories or news snippets, complete with the obligatory lighter, human-interest piece at the end.

My main practical concern was that some of the stories might conspicuously develop during the interview period, introducing a complex interpretative variable into the study. In the event, this problem did not arise: Britain was, unbeknown to both its citizens and its government, on the brink of one of its most obsessional periods in recent history—the conflict with Argentina in the Falkland/Malvinas Islands. From the moment the conflict began, all other news stories, as if by magic, quickly disappeared. Journalists in El Salvador, for example, were hastily dispatched to South America. Television news was reduced to a month-long orgy of bleak speculation, culminating in the war itself: those news stories that preceded it appeared, to most viewers, as if they were frozen in time.

The analysis of *News at Ten* (in Chapter 6) concentrates on four news items, all transcribed below. Two other items are briefly mentioned in Chapter 6: the lengthy lead report on the victory of Roy Jenkins at the Hillhead by-election, and a regular item detailing the number of jobs lost and gained in Britain over the previous week.

The Hillhead item was considered newsworthy because it enabled the (then) leader of the newly formed Social Democratic Party (Roy Jenkins) to get into Parliament. The result was seen (by *News at Ten*) as a blow to the two main parties (Conservative and Labour), and as the dawning of a new force in British politics. The jobs item was simply a listing of jobs lost and gained. As each set of jobs was listed they were flashed up on a map of Britain. This was a regular weekly feature on *News at Ten*, created in response to the rapid rise in unemployment in the early 1980s.

The British Leyland item

BURNET: In industry: BL management and unions have been holding talks (that they hope to settle next Wednesday) to get a new deal in industrial relations. The deal has strong union backing; it would mean better bonuses for productivity, and new procedures for settling strikes. BL's workers, with the help of robots, have hit new productivity records in BL's biggest plant at Longbridge. Our industrial editor, Giles Smith, has been there.

Anchor in studio.

SMITH: Today's deal will, in the view of both sides, be the icing on the cake of remarkable productivity improvements, that have transformed BL's biggest plant from one of the least productive in Europe, to one of the most. In 1980, each Longbridge worker was producing just 7 cars a year. Last year that rose to 16, and so far this year each man has been turning out Metros a minute at a rate of 22 cars a year—an increase of over 200 percent.

Film of assembly lines.

Workers working on cars.

BRIAN FOX: The rest of our competitors aren't going to stand back and watch us—it's not just about us. They don't want us to be first in the world, so we've got to continue to do the things that they do, and try to beat them.

Interviewed on shop floor, with caption: "Brian Fox, Operations Director, BL"

During the last few months it's no secret that over 2,000 people have left Longbridge. We've still got improvement plans, and we're still getting better, so we're continuing to run a voluntary redundancy scheme. I think an important point is, no one has had to leave here; all of it's been achieved by voluntary means.

101

SMITH: Behind the improvement is the wide-scale use of robots. On this automated body framing line, each one gets through 256 spot welds in about as many seconds. Just 34 men work on the line, which would need nearly 150 if the welds were done in the traditional manner. And a Metro body shell comes off the line once every 48 seconds.

Film of robots spot-welding.

FIRST BL WORKER: We have seen our bonus payments coming through and, er, hopefully we hope to see it continue.

Interviewed on shop floor.

SMITH: But you have seen an awful lot of jobs go in the process. Colleagues of yours have had to leave.

FIRST BL WORKER: That is correct and, er, this is a great tragedy, but, um, I think under the circumstances, for us to be competitive with our competitors, we've just got to have this sort of equipment, in which invariably jobs have got to go.

SMITH: How do you feel about the people who've had to go?

SECOND BL WORKER: Yeah, well, the same actually. It's progress. Um, it's better probably to save a few jobs than have no jobs at all.

SMITH: Longbridge is now producing 98 percent of its target—an unprecedented rate for the motor industry. But robots don't go on strike—men can. Only a major industrial disruption would seem able to blow BL off course from its aim of breaking even next year, and making a profit in '84.

Film of robots spot-welding.

Man drives car off shop floor, moves slowly past camera.

This is Cofton Park, scene in the past of mass meetings, that led to the big strikes in the '70s. It's empty now, and Sir Michael Edwards, and whoever is to succeed him later this year, will hope it stays that way, as a result of the procedures already agreed in Longbridge, and today's new industrial relations deal. Giles Smith, *News at Ten*, Longbridge.	Smith standing on a hill (buildings in the background), to camera.

Zoom in to Smith. |

The West Bank item

GALL: Israelis shot and wounded a Palestinian on the troubled West Bank today. Israeli troops have clamped a tight grip on the area after several days of rioting, in which at least 5 Palestinians have been killed. In today's incident at Halhul, Israelis in a civilian jeep fired warning shots, according to an army spokesman, to disperse a stone-throwing crowd. The West Bank has been tense since the Israelis sacked 3 Palestinian mayors. Derek Taylor is there.	Anchor in studio.

Map of the Middle East (whole screen). |
| TAYLOR: If there's going to be trouble, Friday midday is usually the time, as the mosques empty in the West Bank, and crowds gather. That's what happened in Ramula, and a score of Israeli paratroopers sped forward and fired into the air (sound of gunshot). The streets cleared within seconds, and the paras scoured the town to make sure that it stayed that way.

In Nablus, the other of the two West Bank towns where the Israelis turned the Palestinian mayors out of office yesterday, there was desultory sparring (street sounds). | Film of large crowd, army landrover and soldiers across the street.

Close up of soldiers walking up the street.

Men setting up an oil-drum street barricade. Zoom out to reveal soldiers in the foreground. Cut to smoke bomb thrown at building. Soldiers walking along an empty street. |

103

As the military clampdown continued, the head of the Israeli administration in the Occupied Territories was justifying to foreign journalists the dismissal of the mayors, who, he said, are agents of the PLO, the Palestine Liberation Organization.

Inside the press conference.

MILSON: Israel is engaged now, in a very serious struggle, against the PLO. Er, I consider it to be a very crucial struggle for the chances of peace in the Middle East. It is very clear to all of us that the PLO is committed to the tactics and politics of undermining the, er, framework for peace in the Middle East, established at Camp David.

Close up of main speaker, caption: "Mr. Menachem Milson, West Bank Administrator."

TAYLOR: Israel's action though has brought criticism from the other peace partners, Egypt and America. But at the moment the Israelis have got a lever against both of them; that's the fear that an open rift between the peace partners might be enough to lead the Israeli government to delay the hand-over of the Sinai to Egypt due next month. Derek Taylor, *News at Ten*, on the West Bank.

Soldiers on street.

Civilians on street. Taylor, in front of a building, to camera.

The El Salvador item

GALL: The Americans seem to be anticipating an extreme right-wing victory in Sunday's elections in El Salvador, and they appear to have changed their minds about Major Roberto D'Aubuisson, the leader of the Nationalist Republican Alliance, who's been linked with the right-wing death squads. A former American ambassador to El Salvador is reported to have called

Anchor in studio

Picture of D'Aubuisson, covers whole screen.

D'Aubuisson a "pathological killer." American observers of the election have just arrived there. Jon Snow Reports.

Anchor in studio.

SNOW: With a day to go to the election, the American senator and congressmen observing it arrived in a bullet-proof convoy two hours ago. The British delegation, already here for 5 days, has not disguised its resentment that the Americans have joined them so late. The ballot papers being unloaded at polling stations offer the people a choice of centre, right and extreme right-wing candidates. Each has held rallies, while Social Democrats, Socialists and Communists have not—all their candidates are either dead or in exile. The left argues that the death squads would continue to hit them if they returned. Though there are half a dozen parties of the right, the battle is really between two men. President Duarte, in the centre for the Christian Democrats, is Washington's candidate, but both he and the US Embassy here think he has a good chance of losing. His opponent, Major Bob D'Aubuisson on the extreme right, now has, in the opinion of the embassy and many others, a fair chance of winning. Vast amounts of money sent in from the exiled oligarchy in Miami have given him a lavish campaign. He promises to restore much of their land to them, and to defeat the guerrillas with Napalm and gas within 3 months.

Cars driving over a hill.

Black limousine drives past. Caption: "El Salvador this afternoon."

Men lifting ballot boxes from a table.

Banner-waving crowd scenes.

Duarte addressing large rally.

D'Aubuisson waving amid crowd.

Large rally in a sports arena.

Banner-waving crowds.

Six miles outside San Salvador this morning, in the notorious lava pits, lay the bodies of a man, a woman, and a child. This is the spot where the death squads daily

Road by a wasteland. Zoom in to a brief shot of dead bodies. Close-up of an empty pair of boots/vulture. Snow, at the scene, to camera.

dump their victims. Senior American officials have been convinced of D'Aubuisson's connections with the death squads for a long time. The documentation associating him with the killing of Archbishop Romero has been destroyed—but it was seen before that by the previous American ambassador here, Robert White.

Until a few weeks ago, the Embassy made it plain that D'Aubuisson was not a man with whom they could cooperate. But last night, in an about-turn, the US ambassador revealed to selected journalists that a new view prevailed. Filmed at an Aide meeting this morning he said; "we know D'Aubuisson's reputation, he denies the rough stuff, he should be judged on his future actions, not his past performance." Leaving he told us, America would try to co-operate with D'Aubuisson, if he won the election.

Amid the furor stirred up by this new policy, guns blazed away in the district around the Electoral Commission Headquarters. It lasted 24 hours, and there was never any sign of the guerrillas. But they have been active elsewhere today; their radio has warned of considerably more action here tomorrow. Jon Snow, *News at Ten*, San Salvador.

Various shots of the embassy.

Close up of a man speaking at press conference.

Same man, leaving the press conference.

Soldier firing guns into the trees.

The Whitelaw item

BURNET: The home secretary, Mr. William Whitelaw, got a standing ovation today after a speech to Conservative party activists in Harrogate. He spoke in a debate on law and order at annual conference of the party's central council, and to judge from his reception, he has emerged triumphant again, after a

Anchor in studio.

week fending off his critics. From Harrogate, our political correspondent, David Rose.

ROSE: Mr. Whitelaw must have been worried about what sort of reception he'd get today. There had been rumblings from the party's grass roots, and he'd been given a rough time by the party conference on this issue last year. But, in the event, every speaker except one supported him. Mr. Whitelaw defended his record and contrasted it with his predecessors and opponents.	Whitelaw walking onto conference platform. Audience applauding. Whitelaw next to other speakers. Speaker addressing conference. Whitelaw listening. Audience listening.
WHITELAW: It was Labour home secretaries, like Roy Jenkins, who failed to provide the prison places, for whose shortage they now criticize us. I'm tired of those, whether Liberal, Labour or SDP, who, far from supporting the police and encouraging the public to help, concentrate on criticism and complaint.	Whitelaw speaking.
ROSE: He was clearly delighted by the way the debate had gone.	Zoom out to reveal conference hall.
WHITELAW: And may I once again thank you deeply for the support and help which you have given me at a very difficult time.	Whitelaw speaking. Whitelaw sits down.
ROSE: And they rose to him. Afterwards, Mr. Whitelaw told me that he'd been hurt by previous criticism from within his own party. Many of those representatives from the Tory grass roots are worried by the crime figures—but today, few held the home secretary personally responsible.	Zoom out to audience, who slowly rise, applauding. Whitelaw acknowledges applause.

There's no doubt that Mr. Whitelaw has received almost total support from the Conservative Party workers here at Harrogate. This time last week he feared what looked like a tough week of criticism: from first on Monday, Tory MPs, then in the House of Commons yesterday, then here from party workers in Harrogate. But tonight his position looks very much stronger. David Rose, *News at Ten*, Harrogate.

Rose to camera.

2) The respondents

The respondents were recruited from a number of different sources: half from the local neighborhood (a fairly mixed, though predominantly white, middle and lower middle-class area), and half from a mixture of workplaces, voluntary and political organizations. Most of the respondents lived in or near Sheffield, an industrial city in the north of England with a reputation for left-wing political sympathies (the "People's Republic of South Yorkshire").

The respondents were chosen in order to reflect a range of backgrounds and interests. The sample included a diverse collection of occupational groups: a policeman, a teacher, a youth worker, an electrician, a town planner, a typist, a computer analyst, a librarian, a porter, an unemployed steelworker, a mother bringing up children, a clerk, a workshop foreman, a TV news producer and so on. The respondents were aged from 18 to 68 (with a fairly even spread in between), possessed a wide range of educational backgrounds, interests, political attitudes and TV viewing habits, and were split fairly evenly between men and women.

While the sample could, during the analysis, be divided in terms of variables like social class, educational background and gender, my main concern was to investigate the relation between the discourses that structured people's views of the world, and the readings of the news those discourses engendered. I was particularly interested in those areas where the news program induced common responses, actively engaging with viewers to inform their pictures of the news world. Or, to put it another way, I wanted to explore the precise nature of the ideological power of TV news.

3) The interviews

Basic information about a respondent's viewing and reading habits, interests and background was gathered before the interviews. The interviews themselves were carried out in a fairly open and informal style; viewers were encouraged to converse rather than simply respond to questions. Respondents were asked to discuss each news item (as far as they could remember them) in their own terms. The discussion of each item began with respondents recounting what they remembered and what they thought each story was "about." This provided the foundation on which to build a more detailed discussion of the content, based upon the respondents' own semiological agenda.

Once respondents had constructed a preliminary reading, they were then asked (vaguely at first, to jog their memory, then more directly) about those aspects of the story that they had not included in their interpretation. This sometimes led to a more elaborate interpretation of the item, and sometimes simply confirmed that those aspects had been missed because the viewer had found them incomprehensible or insignificant.

Some respondents were very comfortable during the interview, and enjoyed having their opinions solicited, while others were more reticent (particularly at first). Either way, the whole procedure was inevitably a product of my design, not theirs. This had some identifiable effects on how they watched the *News at Ten*: despite my reassurances that they should watch the news program as lackadaisically as they pleased, most respondents felt some obligation to pay closer attention than usual. They were also viewing it undisturbed and without distractions: they watched items that they might otherwise have talked through or ignored.

This environment favored a far higher level of recall than normal, something taken into account during the analysis. As it turned out, levels of recall were still generally very low, which, as I shall argue later, is itself significant.

While all the interviews were tape recorded and transcribed, it was useful to make notes immediately after the interview, picking up on those nuances of communication that the tape recorder would miss. This was particularly helpful in clarifying moments that, when transformed to the monotone of the typed transcript, would become ambiguous. The use of sarcasm or irony, for example, can disappear in the gap between the spoken and the written.

THE *COSBY* STUDY

1) The program

The second study is based upon a popular fiction, one of the most popular TV shows in the United States, *The Cosby Show*. The study forms part of a research project undertaken with Sut Jhally at the University of Massachusetts. The show was chosen partly for its popularity, and partly because it brings a number of issues (most obviously about race, but also about family, gender and class) into play. It has also been the subject of a certain amount of critical attention, much of which is speculative, about audience response.

The episode chosen for the viewing/interview sessions was fairly typical in a number of respects: it develops two interweaving narratives, and resolves them in the style of a very gentle moral tale. The "issue" that is dealt with in this episode, as in many others, is sexism, and the main characters strike familiar attitudes in its telling. Claire Huxtable is a figure of moral authority; her husband Cliff, the focus of the show's comedy, is allowed to vacillate between the wisdom of fatherhood and a childlike, comic self-mockery; their son Theo is the good-natured but typical male adolescent, full of bravado and misconceptions (for his parents to put right); and the two younger daughters, Vanessa and Rudy, are both cute and mischievous.

The Huxtables are an upper middle-class black family, and one of the study's aims was to explore how audiences interpret images and issues of race and class. Race and class are issues that are rarely explicitly raised in the show, although they are both signified very gently. References are made to black culture and black history, for example, but they are invariably apolitical. In this show, we are reminded that the Huxtables are African Americans by the presence of a visiting friend from Trinidad, Dr. Harman. During the show, Cliff teases his friend about his accent, signifying both the unity and difference between two black cultures. The presence of another doctor also emphasizes the Huxtables' own class position: here are professionals mixing with other professionals.

For those familiar with the show, any episode carries with it a multitude of representations from other shows. While respondents were asked to specifically address this episode during the interview, they were also encouraged to use it as a catalyst to talk about *The Cosby Show* more generally.

SUMMARY OF *THE COSBY SHOW* EPISODE

SCENE 1: *Theo's bedroom*

Claire comes into Theo's bedroom (Theo is reading). She accidentally knocks a pile of his books from a table, and, as she picks them up, discovers a copy of *Car and Woman* magazine. A comic discussion follows, as Theo tries to argue, ingeniously but unconvincingly, that his interest is in the technical articles, rather than the scantily clad women draped across the automobiles. Claire condemns the magazine for its degrading images of women, and tells him to throw the magazine out.

SCENE 2: *The living room*

Claire is on the phone. Cliff enters, and she tells him that she has invited their friends, the Harmans, around for dinner on Sunday. Cliff becomes animated, as he looks forward to renewing his rivalry with Mr. (Dr.) Harman, with another game of "petanque" (a backyard version of bowls). Claire chastises him for his childishness, and reminds him of the fuss they caused last time they played. She proposes that they should all simply dine together and discuss "world issues."

Theo enters with a large pile of magazines to throw out (it turns out that his copies of *Car and Woman* are supplemented by issues of *Bikes and Babes*), and Cliff leaves, rather mischievously, to prepare the "petanque court" in the backyard.

SCENE 3: *Sunday, the living room/kitchen*

The Harmans arrive to Claire's enthusiastic greeting. The Harmans have brought their daughter Lindy with them (who has grown up since the Huxtables last saw her). Cliff enters, and engages Dr. Harman in a competitive banter about what will happen later on the "petanque" court. The women protest, and they sit down, Claire asking Lindy about the "Outward Bound" trip she is about to go on.

Theo enters, and is immediately captivated by Lindy (as Cliff tells him, "They grow up, don't they, son?"). He and Claire exit to the kitchen to "check the roast." In the kitchen, he complains to his mother that she gave him no warning that Lindy had turned into a beautiful woman, and, had he known, he would have dressed for the occasion. Claire retorts by scolding him, and makes fun of his sexist attitude.

SCENE 4: *After dinner, the living room*
The family enter the living room, and the two men immediately make efforts to escape to play their game in the backyard. Theo makes clumsy (and slightly comic) efforts to impress Lindy, for which his younger sisters (Vanessa and Rudy) tease him. Lindy offers to show Theo more information about "Outward Bound," and they exit (to the taunts of Vanessa and Rudy). The men finally escape to the backyard to play petanque.

Commercial Break

SCENE 5: *The backyard*
The two men prepare for their game, bantering with one another in a parody of competitive machismo. Even though the temperature is below freezing, both men attempt to display bravado by stripping down to their shirts.

SCENE 6: *The living room*
The two women are playing cards. Lindy is telling Theo about her interest in rock climbing (part of her "Outward Bound" trip), a subject in which Theo suddenly declares a long-standing interest. Claire teases him, speculating on his subscription to *Rock and Woman*. Theo takes Lindy down to the basement so that she can teach him about rock climbing.

SCENE 7: *The basement*
Lindy tries to teach Theo some basic rock climbing techniques, while Theo tries to turn on the charm. Theo decides, against Lindy's better judgment, to show off by climbing up the side of the basement staircase.

SCENE 8: *The backyard*
The final and deciding game. After more competitive (and comic) banter, the last balls are thrown. Both fall at approximately the same distance from the target ball, leading to a dispute about who has won. The two men go indoors to ask their wives to decide which ball is nearest.

SCENE 9: *The living room*
The two women are reading magazines. Their husbands enter and ask them to resolve their dispute, and Claire responds by making fun of their childish predicament. A crash is then heard from the basement, and all four go to investigate.

SCENE 10: *The basement*

Theo has fallen down the stairs, having attempted to do a handstand on the banisters. Doctors Harman and Huxtable use the occasion to joke about each other's medical ability (to attend to Theo).

SCENE 11: *The living room*

The two women are looking out of the front door. Theo enters and Claire describes the scene to him: the Harmans' car would not start, and both men's attempts to fix it succeed only in dismantling the engine, so Lindy, a student of car maintenance, steps in to help them out. This, Claire tells Theo with a smile, is where women should be; under the hood rather than draped across it, while the men are left "sitting on the curb."

2) The respondents

Although similar in style, the interviewing strategy differed from the news project in two ways: interviews were carried out with small groups rather than individuals, and these groups were selected with specific variables in mind. The groups were gathered using an approach borrowed from the Katz and Liebes *Dallas* research: an individual was established as a point of contact, and then asked to invite one to three friends or family members to the interview/ viewing session (in his or her home). While the Katz and Liebes project was structured tightly around groups of three couples, we were keen to include those who did not necessarily live in traditional family groups: the only proviso was that group members should be familiar with one another and comfortable about watching TV together. The aim was to create an easy conversational atmosphere which could, at appropriate moments, be allowed to flow freely without interjection from the interviewer.

The sample was also structured to anticipate or explore certain variables that might influence people's interpretation of the show: in particular, race, class and gender. There were, accordingly, twenty-three black groups and twenty-seven white groups, both sets being subdivided in terms of their social class (using the fairly traditional socio-economic occupational categories). Most groups included men and women, although there were some single-sex groups (of both sexes). The only requirement all the respondents met was that they were (whether frequently or occasionally) viewers of *The Cosby Show*: a stipulation that, in the United States, is inclusive rather than exclusive.

Most of the interviews took place in Springfield (or its suburbs), the major city in western Massachusetts. Springfield is a racially mixed city; predominantly white, but with prominent black and Hispanic populations (particularly in the poorer neighborhoods nearer the city center). Bill Moyers (following a 1990 program on public opinion and the Persian Gulf made for PBS, filmed in Springfield) described the city as "a very good place to find out what's on the mind of America." Although there are some mixed areas in the city, the level of segregation made recruiting respondents from particular racial and socio-economic groups fairly straightforward (the exception being black upper middle-class people who, like the Huxtables, tend to live in predominantly white areas).

3) The interviews

In the news project, all the interviews were carried out by the same person (myself), while the *Cosby* research involved a team of four interviewers. Although this is advantageous in many ways, possible differences in interviewing style forced restrictions into the interviewing process. In order to retain a degree of uniformity, the interview structure was more tightly controlled. Each interviewer was given a set of core questions and a detailed set of guidelines about those areas and issues they should encourage respondents to talk about. We were particularly interested in what viewers had to say regarding issues around race, class, and gender.

The interview framework was carefully designed to maintain, as far as possible, a degree of conversational flow. As in the news study, questions were as open as they could be, particularly during the first part of the interview, to allow respondents the freedom to set their own agenda. Each interview began, for example, with respondents being asked to simply describe the story (they felt) they had just been told. They were then asked a series of general questions, in order to stimulate the conversation: questions like What do you think this episode was about? and What do you think of Claire Huxtable?

These fairly vague and innocuous questions often succeeded in opening up the discussion, allowing respondents the space to introduce attitudes to topics like class, race or gender, attitudes the interviewer could then explore and develop. If this did not happen, the respondents would be asked to comment on these topics more directly. They were asked, for example, how they would feel if the Huxtable family were white, and alternatively, would the show be as good if they were a blue-collar family? Initial responses to these questions were sometimes ambiguous, guarded or even misleading, so answers were carefully explored during the ensuing discussion.

The subject which provoked the most cautious or evasive reactions was race. In order to ease the discomfort people might feel in addressing this issue, white groups were interviewed by white interviewers and black groups by black interviewers, a decision vindicated by the analysis of the transcripts. Attitudes to race were also approached from two different angles: first, in relation to *The Cosby Show*, and second, toward the end of the interview, in relation to more general perceptions of race relations. In order to provide some breathing space between the two conversations, they were divided by a discussion of the commercials shown during the show. The two discussions, as it turned out, were often not only very different but, when analyzed together, extremely revealing.

Following on from the news study, the interviewer noted those moments during the interview that would remain silent once it had been transcribed. Responses made during the show (usually laughter) were particularly interesting, not only in the subsequent analysis, but as a prompting tool that would be raised during the interview itself ("I noticed you laughed when . . . ").

READING TRANSCRIPTS

The analysis of interview transcripts is a painstakingly slow procedure. As Mishler (1986) suggests, each interview has its own logic, its own flow, its own dynamic. It contains ideas that come in multifarious forms, whether coherently expressed or heavily disguised: consequently, we must, as Ang says: "search for what is behind the explicitly written, for the presuppositions and accepted attitudes concealed within them" (Ang, 1985, p. 11).

This level of scrutiny is invariably idiosyncratic: each statement we read must be interpreted within its own particular context. As fascinating as this can be, it becomes a little awkward when we are faced with a pile of fifty transcripts which we want to interpret both collectively and individually. The task of making quantitative sense of such a diverse body of material is not for the faint-hearted. It is a little like wrestling with a jellyfish: it squirms in so many different directions simultaneously that it seems impossible to control. It is at this point that an audience researcher is apt to sigh and reflect fondly upon the comparative simplicity of questionnaire-based interviews, with their built-in uniformity and neatly pre-coded categories of response.

As I suggested earlier, one of the more useful ways to begin to explore the workings of something, whether it's a car engine or a conversation, is to take it apart and put it back together again. While there are some unavoidable risks in so doing (it is sometimes easier to break something apart than to piece it together, leaving us with nothing more than a pile of apparently disjointed fragments), this procedure allows us to discover causes, consequences and connections. An interview is, unfortunately, a rather less precise object than a car engine: it is built both consciously and unconsciously, with and without purpose. There is no one set of specifications, no well-planned structure and no overall concept of design.

There are many plausible ways to try to break down the layers of linguistic ambiguity that compose an interview transcript. The problem, for audience research, is that our semiological objectives force us onto a slippery terrain where precise categories are difficult to construct. The rules of grammar can be broken down into distinct components, like words, clauses and sentences, but the rules of meaning do not always fit into such easy compartments. Meaning, in other words, does not come in any one shape or size.

This intrinsic imprecision teaches the semiologist to be flexible. Barthes accepts the virtue of methodological adaptability in his analysis of a short story by Balzac (Barthes, 1974). His task is essentially the same: to break down a text into constituent units of meaning. To break it down into words would be cumbersome, long-winded and misleading, so he cuts it up into "brief, contiguous fragments" he calls "lexias," and thereby acknowledges that

> this cutting up, admittedly, will be arbitrary in the extreme; it will imply no methodological responsibility ... The lexia will include sometimes a few words, sometimes several sentences; it will be a matter of convenience: it will suffice that the lexia be the best possible space in which we can observe meanings. (Barthes, 1974, p. 13)

The lexia has no essence: it is endowed with meaning by the culture in which it appears. Empty phrases in one cultural context can become rich in another: culture, in this sense, is a wayward variable that refuses to be pinned down to any timeless system of measurement.

If we are to discover the what and why of meaning, we must, like the ethnographer, immerse ourselves in culture, and emerge positively dripping with appropriate cultural references. Only then can we break a text down into segments of meaning, the better to learn the specificities of cultural structures.

In audience research, this process is complicated (or, from another point of view, simplified) by the need to relate one text (the interview transcript) to another (the TV program). The news study, in particular, was based almost exhaustively upon TV viewers' reconstructions and interpretations of a series of TV news items. Each transcript must therefore be related not only to the culture that informs it, but to the words and images that compose the program they are responding to. This brings us directly to the crux of the whole endeavor: the viewer becomes part of history, the moment when a TV message and culture meet.

My own attempts to transform these rather vague methodological guidelines into a coherent research practice began with much floundering. An approach that seemed to elucidate one interview would persistently collapse in the face of another, making comparisons difficult or impossible. Intricately constructed analytical models would be so bent and twisted to allow for each new type of response that they became unrecognizable. Attempts to use some of the semiological tools devised for textual analysis seemed awkward or inappropriate when applied to the interpretations of an actual (rather than hypothetical) audience.

There is, as I have suggested, no one way to proceed in research of this kind. The method I eventually adopted is neither definitive nor complete, but it does allow us to make quantitative sense of a diverse collection of audience readings. It is, when reduced to its bare bones, very simple (although more sophisticated variables can be built into it), consisting of four stages.

1) The first task is to convert the television program into analytical units of meaning. Most of the divisions used in the semiotic study of film and television are far too rigid to be useful in an audience study: while we can distinguish between each shot, for example, most viewers do not actually watch programs in terms of such neat, formal divisions. Barthes's concept of the lexia, on the other hand, is extremely useful. It permits us to break up the program into manageable segments, chunks of meaning that will correspond to the way the audience thinks, talks about and interprets that program.

If this approach is adopted, a problem (which Barthes had no need to consider) immediately confronts the audience researcher: do we divide the program up ourselves, or do we let the audience responses do it for us? It seems logical, in an audience study, to review the transcripts and divide the program up exactly as members of the audience do. This approach is, despite its merits, insufficient on its own. It deprives the researcher of the analytical advantages that come with the luxury of scrutiny. Even the combined efforts of fifty sets of TV viewers will miss or neglect parts of the program, so that a reading based purely on audience interpretations will be incomplete. We need to study the program ourselves to know which parts of the program remain, for most viewers, silent and apparently meaningless. Absences in an audience's interpretation may well be as ideologically significant as presences.

In practice, this means conducting our own close analysis of the program in conjunction with a review of the transcripts. The audience's interpretations become a body of "cultural capital" we can draw upon to explore the program's meaning. Since we also have the benefit of pondering over every nook and cranny in the program's text, we can call upon additional cultural resources, to reach those parts of the text the audience cannot reach. The program can then be divided into units of meaning, or, as Barthes would have it, lexias.

2) Once the program has been splintered into semiological fragments, we can begin to explore how audience members build it up again. Each audience transcript can thereby be systematically inserted into a lexicon of response, a diagrammatic picture that permits us to pose a number of questions. Which words or images are used to inform a viewer's interpretation, and which are not? How do connections between units of meaning correspond to the logic of the TV program? These questions proved to be particularly interesting in the news study, where interpretations were dependent upon those lexias that were or were not incorporated into the reading, leading to a diverse and often unpredictable set of interpretations.

3) The topography of meaning is not flat, it is distinctly uneven: to paraphrase Morrissey, some meanings are bigger than others. There are countless ways to interpret this irregularity; what matters is that we do so in a way that is practical to our purposes. In audience research, we can see lexias as the building blocks in the construction of a more general meaning: units of meaning will coalesce into structures that we can both identify and name. It is the moral woven by a parable, or a theme identified by the literary critic, or the mythologies conveyed by the highly coded world of TV commercials. It is, in its simplest sense, what stories are "about."

These "larger" meanings are usually fairly adaptable, because they are rarely reducible to any individual lexia; consequently, two very different stories can have the same overall meaning. Our ability to make these connections allows us to make sense of the world. So, having mapped out the lexias used to inform a viewer's reading of a news item or a scene in a TV show, we must explore the "sense" behind these patterns.

In most audience interviews, this is obligingly straightforward: most people will talk fairly easily about the overall meaning that encompasses what they have seen. Even if, for example, a news item is dismissed as confusing and difficult to comprehend (as one respondent put it, "I'm not sure what they were on about there"), the respondent avoids drifting into an existential state by drawing upon a vague residual category of meaning (one that does not require them to understand the specificities of the news item). This point will, I hope, become clearer in the analysis of the news audience.

The identification of these overall meanings is an important part of appreciating the patterns of selectivity used by TV viewers to reconstruct television's messages. It also takes us into the wider discursive arena beyond the TV screen.

4) At the heart of this project is the desire to discover those resources of meaning a TV viewer draws from his or her cultural environment, in order to interpret what he or she sees or hears. How, in other words, do the television program and the viewer's ideological repertoire combine to create meaning? As I have already suggested, we are not gremlins perched inside people's brains, happily watching as visible thoughts go squelching by, so we can never know for certain. We can only look for clues.

A transcript from a probing interview is not a straightforward articulation of the cultural and ideological resources used by respondents to inform their interpretations of television. It is, nonetheless, littered with evidence thereof. This evidence will take various discursive forms: discourses about the TV program will mingle with discourses about the world beyond it, in a chaotic patchwork of ideas.

There are many ways to distinguish between the various discourses on display. My initial inclination was to categorize them before trying to interpret the relations between them (see Lewis, 1985). The problem with this approach is that it tends to muffle their sometimes potent ambiguities more than necessary: categories are simply useful ways to structure and organize material—we should be able to erect them when they are helpful and dismantle them when they are not. We are more likely to retain the richness of the material if we begin by simply digging up discourses and labeling them.

This invariably raises the problem of definition: what is a discourse? How big is it? What does it look like? What are its properties? There are, for better or worse, no right or wrong answers to these questions: like the notion of the lexia, it is largely a matter of convenience. Discourses appear in countless different forms, just as meaning itself does, and our ability to appreciate their significance depends upon our cultural competence and understanding. This often involves an appreciation of the logic that binds an idea together. So, for example, when one of the respondents in the *Cosby* study argues that "there really is room in the United States for minority people to get ahead, without affirmative action," we are able to appreciate the links between this discourse and the ideological presuppositions that support the "American Dream."

The process of labeling makes it possible to group discourses recurring in different forms under one heading: this respondent's statement was, for example, labeled under the heading "anyone can make it in the US." The labeling procedure should be as open as possible, lest we prematurely exclude discursive references. We can, therefore, assign a single statement to more than one label: in this case, we should note that the respondent is also making a specific reference to affirmative action, which we can label as: "affirmative action for minorities is unnecessary."

Labeling discourses, like many other semiological tasks, is not an exact science: as painstaking and laborious as it is, it is also clumsy and haphazard. Methodologically speaking, it is easy to criticize but difficult to replace. For all its flaws, it gives us something of great potential value: it permits us to look at TV viewers collectively rather than individually. It allows us to observe the discursive world not as a discrete collection of separate utterances, but as one rooted in cultural commonalities and ideological unities. Individuals become the expression of the cultural world that created them.

Once we have converted the transcripts into jumbled collections of discursive units, we can begin to impose categories and structures upon them. We can relate those discourses that appear to be about the TV program to discourses that might inform these attitudes, and thereby begin to plot paths of discursive determination. These discursive links can then be related to other fields of determination, such as the race, class or gender of the respondent. In the *Cosby* study, for example, the relation between statements about race and *The Cosby Show* and more general discourses about race relations proved to be complex but revealing. These links were further illuminated by charting the racial and class origins behind these determinations.

The success of this enterprise depends upon the semiological sensitivity with which the initial discursive labeling is carried out. We need to acknowledge what people say, but also be aware of the ambiguities that may be concealed beneath layers of evasive or symbolic language. We will need to read not only the spoken lines, but what lies between them. A good example involves one of the most common ambiguities in discussions about television: the use of "realism" as a criterion for liking or disliking a program. It is a criticism that runs repeatedly through most qualitative audience interviews about television (see for example, Ang's *Dallas* study and Morley's work on family viewing), including the two analyzed here. At first glance, the frequency with which viewers use the word *unrealistic* to disparage a program would seem to suggest that realism was a central concern for most television viewers. We would be wrong, however, to accept this statement at its face value.

Most recent studies of TV viewing indicate that most people do not have a very wide range of critical discourses with which to analyze television. The word *unrealistic* often appears as a residual pejorative category to express a dissatisfaction that may have little to do with realism at all. In *Family Television*, for example (Morley, 1986), a number of respondents use the discourse of realism to compare the sitcom *Only Fools and Horses* favorably with the prime-time soap *Eastenders*. Whatever their relative merits, it would be very difficult to actually justify this comparison: *Eastenders* self-consciously comes much closer to all the traditional notions of realism than *Only Fools and Horses*. It is possible that viewers are using the discourse of realism as a way to articulate an unease or dislike of *Eastenders* that they feel unable or unwilling to express more explicitly: a coded form of displaying discomfort or rejection.

Our ability to interpret these statements will depend upon our acknowledgment of these cultural codes. In this instance, we can begin by labeling this discourse about "realism" not only as it appears, but as the generally negative statement that may lie beneath it. We may subsequently discover patterns of response that reveal both the source and content of this criticism.

These four methodological stages, despite their many imperfections, transform an unwieldy collection of transcripts into the raw material ready for a systematic exploration of the relation between a TV program and its audience. While we may not be able to measure it precisely, we have the chance to assess, as we follow

the progress of meaning, the nature of television's power and influence.

I shall use the two studies that follow to focus on different stages
in the construction of meaning. While both provide a commentary
on the ideological role of television in relation to specific programs,
the first concentrates on the intricate relation between a program
and its audience, while the second focuses on the origin of different
interpretations.

6

Behind the News

WHAT'S NEW?

A great deal has been written about television news. This is hardly surprising: TV network news, in both Britain and the US, has become the information source that most people say they rely on to find out what is going on the world. TV news is at the core of any modern democratic system. The quality of the decisions we make within a democracy depends upon the quality of the information we receive.

Television news cannot bear such a responsibility without coming under considerable scrutiny. Suppose it is nothing more than a tissue of lies and half-truths—what then? The cherished notion of democracy would be little more than a sham. Researchers have, accordingly, devoted time and energy to the study of news: analyzing the political economy of news production (see, for example, Murdock and Golding, 1973; Tuchman, 1978; Gitlin, 1980; Herman and Chomsky, 1988) and the style, form and content of news programs (see, for example, Galtung and Ruge, 1973; Hall, 1973; Brunsdon and Morley, 1978; Trew, 1979; Glasgow Media Group, 1980 and 1982; Lewis, 1981/82; Hartley, 1982; Jensen 1987a).

What has all this research told us? At the risk of oversimplifying a varied and sometimes exhaustive body of work, we can identify a general theme. This involves a systematic debunking of the myth that the news is an objective reproduction of social and political realities, produced by diligent journalists with an instinctive flair for the amorphous principles of "news value." The news is, rather, a structure of highly coded messages, shaped by a complex series of codes that derive from the economic and ideological conditions of its production.

Most serious considerations of the broad ideological meaning of TV news have either assumed or concluded that, in some form or another, it favors and sustains the hegemony of those with power. In countries like Britain or the United States, this means the ideas promoted on TV news tend to fall somewhere between the status quo and the political right, with a few occasional bursts of liberalism thrown in. Ideas that subvert the existing power structure (usually somewhere on the political left) are, on the whole, either ignored or treated as a problem. This is not a conspiracy (although we should not pretend conspiracies never happen), but a product of an elaborate and disparate array of social and semiotic determinations. The critical analysis of news has consequently become a campaigning issue on the left in both countries, with organizations like *Fairness and Accuracy in Reporting* (FAIR) and the *Campaign for Press and Broadcasting Freedom* struggling against the ideological tide.

This view of TV news is still, nevertheless, a controversial idea in the big wide world. This is, in part, a function of its complexity; the ideological positions constructed by TV news are filtered through the notions of "balance" and "objectivity." Despite its prevailing logic, the news is still the site of an ideological struggle. Dominant ideologies are not always uncontested or straightforwardly presented—the news, like all forms of television, is ambiguous. It remains to see how this ambiguity is interpreted by the audience.

While rhetorical and textual studies of the news have become increasingly sophisticated, there have been comparatively few recent qualitative empirical studies of the news audience. As Klaus Bruhn Jensen has written:

> It is time to start looking at the way in which people "make sense of the news" by having them "talk about the news" rather than handing them a questionnaire. In so doing, we can understand more concretely how ideology is circulated via the mass media and how it is used by its various audiences." (Jensen, 1987a, p. 25)

It is to this qualitative empirical level that we now move.

NARRATIVE STRUCTURE AND POPULAR CULTURE

The news, despite the number of people who claim to watch it, makes significantly less impact on its audience than most other forms of TV. Studies have confirmed what we might have already suspected—our ability to recall details of the news programs we watch is extremely low. This even applies to TV researchers while they are not wearing their analytical hats. Using his "discrepancy method," Peter Dahlgren found that during his "normal" viewing of a news program, he *felt* as if he was absorbing most of what he saw. He subsequently discovered that this was something of an illusion:

Our spontaneous impressions were often a bit self-assured, and it was not until after repeated viewings of the videotapes and studies of the transcripts that we realized just how much we had missed. (Dahlgren, 1985, pp. 236–7)

We appear to experience the news with our brains switched to somewhere else. This style of viewing breeds certain habits: Patterson points out, for example, that the audience for television news programs is

often an inadvertent one—which in large proportion, does not come purposely to television for news, but arrives almost accidentally, watching the news because it is "on," or because it leads into or out of something else. (Patterson, 1980, p. 57)

This inadvertent viewing is, I will argue, the key to understanding a great deal about the role and influence of TV news. A program half watched is, after all, something of a mystery—who can say which half was watched?

What is it about news that makes so much of it flow through our heads and disappear into the ether, never to be seen or heard of again? If we can answer this question, we may begin to understand what we *do* see and hear, and why. A large part of the answer, as I shall try to demonstrate, lies in an exploration of the way in which audiences engage (or, perhaps more appropriately, disengage) with the narrative structure of television news.

It is often supposed that TV news has a narrative structure much like any other form of television: the very term *news story* would suggest that this is so. Researchers have, accordingly, concentrated on the similarities between television fact and television fiction, rather than the differences. John Hartley, for example, has argued that although

it may seem odd to suggest that the news and television fiction are structured in the same way ... clearly the different [news] stories often do cohere into a pattern—they break with their individual boundaries and collectively signify particular themes, issues and meanings in the world. (Hartley, 1982, p. 118)

While it is true in a general sense, once we begin to look more closely at the narrative structure of news, we can see that, on TV, news stories have a peculiar structure that is all their own.

We can identify two distinguishing features of most fictional narratives, two codes that structure and organize them into the shape of a story. The first we could call the *code of sequence.* This refers to the way a story proceeds, developmentally, from one scene to the next. Scenes do not appear arbitrarily: they follow a precise and logical sequence. The logic of these appearances is usually based upon a chronology, a sequence ordered, in some way or another, by the passage of time. A narrative can also play with history: using flashbacks, or by organizing scenes around a structure of thematic developments. The key to the sequential code is not any special system for ordering, merely that such an order exists. The novel *Catch 22* for example, or the TV drama *The Singing Detective*, even though they move forward and backward in time, both have a carefully constructed logic that guides us from one scene to the next.

There is a difference between a story and a list. The sequential code implies more than an alphabetical or numerical order, it incorporates the idea of *development*. Scenes are not discrete, they are linked by ideas, themes or characters, by things that grow in our consciousness. Part of the story-teller's skill is the use of the code of sequence to control and direct that growth.

The second code of narrative is, in many ways, a form of the first. It is so integral to the structure of contemporary narrative, on television and elsewhere, that it needs to be distinguished and explored. It is the glue that fixes us to the screen, the device that tempts, teases and rewards those of us who keep on watching. It is a system that Roland Barthes has called the *hermeneutic code* (not to be confused with the more general practice of hermeneutics). He defines it thus:

> Let us designate as hermeneutic code all those units whose function it is to articulate in various ways a question, its response, and the variety of chance events that can either formulate the question or delay its answer; or even, constitute an enigma and lead to its solution. (Barthes, 1974, p. 17)

The hermeneutic code is composed of three elements. It begins with a question or enigma, although not necessarily in the traditional interrogative sense. It will not always take the literal form: who, what, why, which, when, where, or how? The enigma will be those traces of mystery inscribed within the words or images of the story.

The opening line of John Le Carre's thriller *Tinker, Tailor, Soldier, Spy* is a fine example:

> The truth is, if old Major Dover hadn't dropped dead at Taunton races Jim would never have come to Thursgood's at all.

The sentence, which introduces us to two characters and two events, plays with our sense of curiosity. Who is Major Dover, why did he drop dead (did he fall or was he pushed?), and what connection has this to Jim's appearance at Thursgood's? We read on, eager to pursue these questions, their enigmatic quality amplified by the context—we are, after all, reading a Le Carre novel.

There is a sense in which hermeneutic code is implicit in any novel's opening line: it inevitably contains elements of the unknown. It is, nevertheless, possible to distinguish between those, like Le Carre's, that are left deliberately incomplete, and those whose sense is self-contained. Isabel Allende's novel *Eva Luna* opens with a statement that, on one level, denies us nothing:

> My name is Eva, which means "life," according to a book of names my mother consulted.

The meaning, unlike Le Carre's, is not elusive but present. While we may want to know more about Eva, the statement stands complete.

The second stage of the hermeneutic code is rather more difficult to define. It is the presence of an absence: the enigma unleashed by the first stage of the code hangs in suspension, suggested but unresolved. It is the teasing moment between the question and the answer, the moment when the heroine pauses to draw on a cigarette before gliding toward the ringing phone, the time spent by the camera as it lingers on the hero's face as he ponders his reply, the tantalizing ticking of the time bomb that threatens the innocent. TV soap operas will often sustain these moments for as long as possible. Characters will spend whole scenes simply discussing the questions that surround another character. These scenes are not dull—they are sustained by the power of the enigma they carry forward, only to further increase our desire for resolution.

It is the resolution, when it comes, that is the third and final stage of the hermeneutic code. The enigma left unresolved is, in most forms of popular culture, a source of frustration and disappointment. The pleasure that resolution brings may be transitory (like many other forms of pleasure), but we desire it nonetheless. Once our curiosity has been aroused, we search for satisfaction.

There are, of course, cultural forms that deny us this pleasure. Conrad's *Heart of Darkness* or Jarmusch's *Stranger than Paradise*, deliberately leave us with questions rather than answers. They seek to replace the temporary pleasure of a story resolved with a more enduring aesthetic pleasure—the kinds of pleasure that make us want to dwell on the story, to reread or rewatch. They are also, in so doing, withdrawing from the world of popular culture to the more rarified domain we endow with the status of "art." Any Hollywood producer will know that the public demand for resolution (and preferably a happy one) is an artistic constraint it is difficult to avoid. Lose the ending and you lose the audience. This may be irritating for those with more avant-garde inclinations, but it is a fact of our cultural life.

The sequential and the hermeneutic codes are common to nearly all forms of popular television. All its dramatic forms, from films to sitcoms, are carefully structured around these codes. In television fiction the hermeneutic code is often multilayered: big questions and little questions intertwine, and answers turn into questions as the hermeneutic code pushes us forward, toward and beyond the next commercial break. The hermeneutic structure is so ingrained into the producer's consciousness that it is used almost automatically.

Television sport has its hermeneutic code already built in (who will win, and how will the game develop?). Those in charge of TV schedules know that live sport is much more popular than recorded highlights. If viewers already know what happened, the aesthetic pleasure of seeing the game with the banalities edited out is offset by the removal of the hermeneutic code. People are prepared to put up with the dull bits that inevitably permeate live sport as long as the hermeneutic code remains intact.

Quiz shows and game shows are, of course, inevitably structures around questions and answers. But we do not even have to "join in" to enjoy them. They are, like sport, contests with winners and losers, and with various nuances of strategy and play. The British show *Mastermind* is an example of a quiz show whose questions are often so difficult or so specific (the contestants spend half the game answering questions about their special subject, esoteric topics such as "the reign of King Louis the XIV" or "nineteenth-century British painting") that the audience have no hope of joining in. The pleasure comes from seeing the characters and the contest develop, as we urge a greengrocer from Reading or a teacher from Manchester toward victory.

Even TV commercials have begun to use the hermeneutic code, thereby demonstrating how much can be done in thirty seconds. The *Whisper* chocolate bar campaign in Britain adopted the ingenious strategy of launching the advertising campaign before they launched the product. The commercial would make references to "The Whisper" (have you heard it?) without actually telling the audience what the product was. The enigma this generated (what on earth is this a commercial for?) was finally resolved in the shape of the product itself. The US campaign for Nissan's *Infiniti* car used a similar approach, introducing the new car to TV viewers without showing us what it looked like or telling us anything about it. While these particular uses of the hermeneutic code are still a little unusual, the more conventional use of narrative codes in commercials (many ads are now split into a developing series of scenes) is becoming increasingly widespread. Rather than persuade or inform us, they seduce us with thirty-second stories.

Perhaps the most pervasive use of the hermeneutic code is in the TV soap opera. Soap operas usually attempt to keep at least three different narratives on the boil at any one time: when one enigma is resolved it is replaced by another. Our curiosity about the lives of the characters must be endlessly satisfied and aroused: loose ends can never be fully tied up because there is always another episode. As Christine Geraghty writes:

> The apparent multifariousness of the plots, their inextricability from each other, the everyday quality of narrative time and events, all encourage us to believe that this is a narrative whose future is not yet written. Even events which would offer a suitable ending in other narrative forms are never a final ending in the continuous serial: a wedding is not a happy ending but opens up the possibilities of stories about married life and divorce. (in Dyer et al., 1981, p. 11)

We become bound in the spell of these television histories, propelled by the never-ending quest for a final closure.

There is, however, one form of television that steadfastly refuses the temptations of narrative codes in general, and the hermeneutic code in particular. It is a form that, by abandoning narrative, abandons substantial sections of the viewer's consciousness. That form is television news.

TV SNOOZE

At a cursory glance, the structure of TV news is a little like soap opera. The cast of characters may be a little larger, but it still relies, to a great extent, upon the vicissitudes of a small group of people (a particular section of the elite) to keep the viewers entertained. Like soap opera, stories will last for days, months or even years. In order to understand the plots, we can draw upon a whole televisual history of information.

The similarities, for better or worse, stop there. It is not simply that news deals with fact (in theory, at least) and soap opera with fiction—the two involve very different styles of story telling. TV news owes its structure not to other forms of television, but to print. Television news stories are like newspaper stories with moving pictures.

The newspaper story routinely presents information in a very particular form, beginning with the most "important" elements, and then filling in the details, paragraphs laid out in declining order of newsworthiness. This serves two functions. It makes the editor's job very much easier: he or she will simply cut the story from the bottom upward. It also makes it possible for the reader to skim through the newspaper, reading the first few paragraphs of each story and dwelling only when something seems especially interesting. After all, if we had to read to the end of each story to get the point, reading newspapers (excluding, perhaps, British newspapers like the *Sun*) would begin to make serious inroads into our leisure time.

Television news takes a similar form, beginning with the "main points," usually presented by the news anchor, and then proceeding to a more detailed report, usually compiled by one or two reporters or correspondents. The TV reporter will sometimes make a small gesture toward more traditional forms of narrative by "wrapping up" the story with some concluding remarks. Like newspapers, the space devoted to stories bears very little relation to their complexity or the amount of information required to understand them. The more newsworthy the story, the more details will be presented.

The curious thing about television news is that the reasons for using this structure no longer apply. TV and newspaper editing processes are different, and the viewer, unlike the reader, is *unable* to skim through TV news. Unless you do a lot of videotaping and fast-forwarding, you are trapped in the chronology of the news program. Nevertheless, having borrowed this structure from newsprint, TV news producers and reporters (many of whom will have started their careers with newspapers) have become so accustomed to it that they are unable to think about doing it any other way.

If we study this narrative structure in more detail, we can see just how strange news "stories" are. The hermeneutic code is not only ignored, it is turned inside-out. History inevitably has an enigmatic quality—we do not know how the future will unfold. Television news takes this history and squeezes the sense of mystery right out of it. The main point of the story comes not at the end, but at the beginning. It is like being told the punchline before the joke, or knowing the result before watching the game, or being told "whodunnit" at the beginning of the murder mystery.

The protagonists in Mel Brooks' film *The Producers* discover that, with creative accounting, more money can be made from a Broadway flop than from a hit. They then set out to find a show so awful that it will be a "sure-fire flop." In the same way, if we decided to design a TV program with a structure that would completely fail to capture an audience's interest, we might come up with a TV news program. The characters in the film succeed in finding a play that is so dreadful that, to their dismay, the audience finds it outrageously funny—the mirthless structure of news carries with it no such risks.

Television news is structured a little like a cubist painting. The cubist painter will try to capture a subject by circling around it. The picture will be a succession of images from different angles, images that merge into one another in a complex totality of points of view. News will also be based around a subject—usually an event—that is represented to us by layering different points of view upon one another. The subject of the story will be a focal point around which the "story" is constructed. The history that precedes that event, that contextualizes it and explains it, inasmuch as it is presented at all, will simply take its place alongside other "points of view." We do not have our interest awakened by an enigma and gratified by a resolution. The scenes that compose the news narrative appear in an almost arbitrary succession. It is a structure that bears more resemblance to a shopping list than to a story.

Most of the news items in this study are, in this sense, fairly typical. They begin with the anchor introducing the subject/event and telling us its "significant" elements. The shorter items will simply end there, like strange fragments from another story told somewhere else. The longer items will then proceed to a reporter on location, who will give us pieces of information about this event. These snippets of information will include details of the event itself, what various members of the elite make of it (see Hall et al., 1978, on the "primary definers" who the news media use to define events), and a brief history of events leading up to it—presented in no particularly order. Major news items will simply extend this process to incorporate a number of different reports. The extra time permitted to major news stories is often filled by a repetition of various elite perspectives (more politicians, more experts, etc.).

These points, I must admit, had never occurred to me until I began to try and make sense of the patterns that emerged from the audience study. The study revealed that most respondents had great difficulty recalling "stories": their discussions tended to revolve around discrete moments in each item. If they did not already know details of events leading up to the item (which applied to most audience members most of the time), they were extremely unlikely to remember anything the item told them about the historical context. This meant that the meaning the news producers intended to convey (the intended meaning) often bore little relation to the meanings constructed by the viewers. The intended meaning usually relied upon the viewer establishing links between pieces of information presented to them. This, in most cases, simply did not happen.

There were numerous examples of this. The British Leyland item was based upon the news of a "new deal" being negotiated between unions and management. This "new deal" was the focal point of the anchor's introduction, and the reporter on location began and ended his report with references to it. The new deal was, however, incidental to most respondents' reading of the item: only 16 percent made any reference to it at all.

The item about the trials and tribulations of the (then) British home secretary William Whitelaw, was presented as a story of a politician who, following a period of harsh criticism from members of his own party, emerges triumphant—after a speech to party workers in Harrogate. Most of the respondents, however, did not focus their discussion on this story of triumph in the face of adversity at all, but on the brief excerpt from the speech of Whitelaw's Harrogate speech. As far as the producers were concerned, the excerpt (of the speech) they chose to show was irrelevant—it was intended to signify nothing more than the event that preceded his "triumphant reception"—yet, to many respondents in the study, it became the cornerstone around which they constructed their whole interpretation of the item. For them, the speech appeared out of the blue, not as a moment in a particular history.

There were, however, one or two news items that deviated markedly from this pattern. What was odd about these exceptions was that, on first examination, there appeared to be nothing to distinguish them from the others. They certainly did not concern subjects that the respondents were especially familiar with or interested in. It was only when I began to consider their narrative structure (and people's response to it) that the explanation began to emerge.

CONTROLLING VIEWERS IN EL SALVADOR—AND LOSING THEM ON THE WEST BANK

We can measure the effect of the narrative structure used by television news on audiences by comparing the responses to two news items; one which (fairly typically) abandoned traditional narrative codes, and one that (less typically) did not. Both items were foreign news stories, both concerned parts of the world most respondents knew very little about, both involved films presented by reporters on location, and both lasted approximately two minutes. The first was a story of trouble between Palestinians and Israelis on the West Bank. The item revolved around three connected pieces of information (laid out, here, in their historical sequence: this was *not* the order in which the news presented the three events, as I shall explain shortly):

1) the sacking of three Palestinian mayors by the Israelis;
2) rioting by the Palestinians in response to this, with a heavy military clampdown by Israeli soldiers; and,
3) criticism by Egypt and the U.S. of the Israeli action (in sacking the mayors), and its effect on future negotiations between these three countries.

The second two pieces of information make little sense without the first, yet only *one-fifth* of the respondents were able to make any connection between the first two, and *only four out of fifty reconstructed all three elements.*

The most surprising piece of information to get "lost" was the first part of the story. This might have been understandable if the reporter had glossed over it, but this did not happen. The whole item appeared to be structured around this piece of information: the only interview shown was with an Israeli administrator, seen "justifying to foreign journalists the dismissal of the mayors." This interview was even mentioned by more than two fifths of the respondents—even though most were unable to make the links necessary to make sense of it.

The failure to make these links had a distinct effect upon the audience. The majority built their reading of the item upon the images of violence shown in the report. Deprived of historical context, these images signified nothing but themselves. The story was, for most of the respondents, just another episode in an endless saga of violence in the Middle East. The specificities of the region's history faded into generalities about the world's "trouble spots." Over two-fifths of the respondents made a direct comparison to Northern Ireland, not because of possible historical similarities, but because the violent pictures looked the same.

Some viewers constructed this meaning with an air of resignation:

Well I think personally, the Israelis and the Arabs and so forth, all that fracas, it's gone on for thousands of years, it'll carry on.

It has been going on a long time. Probably when it first started it took more of an interest—now it's just a thing that's carrying on and carrying on, and a lot of the things you see like that, that you see often, you tend to think: "Oh, it's still there, and not a lot's coming out of it really." I think you sort of look at it and it doesn't mean an awful lot anymore.

Others were more perturbed by the story, but were still unable to go beyond certain scenes to make sense of it:

The violence . . . I don't, I didn't understand anything about why the army are killing.

This frustration led some respondents to try to understand what was going on by imposing their own guesses and assumptions on events. One, for example, suggested:

I don't know, there's just fighting out there, and they're trying to stop it;

without being able to specify who "they" were—the assumption being that somebody *must* be trying to sort things out.

While such a response demonstrates that TV news is, on a fairly basic level, failing to communicate, it also shows that this failure does not create silence. Whether a reading is partial or exhaustive, vague or informed, it is still a reading. Meaning is being constructed and solidified. For most viewers, regardless of what this item may actually say, what it *does* is to feed a residual racism, a world where foreigners fight one another for no particular reason.

This is a style of response that I had, in some form or another, expected to find. When I compared it, however, with readings of one of the other foreign news items, a report on the elections in El Salvador, I discovered something quite different.

The respondents did not, on the whole, express any more familiarity or interest in the El Salvador item than in the previous report from the West Bank. The West Bank item, moreover, revolves around a fairly simple set of connections, while the elections in El Salvador appeared to present a more complicated event. The response, I had anticipated, would be even more confused or fragmented. I discovered quite the opposite.

Although reporter Jon Snow's piece is fairly detailed, the gist of the story revolves around three points (points that, we should note, were largely ignored by the news media in the United States):

(a) Major Roberto D'Aubuisson is a candidate in the El Salvador elections.
(b) He is seen as having a dubious reputation, because he is an extreme right winger and/or responsible for killing Archbishop Romero and/or connected to the death squads, who are responsible for the dead bodies found dumped by the roadside.
(c) The U.S. are willing to support this man, should he win.

Like the West Bank, it contains three pieces of information that the audience is intended to connect in order to make sense of the story. Unlike the West Bank piece (when only four of the fifty respondents were able to make these connections), exactly half the respondents did so. Most of these *also* went on to recall that this represented a shift in the U.S. position. Pieces of information did not fall apart into discrete and disconnected fragments, they merged into a sequence.

While most responses to the West Bank item seemed impervious to connections between events, the discussions of events in El Salvador related not to fragments and images but to a *narrative logic*. Most of those who made the connection between the first two elements of the story, for example, proceeded to make the third. Other fairly sophisticated connections were made by a surprising number of respondents. Nearly half the sample, for instance, mentioned the absence of left-wing parties in the election, and, of these, three quarters explained this absence with references to the persecution of the left in El Salvador (nearly all these respondents subsequently judged the elections to be a charade).

The difference between the responses to the two items suggests a great deal. From the broadcaster's point of view, one discourse is considerably more powerful than the other: one reporter is able to exercise significant control over the viewer's readings, while the other could almost have shown a few clips of rioting on the West Bank and given up. Why did the two items, in practice, signify so differently? The secret of Jon Snow's success is, on one level, fairly simple: like the gifted comic, it's not the subject matter that counts, but the way he tells it.

The West Bank news item has a structure that characterizes the whole genre of television news. Like nearly all news stories, it revolves around an event (see Galtung and Ruge, 1973). The event will be the focal point of the news story. Because most newsworthy events do not occur out of the blue (natural disasters being one exception) this event is a momentary climax reached through the passage of recent history. In this case, the event is a riot, a climactic response to the sacking of the Palestinian mayors. It is a history that has the sequential code and the hermeneutic code built into it. In Scene 1, the Israelis take the controversial step of sacking the Palestinian mayors. What will happen next? How will the Palestinians react? History is silent for a moment as the event sinks in, only to erupt in Scene 2, when the Palestinians take to the streets to protest their anger.

The traditional TV narrative would not have failed to exploit the potential of the hermeneutic code with the availability of such easy material. The news item, on the other hand, resists any temptation to engage the viewer's interest (just the facts, ma'am). The story is told backwards: the climax of the story is introduced first, and only then are we told of the events that preceded it. This structure is laid out in the anchor's introduction, which begins with a number of details about "several days of rioting" and ends with the statement:

> The West Bank has been tense since the Israelis sacked three Palestinian mayors there.

The cause of the rioting, in other words, is only revealed *after* the event. This structure is then repeated by the reporter, who begins with "newsworthy footage" of rioting (and the Israeli clampdown) in Ramula, before it is revealed that

> in Nablus, the other of the two West Bank towns where the Israelis turned the Palestinian mayors out of office, there was desultory sparring.

The cause of the trouble, rather obliquely referred to here, is then developed, and Menachim Milson is shown defending the action.

The eagerness with which we are rushed to the climax of the story completely diminishes the enigmatic power of the causal sequence (the sacking of the mayors). There are no enigmas, no teasing delays and no resolutions in this story. The power of the causal sequence to signify at all is, thereby, also diminished. The viewer, accustomed to hearing the "main points" first, treats this focal point (the violence) as the beginning and end of the story. History becomes nothing more than a further detail. The sacking of the mayors is an event silenced by its position in the narrative.

The *El Salvador* item begins in much the same way, with the anchor immediately directing us to the end of the story:

> The Americans seem to be anticipating an extreme right-wing victory in Sunday's elections in El Salvador, and they appear to have changed their minds about Major Roberto D'Aubuisson. . . .

This power of the introduction to deflate the story that follows is lessened by the rather puzzling presentation: the connection between the two events (the possibility of an extreme right-wing victory and the U.S. *volte face* on D'Aubuisson) is unstated. While this would normally be interpreted as bad journalism, it allows Snow to rescue the narrative, and use his film report to develop it.

Snow makes skillful use of narrative codes throughout his report. He begins by setting the scene of the election—the arrival of the observers, the distribution of the ballot boxes, the political complexion of the candidates on offer, and the enforced absence of the left. He then reports that

> though there are half a dozen parties of the right, the battle is really between two men: President Duarte in the centre for the Christian Democrats, is Washington's candidate, but both he and the U.S. Embassy here think he has a good chance of losing.

The loser having been introduced, the enigma "who, then, is the likely winner?" is established. Only then is D'Aubuisson presented to us, his "right-wingness" being stated both explicitly and implicitly (in relation to his policies). The film then mysteriously moves to a shot of Snow standing by three dead bodies. Snow briefly describes the scene, setting up the enigma—"Why are there dead bodies here, and what has this to do with the election?" This enigma is developed in Snow's next sentence, which answers the first question by referring to the death squads, but, teasingly, leaves the second open. The enigmatic power of the scene is intensified by two more descriptive shots of the same scene (what Christian Metz would call a "descriptive syntagm") revealing close-ups of a vulture and an empty pair of boots.

The camera then focuses on Jon Snow, who resolves the enigma by referring to the evidence linking D'Aubuisson to the death squads, and to the killing of Archbishop Romero. The narrative ends with the U.S. Embassy's "new view" of D'Aubuisson. This revelation (and relevation it is, in the light of the story so far) is, once again, presented without disrupting the narrative flow: Snow leads us gradually into the story's conclusion, treating us to another brief whiff of suspense:

> Until a few weeks ago, the Embassy made it plain that D'Aubuisson was *not* a man with whom they could co-operate. But, last night . . .

the viewer is allowed to briefly ponder on what this "new view" might be, before Snow finally reveals the details to us.

The *El Salvador* report uses narrative codes to draw the audience into the story. It moves viewers along from one scene to another, allowing them to make connections and develop a certain sense of history. The West Bank item does the opposite. Its structure means the story it tells dissolves into a series of isolated events. The viewer, used to the structure of news, sees only the events with the privileged position in the narrative. Of the two, it is the West Bank report that is more typical, and the audience research repeatedly revealed the same structure of response.

What is at stake here is not the capacity of news to produce a reading, but the capacity of its *creators* to prefer one. The narrative still prefers a set of meanings—the West Bank item produced a fairly consistent set of readings—but *not* in the way we, or the program's producers, would have anticipated. Once we begin to understand this point, we can investigate the ways in which TV news actually influences audience response.

THE MEANING OF NEWS

It is becoming clear, I hope, that an understanding of *how* news means is essential if we are to understand *what* it means. The curious structure of TV news dispels any straightforward expectations we might have about the influence of news messages. As we have seen, the substance of an argument can depend upon the form in which that argument is presented. This, I would argue, is a serious problem for the manufacturers of news. If information is presented in such a way that the audience neither sees nor hears it, then there is little point in presenting it at all.

I have, in the past, argued that if news adopted the conventions of narrative codes used in other cultural forms, it would be considerably more successful at communicating its message to people (Lewis, 1985). While I still have no doubt about this—the evidence, after all, would seem to confirm it—these suggestions are sometimes met with horror rather than approval. Why, I have been asked, should we give the makers of news even more power to control people's view of the world?

As it happens, most TV newsmakers are rather too conservative or self-confident about their trade to listen to the likes of me—no matter what the evidence suggests. There is, nonetheless, a vital question to be addressed here: if TV news has, through its structure, relinquished the use of narrative to manipulate the viewer's understanding, does it have less power? Does it, in fact, open up space for viewers to construct their own readings? Does the gap between encoding and decoding pass power from the hands of producers to consumers in a kind of semiotic democracy?

As attractive as this sounds, it would be premature to reach such a conclusion. A close analysis of the material produced by the news audiences in this study inspires a rather different understanding. Suppose we went to a restaurant, and, as we were handed the menu, we were told we could order courses in any sequence we liked. Would Sir or Madam like to start with the chocolate cake, or perhaps the strawberry cheesecake? Most of us would probably respond to such a choice with a distinct lack of enthusiasm. Starting rather than finishing with dessert might be better for our teeth (according to dentists), but it upsets our whole idea of the way we eat a meal. Our freedom to choose, in other words, is constrained by our cultural history.

In the same way, the absence of a narrative to bind us to the logic of a news program does not free us to construct any meaning we like. On the contrary, the responses to the West Bank item suggest that the narrative structure exercised a form of control by default: the narrative positioned some ideas in a place where they would be heard, while reducing others to comparative silence. This led many viewers to construct a very particular reading: the West Bank became just another trouble spot where foreigners, for some long-forgotten reason, interminably beat the hell out of each other. Regardless of its intention, the news item communicated this meaning very powerfully.

A careful examination of the other audience readings also reveals, in a similarly disjointed way, that TV news does, indeed, have a great deal of power. If we are to understand the nature of that power, however, we must abandon many of the suppositions we have used hitherto to evaluate it. This involves understanding the specific structures of determination that operate when we watch the news.

These structures do not appear to be organized around the divisions that are often used to evaluate the content of news. It has been argued, for example, that there is a distinct hierarchy of content based on origin, so that the weight or authority attached to a statement depends who makes that statement. The most powerful voice on the news would seem to be the reporter's own, endowed as it is by the aura of objectivity. The expert comes next, followed by authoritative members of the elite, like corporate managers, government representatives or police chiefs. At the bottom of the pile comes the *vox populi*, the "ordinary person," the woman or man in the street.

This hierarchy certainly exists among newsmakers. News, as many analysts have pointed out, is structured around the views of elites (see, for example, Galtung and Ruge, 1973, and Hall et al., 1978). It is, in this sense, inevitably influential. This does *not* mean, however, that audience treat the voices they hear on the news in the same way. Once they appear on the TV screen, the study suggests that viewers do not seem inclined to give more weight to "high-status" speakers than to "low status" speakers. Viewers tended, on the whole, to remember ideas without remembering their origin. The three speakers on *News at Ten* who, on one level, had the most significant impact on the readings were the (then) British home secretary and two workers on the assembly lines at the British Leyland car plant. These people do not, in the hierarchy of news characters, have a great deal in common. Their impact, it appeared, had less to do with *who* they were than with their position in the news discourse. These are important points, and I will return to them shortly.

Another source of conventional wisdom concerns the relative impact of spoken and visual material. Within the semiological literature, there is a tendency to emphasize the dominance of the verbal over the visual: language is seen as *anchoring* the meaning of the image, attracting the viewer's attention and interpreting it for the viewer (see Seiter, 1987, pp. 25–26, for a useful summary of this position). Broadcasters, on the other hand, are inclined to stress the power of the visual image, the idea that pictures speak louder than words. The CBS news reporter Lesley Stahl has illustrated this point with the story of a report she compiled about Ronald Reagan's campaign strategy. The report borrowed some of the more flattering images from the Reagan campaign, but accompanied them with a critical commentary that highlighted the deceptive nature of these images. She naturally expected a rough reaction from the Reagan camp, but, to her surprise, received only congratulations. The report, she was told, would be seen but not heard: the power of the visuals would silence the dissenting commentary (this point was discussed in detail during the thoughtful documentary *Consuming Images*, broadcast on U.S. public television in 1989).

Both these conflicting analyses contain moments of truth. They become misleading when they are elevated to become structural rules of TV viewing. The readings in the *News at Ten* study suggested that neither the verbal nor the visual level of the program dominated the responses. Some pictures were powerful, some words were powerful—it is not possible to make any comparative generalities. What made images or statements powerful was, once again, their position in the news item and the ideas the viewers were ideologically attuned to receive.

These points are fundamental to any discussions of ideological influence or media bias. This is not to say that the study of content is irrelevant—far from it. In order to evaluate content we need to understand how power is actually structured in the viewing of a news program.

On the basis of the audience study, it is possible to locate three of the axes of power that operate in the contemporary consumption of news.

1) Ideological resonance

The role of ideology in the watching of news is, in some ways, the most pervasive but least tangible element in the whole process. It is informed by a point emphasized in the earlier chapters of this book: meaning is contingent upon the semiological or ideological resources available to the viewer. While this applies to all forms of communication, the structure of TV news makes it particularly important.

Most forms of televisual narrative have a certain power to draw the viewer into a narrative logic, using weapons like the hermeneutic code to attract and maintain the viewer's interest. On the rare occasions when television news uses these narrative codes (as the readings of the *El Salvador* item suggest), it succeeds in communicating a set of ideas that can, ever so slightly, go beyond their existing ideological framework. Some viewers, for example, were shocked by the cynicism of the U.S. Embassy in El Salvador. To reach this state of shock, they were required to make a series of links (between the limitations on the democratic process, the death squads, Major D'Aubuisson and the embassy's about-face). They were, I have tried to show, able to make these links because the narrative structure encouraged them to do so. The *El Salvador* item was, however, illustrative because it was exceptional rather than typical: news does not routinely work in this way. Most items have a narrative form that actively *discourages* the viewer from making connections between ideas.

The structure of news forces viewers to draw more actively upon their own ideological resources to make sense of what is going on. The problem here is that these resources are frequently meager and superficial. Perhaps the only instance when a majority of respondents were able to draw upon a fairly rich variety of discourses, thereby exploiting the ambiguities of *News at Ten*, occurred during the discussion of the jobs item. The item simply listed the number, type and location of jobs recently gained and lost in Britain. To some of the respondents, the item was simply about comparative numbers—was unemployment rising or falling? The fact that the item did not actually give the totals of "new jobs" or "jobs lost" allowed those generally critical of the government to assert that it demonstrated that unemployment was still rising, and those more sympathetic to government policy to suggest that the rise appeared to be tapering off (for the record, the actual totals indicated roughly twice as many jobs lost as gained).

Other respondents were able to draw upon different perspectives with which to interpret the item. The dramatic decline of the manufacturing industry in Sheffield (where the interviews took place) allowed a number of people to absorb a variety of discourses around the issue of unemployment. This enabled them to construct two other frameworks for interpreting what they saw. One group felt that the issue of unemployment was a regional one, with jobs shifting from the north to the south. To these respondents, the numbers were less important than the location of employment patterns. This group subsequently read the item as a story of economic decline in the north and employment regeneration in the south. Another set of respondents were informed by their knowledge of the decline of manufacturing and the rise in the service industries. In these instances, the statistics they commented on involved the categories of jobs lost and gained.

The richness and variety of responses to this news item was the exception rather than the rule. For some respondents the jobs item even came as something of a relief—here, at last, was something tangible for them to talk about. Loomis (1990) found that documentary viewers who found the program difficult would, in a similar way, seize upon those moments they could interpret coherently. The familiarity of these moments, in an otherwise barren televisual landscape, became, Loomis suggests, a source of pleasure.

In news watching, as in other areas of life, knowledge is power. The few respondents who were able to offer what they felt to be an "informed reading" of most items clearly enjoyed the discursive power this gave them. The majority of the respondents, however, were limited to those moments in the news that created some form of *ideological resonance*. During the item from the West Bank, this involved the articulation of a discourse (with rather vague parameters) about the world's "trouble spots": places where, for one reason or another, the inhabitants insisted on fighting one another. The only moment on the item that fitted this ideological framework was the occasion when we were shown rioting Palestinians confronting Israeli soldiers. This scene resonated with the framework and made an impact. The specificities of history, of causes and consequences, were lost completely.

The fragmented narrative structure of news means that the "preferred meaning" of a news item is usually limited to these moments of discursive or ideological resonance. What is also particular about television news is that, unlike many other forms of television, it operates on a discursive level that most people find elusive. It portrays a world that is, in most cases, difficult to relate to (an issue I shall explore in more detail later). One of the consequences of this, I discovered, was that the frameworks respondents used to make sense of a news item frequently originated from the news itself. This, of course, directly raises the issue of power within the news discourse—an issue I shall address in terms of its logic and its structure.

2) The power of association

Many advertisers have long since given up trying to persuade people of the value of their products. TV commercials from the 1950s that do try explicit forms of persuasion ("this is a great car because of X, Y and Z") now look rather quaint. It is much easier, and more effective, to try and create an association in people's minds between the product and an appropriate image or idea. So, for example, diamonds become associated with love and romance, perfume with sex, breakfast cereals with health, soft drinks with feeling good and banks with security. Some of these associations are, to say the least, more appropriate than others. A TV campaign by Pepsi in the U.S. went so far as to try to link Pepsi with the democratic changes taking place in Eastern Europe at the end of 1989. As ludicrous as this association is, it successfully creates a link between a concept of "freedom" and Pepsi Cola.

From the advertisers' point of view, this is an effective way of using a medium like television. Working on a metaphorical level, it enables them to say anything they like about the product, without actually telling any lies. Moreover, a logic based on nothing more than a straightforward association is so simple that, as long as it is repeated enough times, it can enter even the most inattentive TV viewer's consciousness.

Roland Barthes has described this associative form of communication, using the term *myth* (Barthes, 1973). As a form of argument, he defines myth as ahistorical. It ignores the cumbersome requirements of sequence or development: it is an instant logic freed from the constraints of historical analysis. It is, nonetheless, powerful because it is so difficult to refute. It is much easier to *create* an association than it is to deconstruct it.

The manufacturers of news, whatever their intentions, are manufacturers of myth. The narrative structure of news, for most viewers, cannot sustain the links and developments necessary to go beyond crude associations. TV news does not necessarily ignore historical details, it simply fails to persuade the viewer to fit these details together. The West Bank and Whitelaw news items both provided a historical context, but presented it in a way that allowed it to vanish from memory. The power of news lies, therefore, in the power of association.

The readings of the British Leyland item on *News at Ten* provide an interesting example of this. Nearly all the respondents were already familiar with British Leyland (BL). Leyland workers had cropped up on numerous news programs for more than a decade, during news coverage of strikes at their factories in the West Midlands. The specificities of previous disputes did not mean a great deal to most of the respondents—they were, nevertheless, left with residual association between British Leyland and strikes. This was articulated during the interview time and time again:

> I think people haven't got a very good impression of British Leyland actually, after all the strikes, it's a bit of a you know, ... letting you know they are doing well again and things are alright.

> The rate of cars that is coming out now is, by far, it's a lot higher, but there again it's people isn't it? Not as many strikes (laughs).

> Interesting that they are actually doing something successful for a change and not having a strike, usually when BL is on it's because they want to have a strike.

The Glasgow Media Group's well-known assertion that British television news associates workers rather than management with industrial action (strikes are therefore seen as the fault of unreasonable workers rather than of unreasonable management) is clearly borne out by these respondents' attitude toward British Leyland. As two of these respondents imply, the meaning of strike-bound British Leyland is associated not with incompetent management but with militant workers.

This associative logic provided the framework for nearly all the discussions about the item, and it became particularly appropriate during the interviews with two BL workers. Prompted by Giles Smith (the reporter), the two workers stated that, despite the inevitable redundancies, automation at the Longbridge plant was a good thing. As one of them suggested, "It's better to have a few jobs than no jobs at all." These conciliatory views were in stark contrast to most respondents' expectations, making them the focal point of most of the audience discussions. Many used this "knowledge" to conclude that the workers were untypical of the workforce as a whole—a suspicion that spanned a variety of quite different political perspectives:

> I don't think the British Leyland workforce are really like that, I think they are a little bit more aggressive and a little more militant than *they* were, from what I know of the past attitudes of BL workers.

> They certainly didn't seem typical in the face of the usual shop steward attitude at all, I didn't think, but they seemed sensible.

> I think basically . . . I think them two men were plants by the owners, definitely, they were a bit too good.

> Well it seemed like a PR job to me, with the two workers, seemed sort of, well they were two people with the same opinions, they seemed to be a bit sort of stooge like . . .

Others were simply rather surprised:

> I was rather surprised that they were pro-automation, and accepted the fact. . . . I would have thought that they would have sided with the unions and put up a fight against the automation. I was surprised that one of them, especially the second one, said it's better to lose a few jobs than there be no jobs at all.

> I was amazed at the two guys, er, you know, "a few jobs are better than no jobs." . . . You generally think of your average

factory worker as being more or less against too much automation and that kind of thing, and they seemed to be welcoming
it wholeheartedly. I found that a little bit surprising.

If we examine the news item outside these ideological constraints, this focus on an extremely brief interview might seem rather
strange. It was, for example, no longer than an interview with a
member of management (Brian Fox)—yet even those respondents
who remembered seeing the manager interviewed thought it un-
worthy of much comment. What made the workers so memorable,
and the interview with them such a powerful moment in the news
item, was an associative logic created by television itself: British
Leyland equals strikes equals militant workers. While the workers
directly contradicted this logic, their significance in the discourse
relied upon it.

The ability to resist these associative logics depends upon the
existence of an alternative ideological framework. This point was
revealed rather self-consciously by one respondent, who, commenting on one of the Leyland workers, suggested that

> he just seemed rather placid, and the image I've got of BL is
> that "we are going to stick up for our rights and get what we
> want" and "we are going to strike," which is probably another
> image projected by the media, which might not be the right
> image, I don't know, er, but all the mythology I've absorbed
> about BL is not reflected by that chap. No, I don't think he was
> representative at all.

In other words, in the absence of any other information, it is the
media's framework or nothing.

The creation of these associative logics defies, in one sense, all
the sophisticated complexities of textual analysis. It refers us beyond
elaborate semiological constructions to a set of broad associative
frameworks. At the crudest level, these frameworks may be established by simple process of repetition. A good example of this occurred in response to the news about Roy Jenkins' victory at the
Hillhead by-election. This lengthy (nine minute) item consisted of
a series of quotations from a number of politicians: Roy Jenkins,
David Steel, Shirley Williams, David Owen, Cecil Parkinson, Tony
Benn, Francis Pym, Michael Foot, and a series of unidentified Social
Democrats. One of the item's themes (suggested by a number of
these sources) was the notion that Roy Jenkins was now "the alternative prime minister." This idea was repeated seven times during
the item: five times by various Social Democratic Party members,

once in the opening headline and once in a question asked by Peter Sissons.

This theme is not politically impartial: it supported the Social Democrats' claim that, despite their meager representation in Parliament, it was they, rather than the Labour Party, that were the real alternative to Thatcherism. In order to maintain the notion of 'impartiality', it was therefore essential that these suggestions were seen as originating from Social Democrats rather than from *News at Ten*.

Two of these suggestions came, apparently unambiguously, from two prominent Social Democrats, Shirley Williams and David Owen. Pictures of Williams and Owen appeared next to a visual display of their statements (which were read out by Alistair Burnet). The other three authored references to Roy Jenkins as "the alternative prime minister" also came from sources outside *News at Ten*:

> The Social Democrats have been talking today of Mr. Roy Jenkins as the next prime minister.

> Mr. Jenkins arrives at Westminster on Tuesday. His friends expect him to become Mrs. Thatcher's chief opponent—they say, the alternative prime minister.

> Today Mr. Jenkins could have been facing the political wilderness—instead he's being talked of as a future prime minister.

Not surprisingly, given the number of references to it, two thirds of the respondents (thirty-three out of fifty) subsequently constructed this idea as one of the main messages of the item. An associative logic had been almost bludgeoned into them.

What was more startling was that most of them (twenty-five out of thirty-three) were unable to identify the source of the idea. Those that did identify the source were, in most cases, able to do so because of their awareness that this was an idea that the Social Democrats were trying to promote (an awareness usually derived from their knowledge of contemporary political discourses). The others were, on the whole, far less critical of the idea, since it appeared to originate from no particular source. For them, the idea just existed, and *News at Ten* were simply bringing it to our attention. The source of the associated logic is, in other words, lost to the collective memory.

The consequences of this are profound. It suggests that many viewers find it difficult to place those views of the world that are repeatedly put forward on the news, in any critical or qualifying context. Journalists are apt to defend the elite-centered nature of news reporting on the grounds that they are simply reflecting the existing power structure. This was, for example, the response of ABC's flagship current affairs program, *Nightline*, to an exhaustive content analysis that located their guests firmly within a narrow right-wing orthodoxy (described in January/February 1989 issue of the FAIR publication). This is already a decidedly feeble defense (we could use it equally well to defend news media tightly controlled by the state), but we should be aware that it relies upon the ability of audiences to locate the origin of the views they hear and judge them accordingly. In this audience study, only a minority possessed this capacity.

From this evidence, it would appear that some of the criticisms of a straightforward content analysis of news seem unfounded. The failure of the news narrative to offer the viewer anything more than a set of disconnected associative logics would seem to lead us away from sophisticated textual structures and back to basic quantitative questions of content. While there is much to be said for this approach, I would like to qualify it with two important caveats.

The first concerns the route we took to arrive at this position. Only by analyzing the role of narrative (or lack of it) in news in some detail were we able to identify its powerful structural moments. The second refers us back to this narrative analysis. While the research suggests that the narrative structure of TV news discourages the viewer from making connections, it is still active in making some structural moments powerful and others weak. This brings us to a third axis of power in the news: one that concerns its form rather than its content.

3) The distribution of power

I have, throughout this chapter, referred to the gap between the broadcaster's intended meaning of the news item, and the meanings constructed by most members of the audience. To understand the significance of the news event we need, in most cases, to understand the history of events that preceded it. (There are, of course, more than one set of historical contexts, and part of the ideological role of TV news involves which history it chooses to reveal.) The problem (from the broadcaster's perspective) is that for many audience members, this history proves remarkably elusive.

The explanation for this, I have argued, lies in the failure of the news narrative to use narrative codes to forge links between the "history" and the "event." Because the history is invariably presented after the event, the narrative is thrown out of sequence and the hermeneutic code completely subverted. The viewer is then obliged to make sense of the event in isolation. There are, in other words, weak moments and powerful moments in the modern television news story.

The powerful moment in the news discourse is the portrayal of the "event"—or at least the part of the story audiences perceive as the event. Just as newspaper readers will skim the opening paragraphs for the main gist of the news story, so viewers will focus their attention upon its televisual equivalent. The equivalent moment, perhaps surprisingly, does not appear to be the anchor's introduction (see Lewis, 1985, for an account of the "refocusing effect") but the first main *action sequence* in the report. In the story from the West Bank, this consisted of scenes of rioting. The history behind those scenes (which, in fact, appeared to be the intended focal point of the story) was subsequently forgotten. We can trace exactly the same pattern of response during discussions of the Whitelaw item—with even more curious consequences.

The news of Whitelaw's reception in Harrogate would appear, to both broadcasters and researchers, to have a fairly straightforward and clear meaning. The story was "about" the favorable reception given to Willie Whitelaw by Conservative Party workers, following a period when he had been losing credibility with his own party's right wing. The story was, indeed, something of an anticlimax. After a series of attacks upon Whitelaw for his supposedly "soft" approach to law and order—attacks which had become particularly vociferous during the preceding Conservative Party Conference—the broadcast media sent teams up to Harrogate expecting the (then) home secretary to be given a rough ride. As one BBC news broadcaster told me: "We were there to see Willie Whitelaw get mauled, and he didn't. We'd expended all that effort, and so had they (ITN), so we still had to produce something out of it." What resulted on *News at Ten* may not have been terribly newsworthy, but it was not, apparently, ambiguous. Not, at least, until we examine how it was decoded.

The main action sequence in the story involves a brief clip of Whitelaw's speech to party workers, followed by pictures of a gratified politician receiving a standing ovation. *News at Ten*'s story did not concern the actual speech, but the reception given to this beleaguered minister. This was not intended to be a story about the particularities of law-and-order policy, but about the Conservative Party's feelings toward the man responsible for enacting it. The clip from Whitelaw's speech was therefore chosen fairly arbitrarily—as long as it made a fairly coherent "sound bite," it did not really matter what he was shown saying.

The perceptive reader will have already anticipated how such a simple story could be undermined in the telling. Like the West Bank piece, the intended meaning relies upon a history—in this case, the history of Whitelaw's problems in his own party. Without a knowledge of this history, Whitelaw's speech takes on an entirely different meaning, and the speech itself becomes the focal point of the story. Could this news story be told in a way that allows the audience to "lose" this history?

Any other television narrative would have used the hermeneutic code to draw viewers into the story and lead them towards its climax. The story might begin with synopsis of recent history—featuring perhaps, film footage of Whitelaw being criticized or booed by party members. It would then take us to Harrogate, with the question that brought the TV cameras there—will Whitelaw be in for another mauling? We might be tempted to tease the audience a little, developing this enigma before resolving it with pictures of the "triumphant reception." The narrative codes required to tell such a story are not exactly sophisticated, but television news is not, as we have seen, in the business of telling stories.

The enigma that drives the viewer forward, that links the history to the event, vanishes with the anchor's opening line:

> The home secretary, Mr. William Whitelaw, got a standing ovation today, after a speech to Conservative party activists in Harrogate.

He then refers briefly to the speech—without mentioning its content—before returning to the main point: "To judge from his reception, he's emerged triumphant again. . . ." Only in the last clause of the introduction does he introduce the historical context, when we learn that his triumph followed "a week fending off his critics." By then, of course, it is too late: there is nothing enigmatic about this history—its signifying power is negated by its position in the discourse. The reporter's subsequent reference to the story's history therefore falls on largely deaf ears:

> Mr. Whitelaw must have been worried about what sort of reception he'd get today. There had been rumblings from the Party's grass roots, and he'd been given a rough time by the Party Conference on this issue last year. But, in the event . . .

The audience's consciousness is allowed to glaze over this "detail," focusing on what appears to be the main event—the speech. The effects of this narrative structure were clearly revealed in the audience's readings. Of the fifty respondents, forty-one incorporated references to the speech into their readings, thirty-eight incorporated references to his reception and only twelve incorporated references to the story's history. Significantly, those twelve were the same people who were already aware of that history. Of the forty-one respondents who referred to Whitelaw's speech, on the other hand, a large number—thirty-one—went on to mention at least one of the two points he made, despite the irrelevance of these points in relation to the encoded meaning of the story (he begins by criticizing former home secretaries for not building enough prisons, and then refers to the need to support the police and the opposition parties' failure to do this).

So, for a majority of the respondents, Whitelaw's speech was seen as the focal point of the story. For them, this became a story about government policy on issues of law and order—an entirely different reading from the one intended. This was made possible by a failure to incorporate the item's introduction into their readings. Without knowledge of the context of events in Harrogate, it is impossible to understand the significance of Whitelaw's good reception. This, in turn, forces the viewer to shift his or her attention toward what Whitelaw actually said.

This, structurally speaking, is the same pattern of response (or "misreading") generated by the other news items. Within the news narrative, the most powerful moment seems to involve the event, or action sequence. To viewers unfamiliar with them, the details that surround that event—including the historical context—appear to fade away. News is event-orientated in every sense. It is events that make news and events, due to the structure of news, that remain in the viewer's mind. This enables us to develop the debates about the meaning and influence of TV news. We can now begin to tackle these debates with a more sophisticated idea about the quality and structure of television's power.

NEWS FROM ANOTHER PLANET

The majority of the respondents, like most people when asked, felt that television news was reasonably "objective" and "impartial," and that it "did a pretty good job" of reporting the news. Even those respondents who said they found the news "boring" did not seem to hold the newsmakers responsible for their lack of interest. This opinion sits a little strangely with the findings of this research, which suggest that TV news performs, even on its own terms, quite dismally.

This paradox suggests that most people find it difficult to evaluate television news. It is, after all, presented by people who *look* as if they know what they are doing. Just as the sky is blue and the grass is green, it is difficult to imagine how else it could possibly be. The few respondents who were able to articulate a critical view often found it difficult to propose anything more than superficial changes to its form and content. As Brunt and Jordin concluded in their study of *Newsnight* viewers in Chesterfield:

> Where resistance to the media took the form of outright rejection of current affairs coverage, we noted that this might leave viewers still inhabiting the political frames of reference adopted by the media to the extent that they assumed them as their own commonsense wisdom. (Brunt and Jordin, 1987, p.155)

This is, as Brunt and Jordin proceed to argue, largely a question of knowledge. We need to know all kinds of different things to be able to construct an effective critique of TV news. We need, for example, to have an understanding (of events) that goes beyond the range of discourses that the news delivers. How else can we evaluate the information we are getting? We also need to know what we are missing on the news itself—something we are, as Dahlgren (1985) has pointed out, often blissfully unaware of. Those respondents who did admit to feeling confused by the news tended to blame themselves rather than the broadcasters.

Most people feel far more able to comment on the merits of television fiction than on news or current affairs. The respondents in Morley's family study (1986) or Ang's *Dallas* research (1985), for example, offer sometimes detailed critiques of television drama. Once we begin to look at these attitudes more closely, we discover something that is, if we think about it, very odd. One of the reasons why most people feel more able to evaluate TV fiction than television news is because it seems much closer to their own lives, and to the world they live in. The worlds of soap opera or sitcoms are often worlds they can relate to—and if they can't it becomes a direct source of criticism. The world of TV news, on the other hand, might almost be beamed in from another planet.

It is, in this respect, revealing to think about how people talk about different forms of television. One charge that people will often make of television fictions that they dislike is that it is "unrealistic."

Ien Ang's account of "*Dallas* haters" is full of such remarks—as one woman complained, fairly typically: "The characters in it are so unreal" (*ibid.*, p.90). While many TV fictions are engaged in forms of realism, and can subsequently be held accountable, this is a criticism that could most appropriately be leveled at TV news. News, more than any other television form, purports to reproduce reality. We might, for example, accuse TV news in the United States of giving an unrealistic portrayal of Central America, or crime, or President Bush, or simply the world we live in—and yet we prefer to vent our spleen on things we know are fictional.

It is as if we allow the news to occupy a remote and discrete place in our lives—one that lies beyond our critical judgment. It is a distant world and we are alienated from it. This sense of alienation, although rarely explicitly stated in the interviews, crept inexorably into many conversations nonetheless. Perhaps its most identifiable form was a vague but deep-rooted assumption that television, in a general unspecified sense, represented a world, populated by those with power, somewhere in "the establishment."

This feeling was expressed, in different ways, by respondents from a range of political (or apolitical) backgrounds. While a few were able to contextualize this idea within a notion of political bias, most did not. The British Leyland item, for example, was often criticized as a "put up job" or "an advertisement" for British Leyland. Behind this accusation was an assumption broadly linking television with the government and the world of management: the world of "them" rather than "us." What was perhaps most interesting about this assumption was its vague, rather indefinite quality. When questioned as to exactly *why* ITN should want to broadcast propaganda on behalf of British Leyland, most of the decoders could not, or felt no need to, pinpoint any specific set of relations between the two. Rather, both were seen as connected to "the establishment." In the following exchange, for example, the establishment is symbolized by "government" (it has just been suggested the two BL workers were "plants"):

Q: Who do you think planted them? The management?

A: Probably the management. I mean, they *may* have thought it (automation) was a very good thing.

Q: Why do you think television cooperated with that?

A: They're basically dominated by the government, what's on television anyway, everything, er, they have a say in what goes on.

Q: Do you mean a specific part of government, or the institution of government?

A: The institution of government, 'cause I mean, you can't blame any party, the Conservative or the Labour—it's the government in general.

Q: So that's why they would go along with management?

A: Yeah.

This alienation is, perhaps, not that surprising. The world of the news is populated, designed and created by the small cast of elite personnel. It is, for the most part, a world designed, created and inhabited by *other* people, people very distant from the world we know. While there will always be something "otherworldly" about a reality signified through a small box in the living room, there is no doubt that television news frequently fails to make coherent connections between issues/events and the relation of those issues/events to the viewer's own concerns. This allows us to make judgments about the news world that bear little relation to anything else.

Opinion polls show, time and time again, that elections are won and lost because people feel one party is more "able" than another to handle the economy. If we trust one mechanic more than another to fix our car, it is a judgment usually based on evidence that we understand—one charges too much, or maybe did a lousy job last time. Judgments about politicians are rarely applied with such an empirical rationale. A good example is the "problem" of inflation, which has preoccupied broadcasters and politicians at various times in recent history. Public opinion polls have, accordingly, put inflation at the top of the agenda of "important issues facing the country." Yet, incredibly, had opinion pollsters asked the public (or, for that matter, many broadcasters or politicians) *why* they thought inflation was a problem—given that wage inflation in most Western economies has usually kept pace with prices, thereby maintaining most people's standard of living—the vast majority would not have had a sufficient knowledge of economics to be able to answer. We were told it was a problem, so we worried about it and, in some cases, voted for the person we judged best able to solve it.

Many economists, indeed, would have argued that a level of inflation below 10 percent (as it was in Britain in 1979, when Mrs. Thatcher won an election partly on her professed ability to deal with it) was a comparatively minor problem for an economy to live with— particularly if that economy was faced with the possibility of extremely high levels of unemployment. This creates the absurd situation of an electorate making a crucial political decision on the basis of an issue that was either misunderstood or incomprehensible.

Such a curiosity begins to make sense if we see events like "inflation" or "elections" as entities whose significance is located not in our world, but in the alien world of the news. The idea that inflation is a major problem *makes sense* in that world, whether we understand it or not. As Jensen has written:

> It is presupposed that inflation is a problem that "hurts." It is true that the negative evaluation of inflation is relatively uncontroversial . . . Still, such questions as the origin of inflation, the best solutions and the matter of who will benefit most from the economic stability are certainly controversial, but they are not expressed explicitly in the news. Instead it is implied that low inflation is in the common interest. (Jensen, 1987, p. 19)

In the TV world, since everyone seems troubled by it, it *must be* a problem.

It is at this point that we can begin to understand a little more about the associated logics that form the basis of the news discourse. We tolerate the myths that TV commercials promote because we know they work on another discursive level—the metaphor. We don't need to really believe that buying a Pontiac will make our lives breathtakingly exciting to accept the association (between the car and a thrilling lifestyle) made by the TV commercial. It is a contemporary form of poetic license. It appears that we tolerate the myths that we get from TV news because they also work on another discursive level—a level we accept as somehow disconnected from the everyday logic of our own world.

Opinion research on political attitudes seems to demonstrate the confusion this creates with increasing clarity. During the Reagan years in the U.S., polls showed that, on the whole, people were closer to Reagan's opponents (on the issues they identified as important) than they were to Reagan: yet many of them voted for him regardless. The same contradictory phenomenon occurred in Britain under Thatcher: people would often seem far closer to the Labour party on "the issues," but were disinclined to actually vote them into power. On the distant world of TV news, these paradoxical attitudes "made sense," because they were removed from everyday realities. We know, for example, that there is no connection between the attractive couple and the convertible in the commercial, but we retain the image that the car is, in some vague ineffable sense, sexy.

Similarly, we may disagree with Thatcher and Reagan, while simultaneously maintaining the images of them on the news that indicate they were "doing a good job."

There are many examples of this cognitive dissonance. When Walter Mondale ran against Reagan in 1984, polls showed that most people believed both candidates would, if elected, raise taxes. Mondale's decision to come clean and admit that he would do so did not, however, gain him points for honesty. People, regardless of their skepticism, felt more comfortable with a candidate who *disassociated* himself from tax increases. George Bush's campaign team learnt this lesson well, and did almost precisely the same thing ("Read my lips, no new taxes") just as disingenuously in 1988.

To win elections, politicians do not seem to need to offer solutions to people's everyday problems. The world they need to govern well is another, rather different world—the world of TV news. This has far more to do with alienation than it has with democracy. Television news, with its fragmented narrative form, allows this distance to develop. It does not offer the viewer a coherent vision based on historical connections; it deals in a series of disparate associations. As long as these associations appear to float above the ebb and flow of historical reality, they are immune from the contradictions it may expose.

Cultivation analysis has produced evidence that appears to confirm this analysis. A detailed examination of attitudinal data suggests that the more TV we watch, the more we are able to hold contradictory ideas simultaneously. As Morgan (reviewing survey results) puts it:

> Television cultivates a set of paradoxical currents. In a nutshell, heavy viewers think like conservatives, want like liberals, and yet call themselves moderates. They are less likely to vote but quicker to turn against an incumbent. They think elected officials don't care about what happens to them but are more interested in their personal lives than in their policies. They want to cut taxes but improve education, medical care, social security. They distrust big government but want it to fix things for them, to protect them at home and from foreign threats. They praise freedom but want to restrict anyone who uses it in an unconventional way. They are losing confidence in people who run virtually all institutions, including religion, but they express trust in God, America—and television. (Morgan, 1989, p. 250)

It is, perhaps, too much to hold the structure of television news entirely accountable for creating such confusion. What a qualitative study of the news tells us, nonetheless, is that the meaning of television is contingent upon its form—a form that alienates us, as a society, from our own history.

7

The Power of Popular Television: The Case of *Cosby*

REVIEWING *THE COSBY SHOW*

The Cosby Show does not need much introduction. For those readers who have managed to avoid this extraordinarily successful TV show, let me congratulate you for your singularity and offer this brief synopsis.

The Cosby Show is a half-hour situation comedy about an upper middle-class black family, the Huxtables. Cliff Huxtable (played by Bill Cosby) is a gynecologist and obstetrician, and his wife Claire is a lawyer. They have four daughters and a son, and, as the series has grown older, they have acquired in-laws and grandchildren. The show focuses on the Huxtables' attractive New York brownstone home, which provides the set for an endless series of comic domestic dramas. There is little, thus far, to distinguish this television fiction from many others: we are used to a TV world populated by attractive professionals and their good-looking offspring. What makes the show unusual is its popularity, its critical acclaim, and the fact that all its leading characters are black.

These distinctive features have made *The Cosby Show* the subject of much speculation and discussion. At the heart of many of these discussions lies an apparent contradiction. Here we have a country that is still emerging from a deeply racist history, a society in which white people have treated (and continue to treat) black people with contempt, suspicion and a profoundly ignorant sense of superiority. And yet the most popular TV show in the U.S. over the last decade, among black and white people alike, is not only about a black family, but one portrayed without any of the demeaning stereotypes that have characterized images of black people in mainstream popular culture. Commentators have been provoked to try and resolve this apparent curiosity and, in so doing, to muse upon the show's social significance.

The most prevalent critical reaction, particularly during the first few years of the show, was to applaud Bill Cosby's creation as not only a witty and thoughtful sitcom, but an enlightened step forward in race relations. After decades of negative or degrading media images (see, for example, Hartsough, 1989), the Huxtable family presented black characters that black and white audiences could relate to. The celebratory tone of many reviews contained genuine hopes about what such a cultural intervention might achieve in dispelling racial prejudices in the United States.

The history of critical response to popular culture often follows a similar pattern: elaborate praise becomes an increasingly difficult burden to bear, and euphoria is almost invariably followed by a cynical backlash. *The Cosby Show*, for good or ill, is no exception to this rule. Critics have subsequently accused the show of presenting a misleadingly cozy picture, a sugar-candy world unfettered by racism, crime, economic deprivation and hardship. Some have argued that the Huxtables' charmed life is so alien to the experience of most black people that they are no longer "black" at all, but, as Henry Lewis Gates puts it, "in most respects, just like white people" (Gates, 1989). Gates has also argued that these "positive images" can be counter-productive, since they suggest to the world the myth of the American dream, a just world where anyone can make it, and where racial barriers no longer exist:

> As long as *all* blacks were represented in demeaning or peripheral roles, it was possible to believe that American racism was, as it were, indiscriminate. The social vision of "Cosby," however, reflecting the miniscule integration of blacks into the upper middle-class, reassuringly throws the blame for black poverty back onto the impoverished. (Gates, 1989)

At the risk of simplifying critical opinion, most analyses of *Cosby* fall broadly into one of two camps: the show is seen as either socially progressive or as an apology for a racist system that disadvantages most black people. Both views carry with them assumptions about media effects—the debate concerns the nature of this effect. This, in turn, raises questions about the meaning of the show for black and white audiences. The study presented in this chapter will I hope, begin to clarify some of these questions.

COSBY: THE CASE AGAINST

Few would argue that *The Cosby Show* presents a typical or realistic view of the lives of black Americans. The Huxtable family, like their creator, have attained a level of wealth, comfort and success shared by only a tiny minority of black people in the United States. The period which produced *Cosby* also produced a deterioration in the social conditions of most black Americans (see Downing, 1988).

The success of *The Cosby Show* has, according to Gates, led to a curious divergence between media images and social realities. Bill Cosby has broken the mold of black media stereotypes and opened up our TV screens to a host of black performers:

> This is the "Cosby" decade. The show's unprecedented success in depicting the lives of affluent blacks has exercised a profound influence on television in the last half of the 80's . . . "Cosby's" success has led to the flow of TV sitcoms that feature the black middle class, each of which takes its lead from the "Cosby" show. (Gates, 1989)

And yet, outside the television world, there are a plethora of social statistics to demonstrate that many of the advances made by black Americans in the 1960s and 1970s are being reversed in the 1980s and 1990s, so that, as Gates puts it, there is very little connection between the social status of black Americans and the fabricated images of black people that Americans consume every day.

The gulf between television and the world outside is propounded by the Huxtables' charmed lives, a utopian familial harmony that has caused some critics to wince in disbelief. Mark Cripin Miller's description is characteristically derisive:

> And then there is the cuddliest and most beloved of TV Dads: Bill Cosby, who, as Dr. Heathcliff Huxtable, lives in perfect peace, and in a perfect brownstone, with his big happy family, and never has to raise his hand or fist, but retains the absolute devotion of his wife and kids just by making lots of goofy faces. (Miller, 1986, p. 206)

The problem that Gates and Miller are identifying is not simply that the show is an unrealistic portrayal of black family life—few sitcoms, after all, make any claim to represent social reality—but that the Huxtables sustain the harmful myth of social mobility.

The Huxtable family appear to have glided effortlessly into the upper echelons of American society. The show never offers us the slightest glimpse of the economic disadvantages and deep-rooted discrimination that prevent most black Americans from reaching their potential. Michael Dyson, in an otherwise positive assessment of the show, comments that

> it is perhaps this lack of acknowledgement of the underside of the American Dream that is the most unfortunate feature of

the Huxtable opulence. Cosby defends against linking the authenticity of the Huxtable representation of black life to the apparently contradictory luxury the family lives in when he says: "To say that they are not black enough is a denial of the American dream and the American way of life. My point is that this is an American family—an *American* family—and if you want to live like they do, and you're willing to work, the opportunity is there." (Dyson, 1989, p. 30)

But, as Dyson suggests, this is a cruel distortion: "Such a statement leads us to believe that Cosby is unaware that there are millions of people, the so-called working poor, who work hard but nevertheless fall beneath the poverty level." And yet, writes Dyson, "surely Cosby knows better than this."

Whatever Bill Cosby's intention, some critics argue that the end result is extremely damaging. The Huxtables ultimately sustain the idea that "anyone can make it," the comforting assertion of the American dream; a myth that sustains a conservative political ideology that is blind to the inequalities that hinder those born on mean streets and pamper those born on easy street. As Miller puts it:

Cliff's blackness serves an affirmative purpose within the ad that is *The Cosby Show*. At the center of this ample tableau, Cliff is himself an ad, implicitly proclaiming the fairness of the American system: "Look!" he shows us. "Even I can have all this!" (Miller, 1986, p. 210)

This mythology is made all the more powerful, Miller argues, by the close identification between Cliff Huxtable and Bill Cosby. Behind the fictional doctor lies a man whose real life is *also* a success story: fact and fiction coalesce to confirm the "truth" they embody.

Herein, the critics argue, lies the popularity of the show in the United States. The show may appear to herald a new dawn of racial tolerance, a world where white people accept black people into their living rooms as equals. This appearance, according to Miller, hides the more subtle fears of white viewers, to whom black people are still seen as a threat. Cliff, or Bill Cosby, is attractive to white viewers because, as Miller puts it, he represents "a threat contained," offering

deep solace to a white public terrified that one day blacks might come with guns to steal the copperware, the juicer, the microwave, the VCR, even the TV itself;

at a time when

American whites need such reassurance because they are now further removed than ever, both spatially and psychologically, from the masses of the black poor. (Miller, 1986, pp. 213–4)

The thrust of this argument, despite Miller's hyperbole, may provide us with an insight into the ideological state of white people in the contemporary United States. *The Cosby Show* is not simply a source of gentle reassurance, it flatters to deceive. The U.S. is still emerging from a system of apartheid. Even if legal and political inequalities are finally disappearing, economic barriers remain. In an age when most white people have moved beyond the crudities of an overt and naked racism, there is a heavy burden of guilt for all concerned. *The Cosby Show* provides his white audiences with relief not only from fear, but from responsibility.

How far this account of the show's appeal explains its popularity and significance remains to be seen. Suffice to say, at this point, that whatever the audience study reveals about this argument, it moves us well beyond the parameters of traditional TV audience research. It is impossible to design an audience study that, in a simple and straightforward sense, measures the effect of the show on attitudes toward race. An exploration of the show's influence forces us to delve more deeply into the complex interaction between the program and the viewer, and thereby into the delicate ideological supposi-tions that inform the points where they meet, where they create meaning and pleasure.

There are, in the meantime, other things to consider before we can fully appreciate the depth of audience responses to *The Cosby Show*. We have, after all, only covered the more pessimistic aspects of the critical terrain.

COSBY: THE CASE FOR

If we are to engage in a battle over the nature of what gets shown on primetime TV in the United States, we should be well versed in the art of the possible. Any attempt to change the form or content of mainstream television will come up against two powerful bastions of conservatism: the profit-oriented predilections of network and advertising executives, and the well-trained expectations and tastes of TV audiences. We can create innovative programming ideas until we are blue in the face, but if the networks, advertisers or viewers don't respond, then we are wasting our time.

The Cosby Show's focus on a black family and its departure from an accepted assortment of racial stereotypes did not make it an obvious candidate for primetime. ABC turned the series proposal down, and, were it not for Bill Cosby's track record (including, significantly, his ability to sell products on TV commercials), it would probably never have made it on the air. To attack the show because it panders to the needs of a mainstream white audience is to attack its life-blood: the U.S. has a television culture where audience ratings decide whether you live or die. This bottom line gives a television program very little room for maneuver. To have confronted the audience with the uncomfortable realities of racism would have been commercial suicide.

John Downing argues that any evaluation of the show must take account of this conservative cultural climate, and that despite its limitations; "to be as good as it is *and* to have gotten past these barriers is a major achievement in itself" (Downing, 1989, p. 68). Ultimately, Downing acknowledges, the show does let "racism off the hook": it is, nevertheless, a considerable step forward in the history of media representation. There is, Downing argues, "an abundance of black culture presented in the series, expressed without fanfare, but with constant dignity" (*ibid.*, p. 61). The show celebrates black artists, from Ellis Wilson to Stevie Wonder, while political figures like Martin Luther King, or events like the civil rights march on Washington have been interwoven, albeit ever so gently, into the story-line.

The naming of the Huxtables' first grandchildren is a typical example of *The Cosby Show* style. Their eldest daughter, Sondra, decides to call her twins Nelson and Winnie. The episode that deals with this decision highlights the issue of naming, but makes no comment on its overt political connotations. The reference to the Mandelas is made quietly and unobtrusively, relying upon the audience's ability to catch the political ramifications of the statement.

If the subtlety of this approach is a virtue, it is one borne of necessity. During the show's second season, NBC tried to have the anti-apartheid sign on Theo's bedroom door removed. Bill Cosby, with the newly found clout of ratings success behind him, stood his ground and fought successfully to keep it there. What is interesting about this story is not only Cosby's triumph (would the network have capitulated to a show with a few less ratings points?), but the almost pathological fear of certain kinds of political discourse by those in charge of television entertainment. The fuss was made about a sign expressing a sentiment that is, outside the comparatively small "market" of white South Africa, *supposed* to be fairly uncontroversial. The sign made no intrusion into the plot, and many viewers would probably not even notice its presence. The network's desire to remove such a meek symbol of black resistance from the airwaves demonstrates what progressive voices on primetime TV are up against.

The seriousness with which *The Cosby Show* approaches the issue of cultural representation has put it on a pedestal and exposed it to critical scrutiny. As Bill Cosby and program consultant Alvin Poussaint have pointed out, few other sitcoms are attacked for their failure to deal with issues of racism. This is, Poussaint has argued, a particularly unfair strain to put upon a situation comedy. Writing in *Ebony*, Poussaint points out that

> audiences tune in to be entertained, not to be confronted with social problems. Critical social disorders, like racism, violence, and drug abuse, rarely lend themselves to comic treatment; trying to deal with them on a sitcom could trivialize issues that deserve serious, thoughtful treatment. (Poussaint, 1988)

The limits of *The Cosby Show* are, according to Poussaint, the limits of the genre. This is a point, indeed, acknowledged by some critics. Gates, in an otherwise fairly critical piece, accepts that the very structure of a sitcom "militates against its use as an agent of social change" (Gates, 1989).

Despite these constraints, what *Cosby* has confronted, many have argued, is the deep-rooted racism of white Americans who find it difficult to accept racial equality. Dyson, for example, has suggested that one of "the most useful aspects of Cosby's dismantling of racial mythology and stereotyping is that it has permitted America to view black folk as human beings" (Dyson, 1989, p. 29). Here, at last, are media representations of successful and attractive black people who white people can respect, admire and even identify with.

It could be argued that references to discrimination and black struggle would, in this sense, be counter-productive, alienating substantial sections of the white audience and making identification with the Huxtables more difficult. We should also be aware of the particular nature of the television world. The Huxtables' class position may be unusual (for black *and* white people) in real life, but to be an affluent, attractive professional on television is to be "normal." There are, of course, assumptions about the audience embedded in this argument, just as there are in the arguments of those who are critical of the absence of a discourse of racial discrimination.

Some of the more positive evaluations of the show have made the interesting point that the discourse of discrimination that does find its way into the script is not racism but sexism. The show frequently uses humor to expose the inadequacy of the sexist or machismo attitudes of some members of its male cast. Some characters, like son-in-law Elvin or Rudi's friend Kenny (who spouts forth the sexist platitudes of his big brother), are deliberately set up to be undermined. While it is the characters of Claire and her daughters who take the lead in these instances, they are usually supported by the figure of Cliff, who has traveled some way beyond the sexist stereotypes so common in TV sitcoms.

It is unusual to find strong male characters in sitcoms who support a feminist stance taken by female characters. The male in a sitcom who adopts such a position invariably still runs the risk of ridicule. Downing suggests that, while *The Cosby Show*'s challenge to patriarchy has its limitations, Cliff's involvement in these comic episodes plays an important role in legitimating the show's feminist sentiments: "His condemnation of everyday sexism perhaps communicates itself all the more powerfully to male viewers precisely because he cannot be written off as a henpecked wimp" (Downing, 1989, p. 60).

Downing's defense of *The Cosby Show* is not apologetic: it is a reminder that, however we judge it, the show is, in many respects, one of the more progressive forces in popular culture to emerge from the United States in recent years. This may not be saying very much—we are, after all, talking about a televisual history steeped in sexist and racist images—but it is worth remembering before we embark on a journey through the North American audience. Even if the audience study manifests many of the critic's worst fears, there are countless other television messages whose ideological consequences are almost too oppressive or frightening to even contemplate.

GENDER AND PREFERENCES

We should, following the study of the TV news audience, be fairly wary of assuming that there is a basic reading, suggested by the program's form and content, that audiences will acknowledge and interpret. Audiences will, in collusion with the program's structure, "prefer" certain readings, but we cannot assume that a textual analysis will guide us to these interpretations. The unpredictable nature of some of the news audience's readings, for example, led me to radically reconsider how the narrative structure of news actually operates. The structure of TV news does appear to encourage very particular responses, with far-reaching ideological consequences: but these were quite different from the ideological nuances assumed by a more traditional textual analysis.

Bearing this in mind, it is also apparent that *The Cosby Show* and TV news programs are very different creatures. Part of the unpredictability of television news is a function of its disruption of traditional narrative codes. *The Cosby Show*, on the other hand, conforms fairly closely to the narrative patterns that structure most other television programs. The response of the viewers in the news study to the few moments when TV news does use conventional narrative sequences would lead us to expect that a traditional narrative like *The Cosby Show* would engage the viewer in more predictable ways. In short, the "preferred reading" should be easier to anticipate.

The episode of *The Cosby Show* seen by the viewers in this study was not untypical in using the narrative to tell a moral tale. Like many other episodes, the show gently exposes the limitations of traditional male attitudes. We begin with a confrontation between Theo and Claire about the exploitation of women decorating the car magazine Theo is reading. At this stage, while Claire uses her moral authority to win this particular battle, the message is still ambiguous: Theo's comic justifications for reading the magazine are engaging rather than threatening.

Nevertheless, as the plot develops, it is Claire's analysis that is proved "correct" and Theo's that is found wanting. When Lindy (the attractive daughter of the Huxtables' dinner guests) arrives at the house, Theo's attempts to impress her with youthful machismo succeed only in making him look ridiculous. The two other men in the story, Doctors Harman and Huxtable, provide their own display of male competitiveness in a hotly disputed game of petanque in the back yard. The game begins with both men stripping down to their t-shirts, despite the freezing temperatures, in order to show each other how "tough" they are. This, and their childish squabbling during the game, provide a sharp contrast to the mature behavior of the women on the show.

The point is hammered home in the final scene. The Harmans' car refuses to start, and both men, in their attempts to fix it, succeed only in dismantling the engine. The problem is solved by Lindy, who, it turns out, is a student of car maintenance. This allows Claire to point out the scene to Theo, and thereby reveal the moral of the story: a woman's place is not draped across the car hood, but under it.

What appears to be an unambiguous feminist message is partly compromised by those actions that remain unquestioned. Even though both parents work full time outside the home, it is Claire's job, not Cliff's, to make the dinner (Cliff and Theo's attempts in the kitchen in other episodes are sometimes comically inept). When left alone by the men, Claire and her friend are not found "discussing world issues" (Claire's declared intention) but flicking through glossy (fashion?) magazines. The alternative we are left with, according to Downing, is "patriarchy with a human face" (Downing, 1989, p. 60).

Despite these compromising moments, the discourse of feminism is so strongly and consciously signified in the narrative that we would expect most viewers to respond to it, to see the message as coherent rather than contradictory. In the complex semiosis of television viewing, this would appear to be a comparatively straightforward case of a program "preferring" a meaning.

Most people, indeed, reproduced this message fairly unproblematically, with little or no prompting (many referred to it during their initial summary of the program). When asked if the program had any "message" to convey, most groups responded as these women did:

> Basically for me, the moral or the message was, um, don't ever look at women as a symbol or an object, you know, please look at them as people ... they have a brain behind their body ... people that are using a woman as a symbol, you know, laying across the hood of the car—and we are far more important than that.

> Women are able to do things that one would not expect them to be able to do. They can do extraordinary things, like rock climbing. And men sometimes, I don't know, well men should have more open minds about what women can do.

Even some of the men who felt more uneasy with this message agreed (without prompting) that this was what the story was "about." It is, nevertheless, worth noting that this reading was dominant but not unanimous.

A few respondents, when asked about the moral or meaning of the story, interpreted it quite differently. One teenage boy, for example, felt the show's message was to "be yourself" instead of trying to impress girls/people with things you can't really do. Two other male respondents produced variations on this theme, reducing the politics of male sexuality to the notion of improving male technique. One of the most interesting responses came from a group of working-class gay men, one of whom (a transvestite who performed the interview as his female alter ego) suggested that it was simply about gendered behavior:

> The two ladies wanted to get together and the two guys wanted to get together. The two guys wanted to do what they wanted to do and the two ladies wanted to sit down and have coffee and do what they wanted to do.

This interpretation may derive from this respondent's particular concerns: as a man *and* a woman, a feminist discourse is less appropriate to his/her life than an intricate understanding of the differences between male and female behavior. Sexual politics, in this case, is not about oppression, it is about difference.

These readings remind us that we cannot take a "preferred reading" for granted. What they also suggest is that an awareness of some form of feminist discourse is a prerequisite for constructing this particular preferred reading. The fact that only a few respondents failed to construct this reading indicates the prevalence (although not necessarily the power) of a contemporary feminist discourse, particularly among the middle and upper middle-class respondents. This presence will become more notable later on in this analysis, when some significant discursive absences begin to appear.

Whether viewers enjoyed the message is, of course, quite another matter. It is at this point that some gender differences start to emerge: women, on the whole, took more pleasure in the program's feminist moments than men. This sometimes manifested itself at a fairly basic level, women (in both mixed and single sex groups) being much more inclined to laugh at Claire's victorious moments than men. Women were also more likely, during the discussion, to endorse the ideological thrust of the message, and more specifically, to take pleasure in so doing.

Despite this, a majority of men did not feel alienated or excluded by this aspect of the show. The unthreatening gentleness of the message is, as Downing suggests, inclusive—a number of men commenting favorably on the gentle or "good-natured" nature of the message—as one man put it:

I think the issue of sexism was a motif throughout the whole episode. From the issue of poking fun at her son's interest in scantily clad women on cars and bikes to teasing the two husbands about needing to run out and be competitive adolescents instead of sticking around and talking to their wives . . . They're challenging sexist roles, and the whole show is challenging in a kind of good-natured way, a fun kind of way, about sexism and traditional roles.

The challenge, because it is gentle, "good-natured" and "fun," is seen as acceptable and even mildly enjoyable. Claire, after all, still seems to do most of the cooking—a reassuring image for a number of male viewers. The show, in this sense, gives men a friendly nudge. How far it influenced their own perceptions it is difficult to tell: at the very least, it reconfirms the presence of a quasi-feminist discourse.

Only two small subgroups reacted with displeasure: those women who found the show's message too weak; and men, from the opposite perspective, who rejected the feminist message altogether. One woman, for example, pointed to some of its contradictory moments with some irritation:

I think it could have gone one step further, though, because . . . Claire is a bright woman, and it seems to me that she and that other woman could have been sitting talking about important issues. They could have been talking politics or something.

Men who felt the opposite, possibly because they felt constrained by the presence of other women (either in the group or interviewing them), were rather less assertive. Only one (all-male) group explicitly voiced their discontent, arguing that the show was "anti-men":

The whole show, basically, was showing how stupid men were. It was trying . . . (Exasperated) women must write the show.

In both cases, these reactions signified frustration and displeasure, in marked contrast to those who enthusiastically endorsed the program's message. This confirms Condit's findings about pleasure and the preferred reading (Condit, 1989): those who endorse it enjoy the experience, while those who oppose it need to work harder to articulate their rejection, an experience that appears to signify frustration rather than satisfaction. Moreover, those men who shared the assumptions informing male anti-feminism, but who did not construct this reading at all (the story's message being interpreted as a message to men to "be yourself"), were happier viewers, able to relate to what they saw as the moral of the story. The quasi-feminist message fails to disturb because it is not constructed.

Two men (members, once again, of an all-male group) who *were* able to take some pleasure in an anti-feminist discourse used the program to their own advantage. They were, accordingly, able to point to the program's contradictions not from a feminist perspective, but as a way of justifying their position:

MAN 1: Yeah, it's funny, the writing is actually going in two directions, from the standpoint of women's issues, showing women as sex objects, and then getting out there and making it in the male world, if you will, while at the same time the roles the women played were the exact opposite. The fact that women didn't really have a role in the show except as foils for the men, and so I thought they were at cross purposes.

MAN 2: Well, yeah, I mean they probably missed the boat a little there by having the wife go check the roast, because that defeated the purpose of the message which was: "I am woman, hear me roar," or whatever . . . although I don't know, what are they going to do, have Cosby check the roast?

The last remark reveals how unsettling it would be, for these viewers, if Cliff played Claire's domestic role—so unsettling that it is dismissed as inconceivable. These men take some satisfaction in their analysis because it is not an oppositional reading: they do not need to draw upon discourses outside the program's textual limits to construct their interpretation, rather, they use (unlike most other viewers) the program's contradictions as building blocks to inform their own reading. The ambiguity of the program's message is seen to undermine the feminist discourse they reject. This comes much closer to the forms of "resistive viewing" described by Radway and Fiske (see Chapter 3), although, in this case, its ideological thrust moves in a reactionary rather than a progressive direction. What it suggests is this: resistive viewing can be fun, while oppositional viewing is too much like hard work.

Overall, the audience's interpretations of this aspect of the show lend cautious support to Downing's argument that, in terms of gender, *The Cosby Show* represents a gently progressive force in popular culture. Woman enjoy and identify with the strength of Claire's character ("like a lioness") while most more traditional men are cajoled into an acceptance of her strength. The show's advocacy of forms of feminism is also firmly inscribed in its structure: as Downing says, "the only form of discrimination named as such in *The*

Cosby Show is sexism" (Downing, 1988, p. 57). Whether they agree with it or not, most respondents reconstructed this message. This comparative (though incomplete) unambiguity makes the work of the audience researcher fairly straightforward. The task becomes, unfortunately, considerably more complicated when we start to address those forms of discrimination that remain unnamed. It is to these that the rest of this chapter is devoted.

DECODING RACE

It is sometimes easy to forget that race and racial difference involve a great deal more than categories of physiognomy and skin pigmentation. The differences between a black person and a white person in the United States are deeply rooted in their distinct and separate histories, histories encapsulating a host of material and cultural distinctions that render the experience of being white quite different from the experience of being black. Race, in other words, is a social as well as a physical construction.

Racial discrimination, throughout its infamous history, has usually been predicated on a series of perceived symbolic links between skin color and culture. To colonialists, slave owners and promoters of apartheid, this meant a straightforward denunciation of black culture as uncivilized, inferior or threatening. Despite their manifest crudity, these racist attitudes have never been as simple or homogeneous as they sometimes appear. From colonialism onward, the racist discourses infusing white societies have borne contradictory assumptions about the relation between nature and nurture: black people have been seen as simultaneously within the reaches of white society *and* beyond it. The black person's soul was therefore treated as, on the one hand, a changeable commodity, open to the influences of missionary zeal, and, on the other hand, as the heart of darkness, inherently irredeemable.

Once placed in the industrial "melting pots" of the late twentieth century, the struggles and achievements of black people in an oppressive white world have disentangled the fixity of many of the associations between race and culture. The ability of some black people, against the odds, to succeed in a predominantly white environment, has made notions of biological determinism decidedly less fashionable. While such notions have certainly not disappeared, they are now less common currency than ideas that flirt with the principle of racial equality. This does not mean the end of racism; far from it: as an instrument of repression, racism now takes more subtle forms.

In most Western countries, most particularly in the United States, the idea that white people and black people are irrevocably tied to discrete cultures has been seriously compromised by the promise of social mobility: the idea that anyone, regardless of race, creed or class, can make it. These compromises are now enshrined within legal structures that, while they do not guarantee racial equality, at least give the idea of equal rights a certain amount of credibility. Bill Cosby, whether as himself or as Dr. Heathcliff Huxtable, is easily assimilated into this ideology. He is, Miller argues, visible "proof" of the meritocratic mythology that fuels the American Dream, a black person who has achieved success beyond the confines of a racially defined culture.

Racism is, however, a capricious creature, and it has adapted to this discursive climate by absorbing a number of contradictions. The history of racism is now embedded in an iniquitous capitalist system, where economic rather than racial laws ensure widespread racial segregation and disadvantage. This, in turn, encourages white people to believe in an imagined cultural superiority, while simultaneously giving credence to the idea that we are what we become, that culture is not God-given but a social construction.

The Cosby Show is, as I have suggested, both a singular and an ambiguous intervention into this complex ideological terrain. How do white viewers respond to this black family whose images they welcome into their homes? What does the show say to white viewers about race?

THE BLACK AND WHITE *COSBY SHOW*

One of the criticisms that black people have made of *The Cosby Show* is that the Huxtable family behave, as Gates has put it, "just like white people." Although this is a more complex statement than it first sounds (one I shall examine in more detail in relation to the black responses), it raises an interesting possibility: perhaps white people do not actually see the Huxtables as a black family at all? Perhaps they see them not as black, but white—or at least, as colorless? As extraordinary as such a response (in the face of an apparently unambiguous visual reality) may be, it characterizes many of the white viewers in this study. It is possible to divide the white respondents into those who "forget" they are watching a black show, and those who do not. The former response was, in fact, more typical of the white respondents than the latter, although there were several who occupied, to coin a phrase, a rather gray area in between. This "colorblind" response reveals a great deal about white perceptions of race: it is an instance, as we shall see, where people are able to disassociate physical appearance from cultural practices.

The articulation of (what I will call) the "colorblind" discourse took various forms. Some respondents insisted that, when quizzed about the Huxtables' race, as one person put it, "you can't notice it at all." Others were a little more ambiguous, they knew that they were watching a black family, but "forgot" in the face of their familiarity. "You lose track of it," said one woman, "because they're so average." Another respondent described how the Huxtables' color "just sort of drifted" out of her mind while watching. This forgetfulness is not a product of the respondents' stupidity, but of the program's ambiguity, as Barthes has put it:

> Forgetting meanings is not a matter for excuses, an unfortunate defect in performance; it is an affirmative value, a way of asserting the irresponsibility of the text, the pluralism of systems (if I closed their list, I would inevitably reconstitute a singular, theological meaning). (Barthes, 1974, p. 11)

It is possible, in other words, that this forgetfulness is simply a way of sustaining two contradictory interpretations of the same thing. The Huxtables are, for these viewers, both black and colorless—but mostly colorless.

What is it about *The Cosby Show* that allows the color to fade away: what reduces, for many white people, the signifier "black" to a point of relative insignificance? The answer appears to lie in the show's perceived universality. These white viewers were all able to identify the Huxtables as a kind of "everyfamily," as "typical," "everyday" and "average," or, as one person put it, "just like any other family." The world the Huxtables inhabit was described as "just like everyday life" with "jokes about everyday things" or "real true family things." One white interviewee articulated this idea with a revealing anecdote about a family experience in Provincetown (a Cape Cod seaside resort that attracts a largely gay clientele). His wife has just referred to the Huxtables as "a typical family":

> We tell this story all the time. We were in Provincetown, at a nightclub, and there was one of the female impersonators. And his announcer came out and did a little comedy routine. There were a lot of same-sex couples in the audience. He took one look at us in the front row and said, "Oh, the Cosbys are here too!" . . . He had us pegged.

The "Cosbys" (Huxtables) are so "normal," in other words, that they are used to symbolize, in a unfamiliar setting, a state of familial normality. Their "typicality" turns black into white.

Within this reading of *The Cosby Show*, blackness signifies only so far as to show that they (as black people) are, as a number of respondents said, "just like us." Racial difference dissolves, so that, as another suggested, "it would be basically the same show if they were a white family." The assumption behind these judgments is that "blackness" is a social construction, a collection of cultural indicators that can be freed from the physical actuality of being black. Consequently, when you have what one respondent described as "a black family in a white atmosphere," it is possible to forget that the family on the TV screen is a different race.

What makes this response interesting is its particularity to *The Cosby Show*. These respondents were not generally "colorblind": they share a common definition of what "blackness" is, and they recognize it when they see it. This perception manifested itself when respondents were asked to talk about other black sitcoms on TV, shows like *Good Times, The Jeffersons, 227* and *Amen*. While most respondents were able to link these shows together under the general category of "black sitcoms," they did not include *The Cosby Show* in this category (only one person in the whole white sample made such a categorical link). As one respondent put it, "I think they're totally different"—the difference being that these shows, unlike *The Cosby Show*, involve what is identified as "black humor." This comparison is instructive, and I shall return to it shortly.

What does the colorblind response to the Huxtable household signify? What, in ideological terms, does it mean? In the first instance, it appears that *The Cosby Show* has an appeal among white audiences that other black shows do not. These respondents had few problems relating to or identifying with the Huxtables, as the Provincetown story indicates. (Other respondents made similar remarks, one mentioning, for example, that "my sister said that our family reminded her of the Cosby family.") For these respondents, this identification is a source of pleasure, allowing them the vicarious enjoyment of taking part in the pleasant lives of the Huxtables, "because," as one respondent observed, "it relates mostly to usual, regular families and stuff, and their regular problems, and stuff like that."

Would these viewers enjoy the show as much if its "blackness" was signified by its presence rather than its absence? Moreover, is the absence of any discussion or acknowledgement of racism on *The Cosby Show* a prerequisite for these viewers' enjoyment and participation (as viewers)? The answer to this question reveals the limits of the apparently liberal colorblind discourse: these respondents, on the whole, neither *want* to be reminded that the Huxtables are black, nor, still less, of the existence of any form of racism.

A number of respondents were aware, when prompted, that "black issues" were either introduced with the greatest delicacy, or else entirely absent from *The Cosby Show*. While a couple of the more self-consciously liberal respondents were critical of this exclusion, most felt that this was a positive absence. Some expressed this by saying that they watched the show to enjoy it, not to be preached at, while others explicitly stated that the introduction of black issues would "be alienating," and that the show would "lose a lot" if it dealt with racism, with the ominous consequence that they would "probably lose the white audience they have."

To introduce "black issues" would transform the Huxtables from an "everyfamily" (an idea celebrated by this discourse) into a *black* family—an image these respondents would prefer to avoid. One respondent illustrated this perspective thus:

> My speculation is that they're trying to present a family who's just a normal American family. And that, as white people don't talk about racial issues all the time, or confront them, or deal with them, then neither would this family. They're trying to get the point across that it's not an all-consuming issue in their lives . . . It's the only show I can remember where a black family was shown, and they were upper middle class, professional family, having situations that were familiar to most people and race is never an issue.

To be "normal" here is to be part of the dominant culture, which is white (and, interestingly, upper middle-class, a point I shall take up shortly). While it is possible for black people to be admitted to the realm of normality, entry is dependent upon their losing various attributes associated with black experience.

Those black shows that are seen to signify "blackness" more strongly are, accordingly, compared unfavorably to *The Cosby Show*. These other black sitcoms were denigrated by white groups over and over again for being "slapstick," "loud," "full of yelling and screaming," "stereotypical" and more "black" in style and humor. The use of the word *stereotypical*, in this instance, was very particular: a vague awareness of media stereotypes was combined with an equally vague assumption that perhaps these "stereotypes" were, after all, accurate. One respondent made an unusual attempt to pursue this question in relation to news coverage, but went on to acknowledge that it was difficult for her to make a critical judgment:

> You know how they show, in a courtroom, when they accuse someone, and they would probably always be black. And then the white tend to be left out, I think, in terms of crime. And I don't know, is that really what's happening? Or is it just the way the media are reporting it? You have no way of knowing. I have no way of knowing.

For most of the white respondents, there was only a tiny discursive space between an awareness of media stereotypes of black people, and acceptance of those stereotypes. To condemn other black shows for being "stereotypical" was, therefore, very close to condemning them for being too "black."

Some white respondents (particularly in the upper middle-class groups) expressed their dislike for these "stereotypical" shows by not watching them at all. Those that did watch one of these shows appeared to do so without much enthusiasm—particularly when they were compared to the "calm, thought out" *Cosby Show.* A typical complaint made by one group was that they were "less easy to relate to": "They're just not like our family." Just as its absence on *The Cosby Show* allows inclusion, the cultural presence of race on other shows serves to alienate these white viewers. One woman articulated this fairly explicitly, suggesting that you are aware of race when you watch other black sitcoms, "but you don't think about it with *The Cosby Show* ... it doesn't even cross my mind." Or, as another respondent put it, while other black sitcoms have identifiably "black humor," with *The Cosby Show,* "you just think of them as people."

Representations and attitudes about social class are issues I shall be exploring in some detail later in this chapter. Suffice to say, at this point, that ideas about class appear to cut across this color-blind discourse. The Huxtables' perceived universality is partly a function of their class position: as one respondent rather bluntly put it, "They're upper middle-class, not black."

During the interviews, groups were asked to respond to the idea of transforming the Huxtables from an affluent professional into a working-class, blue-collar family. A number of respondents, most particularly (though not exclusively) from the upper middle and middle-class groups, were not at all happy with such an idea. They did not want to see the show, as one respondent put it, "stoop down to another cultural level." To be blue-collar, in the media world, would emphasize their "blackness," whereas as professionals they merge into the "normal" white world of TV. Social mobility, in this sense, becomes a form of sanctity: much like the missionary in the colonial era, "blackness" is understood as a condition from which black people may be rescued.

The ideological thrust of this reading of *The Cosby Show* is ambiguous, and its ambiguity is brought into sharper focus, as we shall see, by the attitudes these respondents strike when discussing race outside *The Cosby Show*. We need, however, to ask another question first: how do those white viewers who *do* see the Huxtables as black read the show?

TURNING UP THE CONTRAST

The colorblind discourse becomes a little clearer in the light of those white respondents who did not articulate it. These viewers gave an unambiguous response to the Huxtables as African Americans: the signifier "blackness" did not lapse into silence—it formed a non-negotiable part of the show's existence. While this response was, overall, less common among white viewers than some variation of the colorblind response, it took a number of different forms, ranging from the progressive to the reactionary. These differences originated in very different attitudes toward black people and race relations.

Those viewers who held a number of overtly racist assumptions, or who were antagonistic in some way toward black people, seemed unable to ignore the Huxtables' color. This, in turn, made it difficult to identify with the show, and watching it became a less enjoyable experience. This response was, in this study, present only in glimpses. The reactions noted by one of the interviewers during the recruiting stage of the research suggested that some people with strongly held racist views would dislike *The Cosby Show* simply because it *was* black (one such person remarked during his refusal to take part in the study that the show was "stupid, stupid, stupid"). Since the sample contained only people who watched *The Cosby Show*, we were, by definition, less likely to hear this kind of response. When an overtly racist judgment was made, it was fairly unequivocal. One interview, for example, was interrupted toward the end by friends of the interview group, who castigated *The Cosby Show* for being "too black," and then proceeded to discuss the show in the abusive language of racism.

A more subtle articulation of this kind of response came from a viewer who was resentful and uneasy about Bill Cosby's support of black institutions and causes. This respondent, unlike all the other white interviewees, put *The Cosby Show* in the same category as other black shows, and while he enjoyed some aspects of these shows, he criticized all of them for their exclusion of white people from their casts. In an inverse version of the discourse of racial stereotyping (used by most black respondents), he proceeded to argue that the only white people who appeared on the show were "fat and stupid," this being evidence of what he saw as *The Cosby Show*'s pro-black, anti-white position.

The differences between this kind of reading and the more liberal colorblind response is instructive: the more overtly racist viewer is less able to make a distinction between "blackness" as a physical and as a cultural category. It is much more difficult for those expressing a more overt form of racism to forget that the Huxtables are black, because skin color is seen to bear an inevitable ideological message. It is a discourse of biological determinism that can only work to amplify the signifier "black." The ability of other respondents to disentangle the physical from the ideological is, by the same token, a prerequisite for their colorblind reading.

A few groups articulated racial awareness in quite a different way. These people also rejected the idea that the Huxtables could be white, but saw their "blackness" as an enjoyable thing. This is a discourse that a number of people expressed with little confidence: as one woman put, "It wouldn't be as funny if it was white. . . . They have a way about them—I don't know what it is." The inexplicable appeal of the Huxtables' blackness, the idea that the show would lose an ineffable something if it became white, was, for some respondents, clearly more difficult to articulate than either the colorblind discourse or the racist discourse. If nothing else, this tells something about the nature of the dominant white culture, and, in particular, what that culture allows white people, or makes it easy for white people, to say about black people.

Only those who were most positive about *The Cosby Show* as a *black* show were able to offer any explanation: one, for example, referred to her enjoyment of black culture, while another felt it was more "fun" and "colorful" because it was a black show ("black moms are cooler"). These people shared two things in common: they tended to be the most progressive in their racial attitudes, and they usually had considerable experience of black people in their own lives. Some of the most emphatic colorblind reactions, conversely, came from those with very little experience of racial integration.

This discourse is both like and unlike the racist discourse. On the one hand, it involves an emphasis upon the signifier "black" that makes it imperative to incorporate a discussion about race into their reading of *The Cosby Show*. On the other hand, it amounts to a celebration rather than a fear or distrust of cultural difference.

It is difficult to tease out some of the more intricate qualities of this discourse: there are moments in the interviews, for example, when it makes fairly ambiguous appearances. In particular, the idea that black people are "funnier" (a number of white respondents made references to Bill Cosby's amusing "body language," an attribute some of them clearly identified as "black") has both positive and negative connotations: it may be celebratory, or it may refer to a more stereotypical discourse in which the black person occupies the position of clown. Like the Shakespearean fool, the clown's virtues cannot extinguish or redeem the otherness of his or her being. It is, in this respect, worth commenting that a number of the most famous black actors in the United States (such as Bill Cosby, Eddie Murphy and Richard Pryor) are also comedians.

IDEOLOGICAL CONSEQUENCES: WHITE ON BLACK

So, on the evidence presented thus far, how has *The Cosby Show* intervened in the ideological construction of white people's understanding of black people? It is, I hope, already clear that we are not dealing with an unambiguous cultural phenomenon.

There is a sense in which *The Cosby Show* does appear, for a number of white viewers, to cultivate a liberal attitude toward black people and racial equality. The colorblind reading that influenced so many white viewers in this study is, in this sense, a major step forward: the show does indeed, as Dyson suggests, allow white North Americans "to view black folks as *human beings*." *The Cosby Show* proves that black people can be just like white people, or, as one respondent put it, "that black people are just like us." The inevitabilities of crude racism have been disentangled, the color of someone's skin can, indeed, signify nothing.

Before we hurl our hats into the air, proclaiming *The Cosby Show* as the vision of the racially tolerant society to come, two weighty caveats need consideration. Both concern the limits of the "colorblindness" induced by the fictional lives of the Huxtable family. We should realize, first of all, that the price of this victory in race relations is extremely high. For many white respondents, the Huxtables' class position distinguished them from most other black people on television, making it possible for white audiences to disentangle them from preconceived (white) notions of black culture

("They're upper middle class, not black"). The Huxtables, in this sense, look like most white families on TV. If it is necessary for black people to become upper middle-class to be rid of white prejudice, then it is a price most cannot afford to pay. The acceptance of the Huxtables as an "everyfamily" did not dislodge the generally negative associations white viewers have of (what is perceived as) "black culture," attitudes quickly articulated when other black TV sitcoms were discussed. *The Cosby Show* caters to a need for familiarity, and, in this sense, their price of acceptance is that they do appear "just like white people."

The show's failure to reveal any of the racist and class barriers that penalize most black people in the United States is part of this process. As the respondent quoted earlier commented, since racism is not an issue for "normal" (i.e., white) people, it is a condition of the Huxtables' "normality" that racism plays no part in their lives. The significance of this absence was revealed during the final part of the interviews, when the interviewers guided the conversation toward more general race relations issues. In marked contrast to the black group members, most white respondents failed to acknowledge the effective existence of racism in the social structure.

The attitude of most white respondents to affirmative action (in employment, education and so forth) illustrated this perception (or lack of it). An affirmative action policy exists as a counterweight to a society in which a group of people have been and are systematically disadvantaged. It is a policy that is only equitable or sensible if you acknowledge that society *does* disadvantage certain people. If we live in a world of equal opportunity, on the other hand, then such a policy is undoubtedly unfair or unnecessary.

The few white respondents who saw the Huxtables as black (excluding the overtly racist respondents) were also likely to be sympathetic to affirmative action. These viewers, because they do not base their reading upon the notion that "we're all the same," are able to appreciate *The Cosby Show* for its cultural difference as well as its familiarity. Difference is acknowledged, not suppressed, and it becomes possible both to recognize the existence of discrimination and to appreciate the need to address the inequalities discrimination sustains.

Most white respondents, however, were quite unaware of the existence of widespread or structural racism, and their rejection of policies like affirmative action was a logical consequence of this. One of the most striking aspects of the discussions on this topic is how perfectly the liberalism of the colorblind response to *The Cosby Show* fits in with such a rejection: as one respondent put it,

> I think that there really is room in the United States for minority people to get ahead, without affirmative action.

Thus it is with the Huxtables and thus, in all its old glory, speaks the "American Dream."

Most of the other white respondents followed suit. Many, having asserted their own racial tolerance (in relation to *The Cosby Show*), were able to develop this discourse in a proclamation of an equal society, a world in which

> they should hire the person who knows what they are doing, whether they are black, white, Spanish or whatever. I don't think they should hire them just because somebody is a certain race.

A Massachusetts Republican (a 1990 gubernatorial candidate), Steven Pierce, when questioned on a TV interview about the lack of evidence to support his claims that gay couples make bad foster parents (WGBH, May 1990), argued that, in the absence of evidence, you should revert to "common sense." As Gramsci noted (Gramsci, 1971), and as Mr. Pierce so neatly demonstrated, "common sense" is often a convenient way of disguising an oppressive ideology as conventional wisdom. In the discussion of racism and affirmative action, "common sense" leads to the assumption that things are as they should be, as one respondent explained:

> We haven't lived through, I mean . . . I didn't really experience a time where I really saw people first-handedly treat blacks the way I know they've been treated, you know? I've never seen anybody ask a black to sit in the back of a bus because they are black, and I know that happened, so it's difficult for me to . . . . I can see where they're coming from when they expect, you know, some things because that happened. But I've never seen it so I don't expect anybody to get any special treatment because of their color.

Common sense, in this case, is to use limited individual experience to deny the existence of widespread racism, and, therefore, the need to do anything to redress it. It was often at this point in the interviews, significantly, that some respondents would lapse into the reiteration of traditional racist stereotypes, informed by anecdotal images of listless black people languishing on welfare, or gliding effortlessly upward on a tide of government assistance and affirmative action programs.

The effort made by popular cultural forms in the United States to come to terms with racism has often focused on sins of the past, from slavery to the early years of the civil rights movement. Most white respondents were, indeed, aware of this history; what is interesting, for this study, is that the acknowledgment of a racist past was used by white respondents to demonstrate historical contrast rather than historical continuity. Racism, in other words, is a disease that has been cured—no further medicine is required. A number of respondents suggested, in this vein, that affirmative action was now anachronistic, that it belonged to a bygone era of discrimination:

> Well, I think it has gone too far, where the white people don't have the opportunities. I think it has come to a point where people should be hired now, not because of their color or their race, but because of what they're able to do. I mean there are people who are much better qualified but can't get hired because they are white, and I don't think that's right. Maybe in the beginning, they needed this . . . but it has gone too far.

This assessment undoubtedly contradicts the actual experience of most black people (as the black respondents repeatedly testified); yet it makes sense in relation to the world of TV drama, a world where, as Gates has observed, black people, like the Huxtables, have enjoyed considerable success in recent years.

The Cosby Show strikes a deal with its white audience: it asks for an attitude that allows a black family to be welcomed onto TV screens in white homes, and in return provides them pleasure without culpability, with a picture of a comfortable, ordered world in which white people (and the nation as a whole) are absolved of any responsibility for the position of black people.

The Cosby Show is, in this respect, caught in a double bind, compromised by the ideological structures that envelop it. It appears to cultivate both the racial tolerance for which it has been applauded *and* the deep-rooted myopia for which it has been criticized. A more radical message is clearly needed to educate white audiences, yet its inclusion runs the risk of dispatching most of those viewers to the safer territories explored on other channels: racism, it appears, is something that most white viewers simply don't *want* to know about. The world, as *The Cosby Show* demonstrates, is a far happier place without it.

The discussion, thus far, has focused upon perceptions of race—perceptions that are, as we shall see later, particular to white rather than black audiences. It is a discussion that cannot be taken much further without detailed examination of the notions of social class that cut across people's understanding of race. The ideological thrust of *The Cosby Show*, I shall argue, depends upon what it says and does not say about class and class structure in the United States.

"DREAM . . . DREAM DREAM DREAM"

Miller's description of the Huxtable home as "the corporate show-case" that displays both the desirability and the availability of the "American Dream" (Miller, 1986, p. 210) raises the specter of a capitalist ideology at work, with *The Cosby Show* as a vision in which the system is celebrated for its fairness. The fact that the Huxtables are an African American family is central to this image: their presence, Miller argues, assures us that in the United States, everyone, regardless of race or creed can enjoy the good life. As enticing as this argument is, we cannot assume (as, I hope, the analysis of the news audience makes clear) that this will be the ideological message constructed by the show's audience. One of the reasons for doing this audience study is, of course, to clarify such things. While the operation of the colorblind reading of the show certainly supports Miller's contention, there are further nuances to be explored.

The "American Dream" is built on the cracks in an otherwise fairly rigid class system. The system ensures that most poor people will stay poor, and most rich people will stay rich, cycles that will inexorably revolve from one generation to the next. The system is, however, not foolproof: the cracks in it may be too small to threaten its survival, but they are large enough to allow a few to slip upward. It is these happy few who are conjured up by the "American dream," whose strange logic transforms them from exceptions to the rule, to create the idea that there are, in fact, no rules.

One of the problems that muddle thinking about racism in the United States (and elsewhere) is the recent successes of its leaders in proclaiming a level of political and legal racial equality, while, at the same time, upholding an economic system that subjugates most black people. African Americans, having been placed at the bottom of the economic pile, are forced to struggle against inequalities in material and educational resources. It is a struggle that, unless the entire system is transformed, few can win. Capitalism, as the organizing principle of this system, allows the United States to forgo racist principles while maintaining white hegemony—a lesson the white minority in Zimbabwe have, to their undoubted satisfaction, quickly learned. This fusion of racial inequalities within a class sys-

tem complicates the discursive picture. To understand racial inequalities, it is necessary to understand, in one form or another, how
the class structure operates. There are two competing discourses
here: one is imbued with the individualistic notion that "anyone
can make it," the other with the contrary awareness of social structures and class barriers. There is little doubt which of the two, in
the United States, is ideologically dominant: Donal Carbaugh's
(1988) discussion of the pervasive discourses of individualism
among audiences on the Donahue show, although it is couched in
different terms, is an interesting example of the power and use of
this ideology. This does not mean that people are completely unaware of structural inequalities in their society, simply that there
are few well-articulated public declarations of this awareness. Most
public declarations, from TV commercials to political speeches, appear to fuel the discourse of the "American Dream."

What role does *The Cosby Show* play in this ideological process?
The answer, suggested by the group discussions, is that while the
show does not implant the logic of the "American Dream" in people's heads, it does appear to nourish and sustain it, albeit in different ways.

The discussion of white groups attitudes toward racial inequality revealed, as we have seen, a widespread failure (or refusal)
to acknowledge the structures that disadvantage most black people.
Only one white respondent, arguing the need for greater educational
opportunity, addressed the issue at this level:

> I think what you've got, what they really got to do is get around
> to training the black people and other minorities so that they
> are just as qualified as the other people are, and give them all
> a chance to go after the positions that are available.

Most discussions about the issue, unlike this respondent, focused
instead upon the presence or absence of direct forms of racial discrimination. What is significant is that the problem was not conceived on the level of social structures, but as a function of personal
interactions. This allowed respondents to argue, for example, that
because "I've never seen anybody ask a black to sit in the back of
a bus because they are black" (in the absence, in other words, of an
overtly racist climate), therefore "I don't expect anybody to get any
special treatment because of their color."

The fact that black people are, on the whole, poorer than white
people is widely acknowledged, yet, for most white respondents, the
reasons for this disparity cannot be articulated. It is worth noting

that it is at this point that space opens up for an unspoken but pernicious racist discourse asserting white superiority.

What is missing almost throughout these discussions is a discourse that articulates an awareness of class structure. Without such a discourse, it is impossible to make any sense of racial inequalities without reverting to straightforward racist explanations. How *The Cosby Show* contributes to this discursive absence relies, to a great extent, on the role it plays within its televisual context.

"IT'S A DIFFERENT WORLD . . ."

An alien researching life on earth would certainly learn a great deal by scrutinizing satellite broadcasts of television from the United States. The inquiring alien might, nevertheless, begin to ponder on various curiosities: who collects the garbage or cleans the streets, for example? Who builds the houses, farms the land, or works on production lines to produce all those delightful gadgets? And, strangest of all, how on earth does the economy sustain all those lawyers and doctors, who seem to be everywhere? Here is a place, the alien might conclude, chronically overpopulated by members of the middle and upper middle-class (see Fiske, 1987).

These curiosities are, in a different way, also rather confusing to us earthlings. We may realize, unlike the alien, that normality in the TV world is rather different from the normality of the world beyond it: but, since we spend so much time watching TV, we are liable to lose our grip on distinctions between the two. *The Cosby Show* is a good example. Here is a show about a professional family whose social class makes them unusual in the real world, but decidedly average among the privileged populace of television. So, do we see them as normal, or as members of a privileged class?

One of the most striking features of this exploration into the audience is most people's ability to do both at the same time: to combine an awareness of the Huxtables' socio-economic status with the idea that they are a "normal," "everyday" family. This paradox manifested itself in interview after interview. This apparent contradiction is only resolved if we make the distinction between the TV world and the world beyond it, so that the Huxtables are (to quote one group) "very typical" and "universal" in one context and "kind of a highbrow, upper middle-class professional family" in another.

The ideological consequences of this slippage between two different worlds are only comprehensible once we dispense with the notion that human consciousness is a rational and coherent place for thoughts to dwell. John Berger's description of the space between seeing and knowing is a useful way of beginning to understand our capacity for cognitive dissonance: we look at the sky and *see* the sun revolving around the earth, yet we know that it is, in fact, the earth that is revolving around the sun (Berger, 1972). In the same way, respondents may know that *The Cosby Show* is (as one respondent described) "only TV," yet they are also able to see it as an extension of the big wide world.

There are a number of examples of this phenomenon beginning to emerge from recent audience studies, where the lines between televisual and non-televisual realities begin to blur. The quotation marks surrounding television fiction start to fade away once those fictions become part of our oral culture (see Chapter 3), so that we allow what we know to be "only TV" to inform our view of the world. Andrea Press describes an interesting instance of this, in response to a viewer's perception of Claire Huxtable, whom she judged to be a more typical lawyer than the lawyer she actually knew. Her only reference point on which to base such a judgment is television, where lawyers—usually attractive, telegenic lawyers, like Claire Huxtable—abound (Press, 1991). Television, after all, tells us about the world—we cannot *always* remember to remain skeptical.

The televisual context that allows respondents to see the Huxtables as privileged in one breath and typical in another allows *The Cosby Show* to transmit a powerful ideological message: it confirms not only the *desirability* of the privileges wealth has bought to the Huxtable household, but the tangible *attainability* of those privileges. This, of course, is the language of the "American Dream." What makes this language so successful in *The Cosby Show*, and so persuasive to different interests, is not so much its clarity as the structure of its ambiguities. It is to these that I shall now turn.

CLOSE TO HOME: THE UPPER MIDDLE-CLASS GROUPS

The group of viewers in the best position to regard an upper middle-class family like the Huxtables as "normal" and "typical" are, of course, those from upper middle-class backgrounds. These respondents, as one might expect, clearly enjoyed the ease with which they felt able to identify with or relate to the show. When the prospect of transforming the Huxtables into a blue-collar family was presented to them, most responded with a sense of unease. Far better, as one respondent put it, to keep it "sophisticated" and "select," to watch (what another referred to as) "classy" people.

187

For these respondents, this class preference was not simply a question of money: it involved a level of cultural competence (or "sophistication") that is understood as class-related. Most were shy about stating this point too explicitly, preferring to talk about those things they have in common with the Huxtables, as in the following exchange:

MAN: I think I enjoy the program more because he is a doctor, she is a professional.

WOMAN: Identifying ...

MAN: We're both professionals. Our kids are going to go to college, their kids go to college.

WOMAN: It's just the situations ...

MAN: For me, watching the program, I enjoy it more ...

WOMAN: ... I can identify.

MAN: because they're kind of like me!

INTERVIEWER: And you feel the same way?

WOMAN: Sure, I think it's just a higher level of humor and situations than the other shows.

MAN: That's right!

Class is understood as more than an economic category, it is the expression of a number of cultural practices that an upper middle-class audience feels it shares with the Huxtables. This incorporates everything from going to college to the "higher level of humor" these respondents associate with class position.

Anther respondent makes the same point rather more explicitly, using *Roseanne* and *The Cosby Show* to symbolize class distinction:

I don't know. I mean, I've turned *Roseanne* on, and I cannot get into that show at all. How it's popular is beyond my understanding. And I'm afraid that if you took this (Huxtable) family down to this level, in terms of their working-class strata, that the humor would be like *Roseanne*. Because what happens when you work in a factory? What do people talk about? I mean, you know, for one day of my life I worked in the kitchen of a nursing home, and the humor was so awful, and I was 16 years old, that I did not go back. Do you know what I am saying? It was just something I could not relate to at all.

Although this respondent's class-consciousness is reflected in the other upper middle-class discussions, few were quite as explicit in articulating their distaste for working-class culture.

The use of *Roseanne* as a cultural symbol is, in this respect, particularly interesting. *Roseanne* was repeatedly identified by respondents (regardless of class or race) as a "working-class" sitcom. It follows that the upper middle-class respondents responding positively to the Huxtables' class position would, like the respondent quoted above, find a "working-class sitcom" like *Roseanne* not at all to their taste. While this was true in some cases, some confounded the logic of this position and responded positively to both *Roseanne* and *The Cosby Show*. This suggests an intermingling of perceptions of class and race: the Huxtables' class position is more important than the Connors' (in *Roseanne*), because their "whiteness" or "colorlessness" relies upon it. To make the Huxtables working-class would push them toward the cultural world inhabited by other black sitcoms, a cultural territory these respondents uniformly rejected.

Whether they like *Roseanne* or not, these groups endow *The Cosby Show* with a cultural value that is explicitly class-related. One group, for example, interpreted the Huxtables' aesthetic tastes directly in class terms: if they were middle or working-class, "you wouldn't expect them to be so cultured," able to "afford the finer things in life" such as "the artwork, the jazz clubs, and I think I remember something about an auction or something where they got that painting." While some of the black groups interpreted these symbols as signifying African American culture, to the upper middle-class white audience they represent a source of cultural identification based on class rather than race.

NOW YOU SEE IT, NOW YOU DON'T

In the face of the cultural exclusivity identified by their wealthier counterparts, how is it that the white working-class and lower middle-class audience were able to identify with the Huxtables, to categorize them, as many did, as "typical" and "average" as "a regular family, having the same problems just like us"? The answer, in short, is that while *The Cosby Show* encourages class-consciousness in upper middle-class viewers, it dissolves it for the more working-class audience. Like a clever politician, the show uses different discursive strategies to incorporate different class interests among its viewers.

There were, in fact, only two moments in the white working-class group discussions when respondents expressed glimpses of regret at the exclusivity of the Huxtables' affluence. They came from two of the poorest respondents in our sample, whose material circumstances were in stark contrast to the easy affluence of the Huxtables' brownstone, and both used clothes as symbols of material wealth. One woman suggested that, though she liked Claire Huxtable, she would "like to see her more in jeans, or actually doing housework or something," jeans being a symbol of ordinariness that she could relate to. A man in another group made a similar point:

> The average person watching the show, they're not all that rich. That's something . . . the kids always have nice clothes on, and I wear dirty jeans because I can't find a clean pair in the morning, whereas if they showed that on *The Cosby Show*, I'd say "I did that," you know.

As mild as these expressions of class-consciousness are, they were fairly untypical. While one or two other working-class groups made class-conscious statements, they did not do so in response to *The Cosby Show*. The woman quoted above, perhaps significantly, reserved her most scathing comments for the commercials shown *during* the show:

> The way they make it look . . . it really irks me. You know, they never show the family with the mother or father an alcoholic, but they show the fancy clothes, the cars, the wine coolers. I mean, why don't they show the father sitting there passed out in a chair and the kids yelling for something to eat?

It is worth noting that, given the more obviously functional role of TV advertising, this criticism would be more appropriately addressed to the makers of *The Cosby Show*. The fact that it was not suggests that there is something else going on.

Most lower middle and working-class viewers were able to articulate a separation—one that the upper-class respondents were unable to make—between cultural competence and social class. The Huxtables' class position is, in economic terms, undisputed. In a cultural sense, on the other hand, it appears to be much more ambiguous. This is, as I have suggested, partly a function of the television environment, where to be upper middle-class is to be normal. The normality of being upper middle-class on TV diminishes the exclusivity of various class-related cultural symbols.

It is also a product of Bill Cosby's comic skill and his ability to focus upon ubiquitous topics, a skill one respondent defined thus:

> I think you see yourself in those positions the way that show is. It takes everyday-life type of things and it's funny, because a lot of things that happen in everyday life are funny.

This ingenious ambiguity allows the development of a discourse that identifies the Huxtables as upper middle-class in a material rather than a cultural sense: they have the pleasures and comfort associated with wealth, and yet their values and behavior make them "just a regular family." So, as one respondent put it; "they don't have the lifestyles you expect with the incomes they have—they keep themselves down to earth."

This idea was sometimes articulated by drawing comparisons with what were identified as negative aspects of upper middle-class culture, which was characterized as "pseudo-intellectual" and difficult to relate to. As one man put it, in relation to Cliff:

> I guess he doesn't really seem professional, you know, not the way a doctor would be. Like when you go to doctor's office, it's totally different. . . . I work for the phone company and the ones I meet are very uppity and they really look down on the lower class.

The upper middle-class respondents, predictably, included Bill Cosby within their own cultural milieu. This discourse allows working-class/lower middle-class respondents to do precisely the same thing.

It is possible that, for working-class respondents, the fact that the Huxtables are black facilitates the separation between cultural competence and wealth, since the cultural indicators signifying upper middle-class culture are invariably white. For these viewers, their race may be a signifier of class rather than color.

Either way, it is a reading of the show that makes the possibility of upward mobility more conceivable, since the Huxtables were, as one group put it "role models," but "at the same time very human, having the same problems as everyone else." Upward mobility is defined strictly in economic rather than cultural terms, and the Huxtables' "down-to-earth quality" makes them an appropriate symbol of (as one respondent put it) "something to aspire to." One potentially upwardly mobile woman referring to her friends in college, put it fairly explicitly:

> There's more business majors and there's more engineering majors and things like that, because they want to make a lot of money so that they can live like the Cosbys.

What is, perhaps, most interesting about this comment is that she proceeds to lament this materialistic desire to go to college "so that you can get a good job ... rather than to get a good education." The desire to "live like the Cosbys," in other words, is an economic rather than a cultural goal.

The educational and cultural competencies that support class barriers are thereby dissolved, the Huxtables being both wealthy and a "normal," "regular" family. They represent an attainable and desirable conflation of economic and cultural well-being. If the Huxtables were seen as upper middle-class in a cultural sense, with values and concerns distinct to that lifestyle, this would not be possible.

The Cosby Show, once again, succeeds in having it both ways. Whether the viewer is close to the Huxtables' class position or not does not matter, because it is possible to see your cultural values reflected from either position. Both audiences are able to feel they have what it takes to identify with a program that (in the words of one respondent) "shows the best things about this country": one because the *The Cosby Show* is seen as "sophisticated" and "select," the other because it is not. Class barriers (in the form of an upper middle-class cultural elitism) are witnessed only by those unthreatened by those barriers. To everyone else the show exhibits the universality of the "American Dream."

In the absence of the more critical discourses of class or racial consciousness, this aspect of *The Cosby Show*'s ambiguity sustains the meritocratic mythology that allows a population to accept enormous differences in wealth. In this sense, while neither Gates nor Miller anticipates these ambiguities, they correctly identify the show's main ideological drift. The show is, to some extent, forced into this logic by the language of mainstream television in the United States: to be accepted as "normal" by white audiences, the Huxtables must be "normal" on television's terms. They must be part of the upper middle-class media world to signify that they are "just like white people." But this is not the whole story. While a majority of *The Cosby Show*'s viewers are white, a large number are not. It is possible that African American audiences interpret the show in different ways with very different ideological nuances, and it is to this possibility that I now turn.

THE BATTLE OF IMAGES

There are strands of post-modernist thought that suggest the lines between the simulacra of the media age and the real world are becoming increasingly blurred. There is a great deal to be said for this idea: the slippage between the class status of the Huxtables in the world on and off screen, for example, gives credence to this neo-existential vision. There are times, however, when the more dedicated followers of this post-modernist fashion start to lose a grip on the nitty-gritty, when respect for the solidity of forces of social determination begins to float away into the ether.

In audience research, this has involved a tendency to dismiss the importance of crude materialities like class and race, to question the power of these materialities to shape people's perceptions of television, popular culture and the world in general. While it would be foolish to ignore the complexity of these causal relations, it is equally foolish to ignore causality altogether. In this study, these forms of determination manifest themselves in a number of ways, and they do so most profoundly when the audience is broken into black and white. Black people and white people, in short, watch *The Cosby Show* very differently.

These differences, as we might expect, become most obvious when discussing the nuances and meanings of race. It is possible to identify two powerful competing discourses expressed by the black groups in this study: one suggesting that *The Cosby Show* is "too white" to represent the interests of black people, and another that sees the show as a positive intervention in the generally hostile world of the media. These discourses, almost completely absent during discussions with white groups, played a significant role in black perceptions of the show.

A number of black groups referred explicitly to the "too white" criticism of the show, although very few actually endorsed it. On the contrary, the attitude that prevails throughout the interviews with black groups is one of enormous pride and approval in the way they, as black people, are portrayed. Denise Hartsough, in a well-documented review, quotes Richard Carter to comment on the power of this sentiment:

> Even a black journalist highly critical of *The Cosby Show* begins his article by saying: "I don't know a single black person—and

I know thousands—who doesn't admire Bill Cosby for his talent
... And we appreciate his show. Since we've got so little, we'd
be crazy not to." (Hartsough, 1989, p. 10)

As Carter implies in his final remark, this attitude is informed by
a discourse critical of the way in which black people have been the
victims of media stereotypes. It is discourse that, regardless of age,
class or gender, provides the powerful backdrop for most of the black
group discussions in this study.

The effect of this discourse on perceptions of the Huxtables is
fairly dramatic. For most black respondents, it makes the colorblind
response seem faintly ludicrous: the following couple's response to
the question: how aware are you that the Huxtables are black? is
fairly typical:

WOMAN: (in mild disbelief) "How aware? How aware"?

MAN: What do you mean? Just look ...

WOMAN: Just look at them and you can see that they are black.
You're not talking to white folks now (laughs). What kind of
question is that for black folk?

BOTH: Just look at them and you know they're black.

The woman in this group proceeds to ridicule what she sees (as we
have seen, quite correctly) as the liberal white colorblind response
to Bill Cosby, typified by a white teacher she knows:

That sounds like what their white teachers say about (the show):
"I don't know he's black." I say: "What! Can't you see he's
black? What do you mean you're not aware he's black!" She
thought she could say something so wonderful: (imitating her
voice) "Oh no, I'm not aware he's black." I said: "Uh uh, I
want you to be *very* aware that he's black."

Her last remark is an important one. *The Cosby Show*'s meaning
is informed by its place in the battle for positive media representations (of black people). This not only highlights the signifier
"black" for these groups, it gives it a crucial significance. The colorblind discourse, for this respondent, is counterproductive: it allows
the traditional stereotypes to be circumvented rather than replaced.
It allows white people to see *The Cosby Show* outside stereotypical

representations *without* dislodging the effect of those representations.

This reading works to highlight those moments when the show's "blackness" is signified—moments invisible to many white viewers. Most black respondents, accordingly, had little difficulty in identifying these moments. While there were many variations, the following responses were fairly typical (it is also interesting to note that some of these cultural references were interpreted by upper middle-class white respondents very differently):

(If they were white) they couldn't play it the way they play it. Some lines they could not use if it was a white family.

I think the show would be different if the show was white by the mere fact that I can't help but see they are African American people. I look around and I look at the artwork in their house, I listen to the slang, the black English that is used in the show, which is extremely important. I mean those are things I happen to look at: it's the whole environment of the show which makes it black. I mean I've never seen a white program on TV that has made the effort to put other images up other than white images.

The background reminders of black culture are, for most black viewers, seen in the foreground. The anti-apartheid poster or the pictures of jazz musicians on the Huxtable childrens' walls become potent symbols: "I mean it's like you . . . you can see the apartheid . . . you will see, like, Wynton Marsalis, you know a poster of him's up there."

The importance of black cultural symbols in this interpretation tends, in some ways, to diminish the connotations of class; it inverts the judgment made by many white viewers: they are black, not upper middle-class. There were, accordingly, less obvious class differences between the black group readings, although both black and white working-class viewers shared the perception that the Huxtables' "down-to-earth" quality made them, in a cultural sense, "classless." For black respondents, this interpretation simply reinforced the feeling of a common cultural identity based on race. The Huxtables are "average" and "everyday" because of a common culture, this culture not being so much universal, but, as one working-class black woman put it, universally black:

One is a doctor, one is a lawyer, but they are both real people. I don't think it necessarily has to do with your occupation, but how you present yourself and if you know your identity and culture. I think that definitely transcends the class thing. . . . I always feel with the Cosbys that they are down-to-earth people.

When this kind of reading is compared to the colorblind response, it becomes clear that "the whole environment of the show" (identified here as black) is a source of its ambiguity: it suggests a set of cultural indicators whose racial meaning pulls, depending on its audience, in two opposite directions. In short, most white people see an upper middle-class family, and most black people see a black family, while both see them as a normal group of people they can identify with.

This structured ambiguity might lead a cynic to comment that the show is perfectly designed to maximize its audience: the symbols of black culture are strong enough to incorporate a black audience and weak enough to entice a white audience. The tightrope walked by *The Cosby Show* carries it aloft to the kinds of ratings network executives dream about.

Despite the undoubted truth embedded in this cynicism, we should not allow it to obscure the show's positive value to most black people and a small number of white people, who enjoy it as a quiet, gentle celebration of black culture, an oasis, initially at least, in a white cultural desert.

COSBY'S CLASS ACT

The white groups were, by and large, unaware of the realities of racism and the need for affirmative action. The black groups, on the other hands, shared no such illusions. For most black respondents, racism was as great a problem for them now as it ever was; as one respondent put it; "We may be back (where we were) . . . because Reagan did a job on us. He did a big, bad job on us." Others commented on the more subtle nature of racism today, as this woman did:

It is camouflage, you know. It's like when men are in the army and they are taught how to fit into their environment, how to camouflage yourself so to look like a part of that environment—but you are not. And it's the same thing, and no matter how you look at racism, you can't dress it up, you can't put it on a silver platter and serve it: it's racism, it's nasty and ugly and America was built on it.

Similarly, the only criticisms of affirmative action policies were in terms of public relations or effectiveness—few questioned the need for it (only two black respondents said that it was unfair or that "anyone can make it," and both were hotly challenged by other group members).

It is within this discursive climate that *The Cosby Show* begins to play a rather contradictory role. The show's success, for most of these respondents, represents a victory, a victory of which they, as black people, feel a proud part. The Huxtable family show the world what black people can achieve. This response, as we have already seen, was fairly typical:

> Another reason I kind of like it is because it escapes that whole thing of every black family you ever saw on TV was as poor as a rat's ass. I mean, that is all you got, I mean: "How we ever going to make it, daddy died and left me with three kids."

Although black viewers were divided on how representative the Huxtables were as a black family, the need to counter traditional stereotypes often overcame such perceptions. Even if they *were* untypical, in other words, it did not matter—*The Cosby Show* is still an important victory in the battle of images. Or, as another respondent put it:

> I think the overall concept itself: what's wrong with showing a black family who has those kind of values? I almost said white values, but that's not the word I want. There is no monopoly on that kind of thing that's owned by white folks.

The absence of poverty, struggle or any class or racial barriers is seen as a good thing, because black viewers are tired of being associated with negativity. The positive images provided by *The Cosby Show* remain uncluttered by awkward caveats. And yet, as these comments suggest, it is a picture that contradicts the harsh realities that black viewers describe when they are talking about racism in general.

This contradiction created a tension that ran through a number of the black interviews. For some, it created a dilemma between the need to show the reality of struggle and the need for positive images. This dilemma was sometimes informed by a class-consciousness that rarely surfaced in white discussions of the show. One viewer, for example, when asked if he would prefer the Huxtables to be working-class, responded thus:

> I would. I would enjoy it a lot better . . . I would enjoy it more
> if they were struggling per se . . . I mean it seems as though
> Theo is destined, I mean, you know his father's got a legacy
> he's going to hand down. I mean he's got everything already.
> He's got the school planned out for him. You know. No ques-
> tion. It's like white America. It's a silver platter syndrome . . .
> And I don't think it's like that . . . I mean I like to see the
> struggle a little bit because it's not all like that for black America.
> It's not like that. There's racism. There's the economic situation.
> I mean it's just not that easy, and I think they make it seem
> as though "it's here, black America."

The Cosby Show, in other words, misleads the viewer into supposing
that the struggle, for most black people, is over. These fears are, as
we have seen, extremely well founded. At the same time, this respondent is concerned by the direction in which this argument takes
him:

> It's almost like sending mixed messages. There's part of me
> that says, in a way, I don't want white America to see us, you
> know, struggling or whatever.

The tension between the desire for positive images and the
desire for some form of social realism created contradictory attitudes toward other black sitcoms, which were often judged as, on
the one hand, more stereotypical than *The Cosby Show*, but also as
more "what a black family was really like." One woman, for example, even after suggesting that *The Cosby Show* is more "middle-
class white" than other black shows, goes on to say:

> I'm conscious of them being a black family, and proud of them,
> the way they carry themselves. Yes, yes. I'm very conscious of
> the black and feel it lets whites know blacks live good too.

In this case, and in some other groups, these tensions were left
hanging, stated but unresolved. In other groups, they were the subject of disputes between group members.

It is clear, when these interpretations are compared to the white
audience readings, that *The Cosby Show* plays a very different ideological role when African Americans watch it. The black viewers
have, first of all, a critical view of how the media represents them,
and *The Cosby Show* is seen by most as a positive intervention on
their behalf. Second, while many white viewers do not have a critique of institutional racism or a sense of class-consciousness in their

discursive repertoire, many black viewers—regardless of social class—do. The lure of the "American Dream" reading of the show was so tempting to most white respondents because they were not equipped, discursively speaking, to resist it. Many black respondents, on the other hand, were at least partially aware of the absences in *The Cosby Show*, and interpreted it in that context.

For this audience, there really is no need to show *why* most black people do not live like the Huxtables: they can therefore enjoy the positive images without the same ideological consequences. The only problem with this analysis is that it overlooks a discourse a number of black respondents used to resolve the contradiction between the need to portray the realities of racism, and the need to present positive images unburdened by such realities. While these respondents revealed their awareness of the disadvantages faced by most black people during the last part of the interviews, they *suppressed* it during their discussion of *The Cosby Show*. This allowed them to challenge the very notion that the show was unrealistic, on the grounds that the Huxtable family were not, in fact, that unusual:

> I mean for every person who doesn't know that setting, there is an African American who can say, "I know somebody who is a doctor" or, "I know somebody who's a lawyer."

These respondents are fully aware of the critique made by other black viewers, and they usually addressed their discussion to that critique:

> Well, I know there has been a lot of criticism of *Cosby* because people would say that it was not realistic—but it is realistic to have a doctor and a lawyer (but the neighborhood that I lived at, maybe it's a little difficult for them to imagine that there are families like this). It's good for me because we are not always showing poverty, despair—we are showing the progress that our race has achieved, and that is what makes it real—we have achieved progress. We have black millionaires all over the place. It is not uncommon to have a black man and a black woman, both professionals, making a lot of money living together, it is not uncommon these days. But I think in terms of the media and television it is uncommon because they choose not to show blacks in this light. They like to show blacks in crime and in despair, or in negative situations and that is why I think a lot of people say it is unreal.

This sanguine view of the position of black people ("We have black millionaires all over the place") is, as Gates argues, profoundly mis-leading. It is possible, as Gates argues, that this view is the product of the increasing number of successful African Americans (like the Huxtables) on television.

While this discourse is very close to the statements made by many white respondents, it is not equivalent. For most white view-ers, this view of the world informed their belief that policies like affirmative action were no longer necessary. This respondent (as well as the others who took this position), on the other hand, had strong feelings to the contrary. This defense of *The Cosby Show*'s realism, in other words, goes directly against many of the statements made later in the interview about the state of race relations in the United States.

Reading between the lines of the interview transcripts, it ap-pears that the origin of this discourse, at least in part, is a desire to promote black people generally. *The Cosby Show* thereby encourages a certain amount of wishful thinking, to this end. While these re-spondents' awareness of the disadvantages black people face in the U.S. makes them, to some extent, less susceptible to the seductive language of the "American Dream," their uncritical reading of the show's "realism" demonstrates how the desire to promote positive black images can be counter-productive. If African American view-ers, aware of the barriers of class and race, can be seduced into suppressing that awareness, then this is a telling testimony to *The Cosby Show*'s ideological power. Once the Huxtables' easy ride to success becomes not just entertainment but a social reality, the larger white audience has been let almost entirely off the hook.

THE AMBIGUITIES OF AMBIGUITY

Roland Barthes's languish through ambiguity in *S/Z* and *The Plea-sure of the Text* is a rallying cry for a literary and cultural "glasnost": plurality of meaning is celebrated, while those who would bring an end to proceedings by fixing the text to any one meaning are derided as killjoys. It is an approach that punctures the pomposity of tra-ditional textual criticism and opens up new horizons in the analysis of culture. It is not, however, a sociological description: it informs an analysis of culture, not cultural consumption. Urging the cultural analyst to appreciate ambiguity is very different from assuming this is how most cultural consumers behave.

Most forms of ambiguity are seldom tolerated in popular cul-ture. The semiological coyness of the avant-garde, with its refusal to guide the audience in any particular direction, is usually appreciated in comparative obscurity. Most of us may enjoy being teased with ambiguity for a while but if matters remain unresolved for too long, we are liable to become frustrated or bored. The TV show *Twin Peaks* is a case in point. The series began as a fairly conventional mystery drama, but, as it developed, it departed from some of the genre's conventions and became increasingly difficult to interpret. The viewer did not know whether to approach the story as Sherlock Holmes or Sigmund Freud. What the show gained in cult status, it lost in viewing figures. Had the show abandoned the stability of its "mystery" narrative altogether, it would have been dropped, even more quickly, into the annals of television history. Most audiences, in short, like to know what's going on.

Ambiguity is, however, not restricted to the eye of the beholder. Some of the most successful forms of ambiguity are those that do not declare themselves: this is ambiguity in disguise, pleasing different audiences in different ways. Madonna's ability to appear as a sex kitten to one audience, and as an assertive and strong woman to another, increases not only her mystique but the size of her audience. Bruce Springsteen's voice is, to some, radical and progressive, while to others it captures a patriotic working-class machismo. As long as people hear what they want to hear, he is able to capture both constituencies and sell a lot of records. Ambiguity, here, is a conjuring trick for marketing executives to exploit. If we are serious about exploring the ideological meaning of cultural forms, it is something we need to understand.

If we have learnt anything about *The Cosby Show*'s success thus far, it is that it is built on layers of ambiguity. The Huxtable family's straightforward appearance conceals a long and varied cast of characters: to some they are black, to others they are not; in one moment they are privileged, in another they are average. Ambiguity is least likely to be found (although it can be found then too) when *The Cosby Show* declares itself, ever so gently, on the issue of sexism. On the issues of race and class it remains very quiet, and throws open the doors to multiple meanings.

I have tried to chart the ideological effects of these ambiguities, to place them within the broader ideological contexts where meanings take on significance. What has become clear along the way, I hope, is that we can neither deride the show as reactionary nor praise it as progressive without suppressing some of its ambiguities. To many white people it informs a discourse of racial tolerance, a liberal acceptance of black people as equals. To its African American audience, and even some white viewers, it is a jewel in a pale and insipid sea of whiteness, an assertion of black cultural pride that confounds traditional media stereotypes.

At the same time, it panders to the limits of white liberalism, allowing white audiences the sanctimonious pleasure of viewing the world through rose-tinted spectacles, as *Harper's Magazine* puts it:

> The success of this handsome, affluent black family points to the fair-mindedness of whites who, out of their essential goodness, changed society so that black families like the Huxtables could succeed. Whites can watch *The Cosby Show* and feel complimented on a job well done. ... On Thursday nights, Cosby, like a priest, absolves his white viewers, forgives and forgets the sins of the past. (*Harper's Magazine*, 1988, p. 50)

In so doing, it flatters to deceive, and adds credence to discourses that work only to sustain a system of racial inequality.

Could *The Cosby Show* be different? What would happen if it took on racism in the way it has taken on sexism? The ideological room for maneuver is, unfortunately, very small. In the age of the remote control device, an audience's tolerance for images that disturb them is limited: to tamper too much with the delicate semiology of *The Cosby Show* risks losing precisely the viewers who have the most to learn. There is, nevertheless, a little space in which to move forward, but it means treading very carefully and very softly.

8

Conclusion

There are many different arguments running through this book, addressing a variety of theoretical and empirical issues. Although it was been necessary to pursue many different concerns at different times, there is one particular theme that I would like, very briefly, to return to.

If this book has any one underlying preoccupation, it is with the ideological role of television in contemporary culture. Cultivation analysis has made some headway in exploring this question on a macrocosmic level: my concern has been with the more specific intricacies of how, when we watch TV, meanings are actually constructed. The two empirical studies, despite their methodological similarities, reveal substantial differences in response: taken together, what do they tell us about television's ideological influence?

Both studies dispel two related notions. The first is the idea that television's ideological power rests upon the ability of its authors to infuse programs with a preferred meaning. The second is the notion that ambiguity reduces a program's ideological power, passing control, instead, to the audience. To comprehend the power of television, I have argued, we must appreciate its influence regardless of intention and in the face of polysemy.

The first study suggests that the almost perverse narrative structure of television news tends to create a significant gap between the producer and the consumer. The structure of news items, in many cases, leads the audience in directions that neither newsmakers nor news analysts would have anticipated. News items are not communicating the messages they are intended to convey. This failure is, in some cases, quite dramatic. This does not mean, however, that news has *no* influence or that its audience is empowered to choose their own meanings.

The news producer may have relinquished some control, but the news discourse works semiotic spells of its own. Audiences are still guided (albeit by default) toward the construction of certain meanings, and these meanings have ideological consequences. The news item from the West Bank, for example, despite the more honorable intentions of the reporter, succeeded in pushing many viewers toward an implicitly racist response toward "foreigners." It also pushed them away from any historical understanding of the Palestinian/Israeli conflict.

In a more general sense, the structure of news appears to engender a deeply ahistorical view of the world. This is not so much a failure of omission as a breakdown in communication: even when historical context is provided, it is inserted into the narrative in such a way as to render it, for many viewers, almost completely silent. This ahistoricism is not ideologically innocent: it is a fertile breeding ground for political mythology. News becomes myth, and, as Barthes puts it;

> Myth deprives the object of which it speaks of all History. In it, history evaporates. It is a kind of ideal servant: it prepares all things, brings them, lays them out, the master arrives, it silently disappears: all that is left for one to do is to enjoy this beautiful object without wondering where it comes from. (Barthes, 1988, p. 151)

The beauty of these objects is not in their display but in their simplicity. Attitudes are left floating on a pool of association, freed from the constraining logic of our social history. Problems like crime, unemployment, poverty or pollution are dislodged from the social, cultural and economic conditions that created them: politicians thus are able to offer "solutions" without ever referring to these conditions.

This way of seeing the world, Barthes suggests, usually (though not automatically) sustains the political right rather than the political left. Politicians on the right have certainly been singularly effective, in recent years, in constructing a political agenda based on the associative discourse of advertising, associating themselves with symbols of freedom, patriotism and prosperity. The ahistorical influence of TV news has been invaluable in this ideological process, leaving the left floundering in an attempt to reestablish the importance of social and economic causality.

Whether the failure of newsmakers to understand the semiotic processes involved in watching the news makes them less culpable is for you to judge. The point I want to emphasize here is that the power of the news is not always willful. We would not disregard the long-term side effects of a drug simply because they were not anticipated.

The second study suggests that TV fiction, because of its use of more conventional narrative codes, is, in the first instance, a more predictable form of television. *The Cosby Show*, in this study, was fairly successful in communicating a consciously inscribed message (about sexism). Its ideological significance is, nevertheless, ambiguous. In terms of issues around race and class, it can mean one thing to one audience and something else to another.

This polysemy does not lessen the ideological influence of *The Cosby Show*, but it does complicate it. However tempting it may be, we cannot advance a discussion of the show's ideological significance without recognizing this complexity. This kind of recognition is, unfortunately, still unusual in most discussions of popular culture: it is more commonplace to find simpler forms of advocacy, in an attempt to find *the* interpretation or *the* meaning. It is as if we have become seduced into thinking that popular culture must be univocal to be powerful or hegemonic. The hegemonic power of *The Cosby Show*, it turns out, actually depends upon its ability to resonate with different audiences in different ways.

We should also avoid the trap of equating the ambiguity of television with audience power. The audience members in the Cosby study did not construct a range of readings, and then choose the one they liked best. The differences between the interpretations of black viewers and those of white viewers was not a matter of choice, it was a product of the different ideological environments each inhabited. Just because audience research affords us a glimpse at both interpretations does not mean audiences are granted the same right. An ambiguous TV program can be just as manipulative as an unambiguous one, it simply moves in multifarious ways. It is a very modern kind of omnipotence.

References

Adorno, T., and Horkheimer, M. (1977) "The Culture Industry: Enlightenment as Mass Deception" in J. Curran, M. Gurevitch and J. Woolacott (eds.), *Mass Communication and Society*, London: Edward Arnold.

Allen, R. (1985) *Speaking of Soap Operas*, Chapel Hill: University of North Carolina Press.

Allen, R. (ed.) (1987) *Channels of Discourse*, Chapel Hill: University of North Carolina Press.

Allor, M. (1988) "Relocating the Site of the Audience," *Critical Studies in Mass Communication*, no. 5.

Althusser, L. (1971) *Lenin and Philosophy*, London: Verso Books.

Ang, I. (1985) *Watching "Dallas"*, London: Methuen.

Angus, I., and Jhally, S. (eds.) (1989) *Cultural Politics in Contemporary America*, New York: Routledge.

Aufderheide, P. (1986) "The Look of the Sound" in T. Gitlin (ed.), *Watching Television*, New York: Pantheon.

Barrios, L. (1988) "Television, Telenovelas, and Family Life in Venezuela" in J. Lull (ed.), *World Families Watch Television*, California: Sage.

Barthes, R. (1967) *Elements of Semiology*, London, Jonathan Cape.

—— (1974) *S/Z*, New York: Hill and Wang.

—— (1975) *The Pleasure of the Text*, London: Jonathan Cape.

—— (1977) *Image-Music-Text*, Glasgow: Fontana.

—— (1988) *Mythologies*, New York: Noonday Press.

Berger, J. (1972) *Ways of Seeing*, Harmondsworth, UK: Penguin.

Blumler, J., and Katz, E. (eds.) (1974) *The Uses of Mass Communications*, California: Sage.

Blumler, J., and McQuail, D. (1970) "The Audience for Election Television" in J. Tunstall (ed.), *Media Sociology*, London: Constable.

References

Bourdieu, P. (1980) "The Aristocracy of Culture," *Media, Culture and Society*, no. 2.

Brewster, B., et al. (1981) *Cinema and Semiotics*, London: Society for Education in Film and Television.

Brunsdon, C., and Morley, D. (1979) *Everyday Television—Nationwide*, London: British Film Institute.

Brunt, R., and Jordin, M. (1986) "Constituting the Television Audience: A Problem of Method," Paper presented at the International Television Studies Conference, London.

—— (1987) "The Politics of 'Bias': How Television Audiences View Current Affairs" in J. Hawthorn *Propaganda, Persuasion and Polemic*, London: Edward Arnold.

Carbaugh, D. (1988) *Talking American*, Norwood, NJ: Ablex.

Carswell, E., and Rommetveit, R. (eds.) (1971) *The Social Context of Messages*, London: Academic Press.

Chaney, D. (1972) *The Processes of Mass Communications*, London: Macmillan.

—— (1983) "The Department Store as a Cultural Form," *Theory, Culture and Society*, vol. 1:3.

Christians, C., and Carey, J. (1989) "The Logic and Aims of Qualitative Research" in G. H. Stempel and B. H. Westley (eds.) *Research Methods and Mass Communication*, Englewood Cliffs, NJ: Prentice-Hall.

Cohen, S., and Young, J. (1973) *The Manufacture of News*, London, Constable.

Collett, P., and Lamb, R. (1986) *Watching People Watching TV*, London: Report to the Independent Broadcasting Authority.

Condit, C. (1989) "The Rhetorical Limits of Polysemy," *Critical Studies in Mass Communication*, vol. 6, no. 2.

Coward, R., and Ellis J. (1977) *Language and Materialism*, London: Routledge and Kegan Paul.

Curran, J. (1990) "The New Revisionism in Mass Communication Research: A Reappraisal," *European Journal of Communication*, vol. 5.

Dahlgren, P. (1985) "The Modes of Reception: Towards a Hermeneutics of TV News" in P. Drummond and R. Paterson (eds.), *Television in Transition*, London: British Film Institute.

Downing, J. (1988) "*The Cosby Show* and American Racial Discourse" in G. Smitherman-Donaldson and T. van Dijk (eds.),

Disclosure and Discrimination, Detroit: Wayne State University Press.

Drummond, P., and Paterson, R. (eds.) (1985) *Television in Transition*, London: British Film Institute.

Dyer, G. (1982) *Advertising as Communication*, London: Methuen.

Dyer, R. et al. (1981) *Coronation Street*, London: British Film Institute.

Dyson, M. (1989) "Bill Cosby and the Politics of Race," *Zeta*, September.

Eco, U. (1972) "Towards a Semiotic Inquiry into the Television Message," *Working Papers in Cultural Studies*, no. 3, Center for Contemporary Cultural Studies: University of Birmingham, UK.

Eco, U. (1981) *The Role of the Reader*, London: Hutchinson.

Fiske, J. (1986) "Television: Polysemy and Popularity," *Critical Studies in Mass Communication*, no. 3:4.

—— (1987) *Television Culture*, London: Methuen.

—— (1989) *Understanding Popular Culture*, Boston: Unwin Hyman.

Fiske, J., and Hartley, J. (1978) *Reading Television*, London: Methuen.

Galtung, J., and Ruge, M. (1973) "Structuring and Selecting News" in S. Cohen and J. Young, *The Manufacture of News*, London: Constable.

Geraghty, C. (1981) "The Continuous Serial: A Definition" in R. Dyer et al. (1981), *Coronation Street*, London: British Film Institute.

Gates, H. L. (1989) "TV's Black World Turns—But Stays Unreal," *New York Times*, Nov. 12.

Gerbner, G., and Gross, L. (1976) "Living with Television: The Violence Profile," *Journal of Communication*, no. 28:3.

Gerbner, G., Gross, L., Morgan, M., and Signorielli, N. (1980) "The Mainstreaming of America," *Journal of Communication*, no. 30:3.

—— (1986) "The Dynamics of the Cultivation Process" in J. Bryant and D. Zillman (eds.) *Perspective in Media Effects*, Hilldale, NJ: Erlbaum.

Gitlin, T. (1980) *The Whole World Is Watching*, Berkeley: University of California Press.

References

Gitlin, T. (1986) (ed.) *Watching Television*, New York: Pantheon.

Glasgow University Media Group (1976) *Bad News*, London: Routledge and Kegan Paul.

—— (1980) *More Bad News*, London: Routledge and Kegan Paul.

—— (1982) *Really Bad News*, London: Writers and Readers.

Goodwin, A. (1987) "Music Video in the (Post) Modern World," *Screen*, vol. 28, no. 3.

—— (1988) "Music Television: Stars, Sounds and Stories," Paper presented at the International Television Studies Conference, London.

Goodwin, A., and Whannel, G. (eds.) (1990) *Understanding Television*, London: Routledge.

Gramsci, A. (1971) *Selections from the Prison Notebooks*, London: Lawrence and Wishart.

Gray, A. (1987) "Reading the Audience," *Screen*, vol. 28, no. 3.

Hall, S. (1973) "The Determination of News Photographs" in S. Cohen and J. Young, *The Manufacture of News*, London: Constable.

—— (1980a) "Encoding/decoding" in S. Hall et al., *Culture, Media, Language*, London: Hutchinson.

—— (1980b) "Cultural Studies and the Centre" in S. Hall et al. (eds.), *Culture, Media, Language*, London: Hutchinson.

—— (1988) *The Hard Road to Renewal*, London: Verso.

Hall, S. et al. (1978) *Policing the Crisis*, London: Macmillan.

Hall, S. et al. (eds.) (1980) *Culture, Media, Language*, London: Hutchinson.

Halloran, J., Elliot, D., and Murdock, G. (1970) *Demonstrations and Communications*, Harmondsworth: Viking Penguin.

Hartley, J. (1982) *Understanding News*, London: Methuen.

Hartmann, P., and Husband, C. (1973) "The Mass Media and Racial Conflict" in S. Cohen and J. Young (eds.), *The Manufacture of News*, London: Constable.

Hartsough, D. (1989) "*The Cosby Show* in Historical Context: Explaining Its Appeal to Middle-Class Black Women," Paper presented to the Ohio State University Film Conference.

Hawkes, T. (1977) *Structuralism and Semiotics*, London: Methuen.

Hawthorn, J. (ed.) (1987) *Propaganda, Persuasion and Polemic*, London: Edward Arnold.

Heath, S. (1981) "The Work of Christian Metz" in *Cinema and Semiotics*, London: Society for Education in Film and Television.

Henry, P. (1971) "On Processing of Message Referents in Contexts" in E. Carswell and R. Rommetveit (eds.), *The Social Context of Messages*, London: Academic Press.

Herman, E., and Chomsky, N. (1988) *The Manufacture of Consent*, New York: Pantheon.

Hirst, P. (1979) *On Law and Ideology*, London: Macmillan.

Hobson, D. (1980) "Housewives and the Mass Media" in S. Hall et al. (eds.), *Culture, Media, Language*, London: Hutchinson.

—— (1982) *"Crossroads": The Drama of a Soap Opera*, London: Methuen.

Hodge, R., and Tripp, D. (1986) *Children and Television*, Cambridge: Polity Press.

Hovland, C. (1959) "Reconciling Conflicting Results Derived from Experimental and Survey Studies of Attitude Change," *The American Psychologist*, vol. 14.

Jensen, K. B. (1987a) "News as Ideology: Economic Statistics and Political Ritual In Television Network News," *Journal of Communication*, Winter.

—— (1987b) "Qualitative Audience Research: Toward an Integrative Approach to Reception," *Critical Studies in Mass Communication*, no. 4.

Kaplan, E. A. (1987) *Rocking Around the Clock*, New York: Methuen.

Katz, E. (1959) "Mass Communications Research and the Study of Popular Culture," *Studies in Public Communication*, vol. 2.

Katz, E., and Liebes, T. (1985) "Mutual Aid in the Decoding of *Dallas*" in P. Drummond and R. Paterson (eds.), *Television in Transition*, London: British Film Institute.

Klapper, J. (1963) "Mass Communications Research: An Old Road Revisited," *Public Opinion Quarterly*, vol. 27.

Kristeva, J. (1981) "The Semiotic Activity" in *Cinema and Semiotics*, London: Society for Education in Film and Television.

Laclau, E., and Mouffe, C. (1985) *Hegemony and Socialist Strategy*, London: Verso.

Lazarsfeld, P., Berelson, B. and Gaudet, H. (1944) *The People's Choice*, New York: Columbia University Press.

References

Lazarsfeld, P., and Katz, E. (1955) Personal Influence, Glencoe, NY: Free Press.

Lewis, J. (1981/82) "The Story of a Riot," *Screen Education*, no. 40.

—— (1983) "The Encoding/Decoding Model: Criticisms and Re-developments for Research on Decoding," *Media, Culture and Society*, no. 5.

—— (1985) "Decoding Television News" in P. Drummond and R. Paterson (eds.), *Television in Transition*, London: British Film Institute.

—— (1990) *Art, Culture and Enterprise: The Politics of Art and the Culture Industries*, London: Routledge.

Lewis, J., Morley, D. and Southwood, R. (1987) *Art—Who Needs It?*, London: Comedia.

Lodziak, C. (1986) *The Power of Television*, London: Frances Pinter.

London Strategic Policy Unit Report (1987) *No Business Like Show Business*, London: London Strategic Policy Unit.

Loomis, A. (1990) "Semiotics and Ideology: A Textual and Audience Study of a Documentary Video Text," Master's thesis, University of Massachusetts.

Lull, J. (ed.) (1988) *World Families Watch Television*, California, Sage.

McQuail, D. (ed.) (1972) *The Sociology of Mass Communications*, Harmondsworth: Penguin.

McQuail, D., Blumer, J., and Brown. J. R. (1972) "The Television Audience: A Revised Perspective," in D. McQuail (ed.) *Sociology of Mass Communications*, Harmondsworth, UK: Penquin.

Metz, C. (1981) "Methodological Propositions for the Analysis of Film" in *Cinema and Semiotics*, London: Society for Education in Film and Television.

Miller, M. C. (1986) "Deride and Conquer" in T. Gitlin (ed.), *Watching Television*, New York: Pantheon.

Mishler, E. (1986) *Research Interviewing*, Cambridge: Harvard University Press.

Morgan, M. (1989) "Television and Democracy" in I. Angus and S. Jhally (eds.), *Cultural Politics and Contemporary America*, New York: Routledge.

Morley, D. (1980) *The Nationwide Audience*, London: British Film Institute.

—— (1981) "The Nationwide Audience: A Critical Postscript," *Screen Education*, no. 39.

—— (1986) *Family Television*, London: Comedia.

—— (1988) "Domestic Relations: The Framework of Family Viewing in Great Britain" in J. Lull (ed.), *World Families Watch Television*, California: Sage.

Mulgan, G., and Worpole, K. (1986) *Saturday Night or Sunday Morning?*, London: Comedia.

Murdock, G., and Golding, P. (1973) "For a Political Economy of Mass Communications," in R. Milliband and J. Saville (eds.), *Socialist Register*, London: Merlin.

Nordenstreng, K. (1972) "Policy for News Transmission" in D. McQuail (ed.), *The Sociology of Mass Communications*, London: Penguin.

Patterson, T. (1980) *The Mass Media Election*, London: Praeger.

Pechaux, M. (1971) "A Method of Discourse Analysis Applied to Recall of Utterances" in E. Carswell and R. Rommetveit (eds.), *The Social Context of Messages*, London: Academic Press.

Pollock, F. (1976) "Empirical Research into Public Opinion" in P. Connerton (ed.), *Critical Sociology*, Harmondsworth: Penguin.

Poussaint, A. (1988) "The Huxtables: Fact or Fantasy," *Ebony*, October.

Press, A. (1991) *Women Watching Television*, Philadelphia: University of Pennsylvania Press.

Radway, J. (1984) *Reading the Romance*, Chapel Hill: University of North Carolina Press.

—— (1986) "Identifying Ideological Seams: Mass Culture, Analytical Method, and Political Practice," *Communication*, vol. 9.

Richeri, G. (1985) "Television from Service to Business: European Tendencies and the Italian Case" in P. Drummond and R. Paterson (eds.), *Television in Transition*, London: British Film Institute.

Robinson, J. P. (1972) "Mass Communication and Information Diffusion" in F. G. Kline and P. G. Tichenor (eds.), *Current Perspectives in Mass Communications Research*, London: Sage.

Rommetveit, R., et al. (1971) "Processing of Utterances in Contexts" in E. Carswell and R. Rommetveit (eds.), *The Social Context of Messages*, London: Academic Press.

Root, J. (1986) *Open the Box*, London: Comedia.

Rosen, R. (1986) "Search for Yesterday" in T. Gitlin (ed.), *Watching Television*, New York: Pantheon.

Saussure, F. de (1974) *Course in General Linguistics*, London: Fontana.

Schlechtweg, H. (1989) "TV's Class Act: The Semiotics of *Roseanne*'s Audience," Paper presented to the North East Popular Culture Association, Vermont.

Schroder, K. (1988) "*Dynasty* in Denmark: Towards a Social Semiotic of the Media Audience," *The Nordicom Review of Nordic Mass Communications Research*, no. 1.

Schwichtenburg, C. (1989) "Music, Motion and Style in Music Video: The Question of Female Pleasure," Paper presented to the Conference on Culture and Communication, Philadelphia.

Seiter, E. (1987) "Semiotics and Television" in R. Allen (ed.), *Channels of Discourse*, Chapel Hill: University of North Carolina Press.

Sigman, S. J., and Fry, D. L. (1985) "Differential Ideology and Language Use: Readers Reconstructions and Descriptions of News Events," *Critical Studies in Mass Communications*, vol. 2, no. 4.

Silverstone, R. (1981) *The Message of Television*, London: Heineman Education.

Stephenson, W. (1967) *The Play Theory of Mass Communication*, Chicago: University of Chicago Press.

Straw, W. (1983) "Viewing the Media Audience as Active: Issues and Problems," Paper presented at the Canadian Communication Association, Vancouver.

Thompson, G. (1979) "Television as Text" in M. Barrett et al. (eds.), *Ideology and Cultural Production*, London: Croom Helm.

Trenaman, J. (1967) *Communication and Comprehension*, London: Longmans.

Trew, T. (1979) "Linguistic Variation and Ideological Control" in R. Fowler et al. (eds.), *Language and Control*, London: Routledge and Kegan Paul.

Tuchman, G. (1978) *Making News*, Glencoe, NY: Free Press.

Willeman, P. (1978) "Notes on Subjectivity," *Screen*, vol. 19, no. 1.

Williams, R. (1974) *Television, Technology and Cultural Form*, London: Fontana.

Wright, C. R. (1960) "Functional Analysis and Mass Communication," *Public Opinion Quarterly*, vol. 24.

Index

Index